LCAAM

WEEK LOAN

Global Financial Markets

Global Financial Markets

Issues and Strategies

EDITED BY DILIP K. GHOSH AND
MOHAMED ARIFF

Foreword by Salleh Majd

Westport, Connecticut
London

Library of Congress Cataloging-in-Publication Data

Global financial markets : issues and strategies / edited by Dilip K.
 Ghosh and Mohamed Arrif ; foreword by Salleh Majd.
    p. cm.
 Includes bibliographical references and index.
 ISBN 1–56720–572–0 (academic)
 1. Capital market—Asia. 2. Financial crises—Asia. 3.
Finance—Asia. 4. International finance. I. Ghosh, Dilip K. (Dilip
Kumar), 1942– II. Mohamed Ariff, 1940–
HG5702.G55 2004
332′042—dc22   2003026527

British Library Cataloguing in Publication Data is available.

Library of Congress Catalog Card Number: 2003026527
ISBN: 1–56720–572–0

First published in 2004

Praeger Publishers, 88 Post Road West, Westport, CT 06881
An imprint of Greenwood Publishing Group, Inc.
www.praeger.com

Printed in the United States of America

The paper used in this book complies with the
Permanent Paper Standard issued by the National
Information Standards Organization (Z39.48–1984).

10 9 8 7 6 5 4 3 2 1

Contents

Foreword

Globalization is a process unleashed a long time ago—maybe with the evolution of offshore banking or from the dawn of the reality that started the international trade as the vehicle for triggering welfare gain for the parties involved in the exchange of goods and services. We do not attempt today to understand where the global view came into being, but we veritably recognize that we all live in the global village we all have knowingly or unknowingly created. The plague in Bangkok or the flu in Jakarta must have its contagion effect in Malaysia and in the United States, and it is a reality we must recognize and responsively react to with care and caution. The recent act of terrorism on September 11, 2001 and the war on terrorism are not limited to the countries directly hit, but the financial spillover is indeed worldwide. The interconnectedness of the nation-economies is so overwhelming that no single country can effectively ignore the serious problems in another country, near or far. Trade and investment at transnational levels today make it impossible to insulate one economy from the devastating blow in the other economy or economies. Had it not been so true, the Thai problem of the plummeting baht would not have caused crisis in Indonesia, Korea, or Malaysia. So we know the reality of interdependence.

In this interdependent state of our global economy and the market structure we are operating through, many issues have appeared and many strategies need to be devised to cope with the issues and the problems. The Asian crisis in the recent past has awakened us all, and all of us now know that unmanaged capital flows and unregulated credit flows can bring havoc to the national economy as much as it can bring unsettling chaos to the global economy. Many efforts have been made to examine the genesis and the generic solution to the problems of currency market's free fall and stock markets' knife-edge walk. In this book, Professor Dilip Ghosh and Professor Mohamed Ariff have made a selective approach to the study of the problems that arose in the crisis-ridden Asian economies and have linked those studies within the framework of the global economy. However, some of the studies go beyond the issue of endemic value, and thus lend enduring strength of theoretical rigor and virtue. The empirical studies contained in this book also offer guidance and direction to regulators and policy makers. It is a wonderful work, and I hope it will give better light for us to see many things through these theoretical arguments and empirical evidence.

Salleh Majd, President
Kuala Lumpur Stock Exchange

Introduction

We often say we live in a global village. It is, however, hard to pinpoint when globalization began in a serious way since international trade has been a way of life for a long time. Yet, if one has to pick a time when globalization began, one may make the remark that it started with the beginning of offshore banking or maybe from the time when Japan's capital market made its debut by issuing bonds and moving away from the traditional banks as the agency for financial operations—intranational and international. From the 1970s onward, many of the Asian countries began to form a nucleus of economic power as a regional block to be reckoned as a unit in the world economy. Japanese growth, Korean resurgence, Malaysian marvels, Chinese size and potential impact, and many other realities and the realization of anticipated growth brought Western capital to the Western bloc. The growth and stunning visibility of these nations, the pace of technology, cybernetic innovations, and information superhighways tied the knot and made the world a single unit in many significant senses. The global economy was born, and every nation is a part of that Olympian globe, and every economy is connected to this cosmic entity even through the chaotic tubes and tunnels of trade, capital flows, cultural exchanges, and what not.

Today, if one country gets sick, other countries often get infected, and we have chosen to characterize such phenomena as contagion. In the recent past, when Asian countries went through a financial hemorrhage, it was not just a local or regional phenomenon only, it was felt everywhere. The International Monetary Fund, the World Bank, and the Western leaders were equally worried as Dr. Mahathir of Malaysia and other leaders in that part of the world. Accusations and counteraccusations flew back and forth, private greed and public mismanagement of the economic nerves were blamed for the so-called crisis, but the truth became a veritable reality that all nations suffered, and the gainers, if any, in this financial debacle did not gain as much or at all. Immiserizing growth has taken a new meaning now in this age of global markets.

In the wake of the recent Asian crisis and other crises many efforts have been made to analyze the reasons for such economic failures and at the same time scholars have engaged in debates and research on the linkages of nation-economies in relation to others. It is often noted that the free fall of the Thai baht caused the Indonesian rupiah to follow the slide and it did not take much time for Malaysian ringgit or Korean won to follow suit. We know the exchange rate mechanism (ERM)—country crisis, Mexican plight, and many others before and after the Asian crisis. The question is overwhelming then: what are the issues and what are the strategies for the global structure of financial markets in which each economic agent operates without any alternative? This book is an attempt to bring some thoughts on this question concerning various issues and strategies.

No one can even pretend to believe that all the questions can be answered in one study, and we do not dare make such a claim. Numerous studies, symposia, colloquia, and conferences have colored the landscape of intellectual debates and discourse at academic circles, at think tanks, in corporate boardrooms, and at government policy forums. Old frameworks—theoretical structures and analytical vehicles—have been employed with new and fresh thinking in various quarters. Here we have attempted to examine many issues—some of which even appear to be seemingly unrelated, and we provide some analytical results, based on theoretical arguments and/or empirical investigation.

This book is a reflection on many issues and concerns that have surfaced over the last decade of the past millennium at normative, practical, and theoretical levels. The fifteen chapters in this book provide some answers to many questions, highlight and explain many of those issues, and attempt to spell out many strategies to deal with those issues. The first chapter is a theoretical exposition of agiotage—the business of exchange rate and interest rate—and arbitrage in that framework of exchange business. It does not, however, confine itself to the theoretical structure of iterative covered arbitrage—it shows how an investor can beat a currency collapse and ride over a financial turbulence strategically and effectively, even without assuming any risk in the process. Then the analysis of the financial crisis of Asia is depicted, discussed, and debated in the context of emerging financial markets which have attracted so much attention on the part of investors, analysts, government leaders, and supranational organizations such as the International Monetary Fund (IMF), World Bank, Bank for International Settlements, and so on. Crisis or currency market collapse has raised many questions, and in that context the issue of political risk appears to be quite important. Most of us have a good sense of economic risk—translation and transaction risks—but the need to go beyond the business environmental risk index (BERI) has assumed added significance. Here we discuss political risk—its measure and magnitude and the impacts thereof—in some of the selected economies. Since Asia was a big story in the late 1990s because of its fragile financial situation, and Malaysia became more combatant and vociferous, it became imperative that we chose to discuss the foreign exchange risk exposure of Malaysian multinational corporations in that period of crisis.

Globalization is a process with enormous potential and benefits to the economies involved in this network of international flow structure sustained by trade and investment. Of course, interdependence has its pitfalls, too—particularly in periods of friction and turbulence. So we have chosen, in this context, to discuss a country-economy that was not directly linked to any crisis as such, and yet could have felt the quake from a distance. It is Egypt, a country with young stock exchanges in Cairo and Alexandria, involved in the process of globalization of its capital markets. Its experiences—its pains and gains—are examined against the backdrop of emerging capital markets in the age of globalization. We ask questions about optimality and efficiency or lack thereof, and the profitability of trading rules in currency markets, and then examine those issues within a framework of operational experiences.

International trade and financial operations are explained in terms of fixed exchange and floating exchange rates. Prior to the Asian crisis, some of the currencies were pegged to a basket of currencies or to the U.S. dollar, but the free fall of the Thai baht and the roller coaster ride of the Malaysian ringgit, and, finally, the pegging of the ringgit at RM 3.80 to a dollar called for an impact analysis. Here, we make such an effort, and provide some answers to our question about exchange rate pegging. Persistent dependence on foreign exchange rate is studied, and we also discuss optimal foreign exchange spread from a dealer's point of view. The relationship between exchange rate and inflation rate has been examined in the existing theoretical literature by the *Open Fisher Principle*, which has advanced our knowledge of this relationship, so vital for many calculations. Here we discuss the issue in light of the empirical evidence from Malaysia. In response to financial collapse many of the countries took many measures to alleviate the incipient pain and to restore tranquility in the economic system. Some of the afflicted countries took measures dictated by the IMF—countries such as Indonesia, Thailand, and Korea—yet Malaysia went its own way and put its National Economic Recovery Plan (NERP) in place to bring economic order back into the national life. Many studies have examined the rescue packages of the IMF and the resultant effects to restore equilibrium, but hardly any effort has been made to review the nonchalant go-alone plan of the Malaysian government. Here an assessment is made of the efficacy of the Malaysian recovery plan.

The book also looks into regulatory reforms in the banking industry and examines how reforms and regulations changed the operational smoothness in the postcrisis era. Bank operating strategies and the impact of the financial crisis are also thrown into clear relief and thus we hope we provide some normative guidance in regard to understanding the behavior of banks. The deregulation and performance of foreign banks are also subjected to academic scrutiny in the light of international evidence. Transfer pricing is a reality in global economy, and we try to assess transfer pricing and investment initiatives, and to study the Asian and North American linkages.

The book concludes with two studies. In the age of the euro, and in the context of some interest in instituting the Asian version of another composite currency unit like the euro, the question of the optimum currency area has come into focus. Is the euro a practical paradigm for an optimum currency area? This is a subject of chapter 14, one of the book's concluding chapters. At the very end of the book, in chapter 15, we review the Asian crisis, and ask where it came from and what has been going on since then. Global markets are a catenary turnpike, and we travel on it all the time. An understanding and familiarity of the turns and curves of this path is an important knowledge for our future moves. We hope this book is a reasonable introduction to the comprehension of the markets on a global scale.

Acknowledgments

This book owes its origin to *The Inaugural International Conference on Banking and Finance* in August of 2000 at Kuala Lumpur, Malaysia. Upon creative thinking in the aftermath of the Asian financial crisis, we decided to bring scholars from various parts of our globe to think afresh on the issues of the time for topical value and practical insight. With lots of hard work, a bit of luck and numerous phone calls and e-mail correspondence we could assemble a large number of participants. They came with their papers and presented them with style and rigor.

CHAPTER 1

Agiotage and Arbitrage: Could They Work for an Investor in Asian Financial Crisis?

Dilip K. Ghosh and Shyamasri Ghosh

INTRODUCTION

Agiotage is the business of dealing in the exchange of different currencies, and arbitrage is the exploitation of the misalignment of market quotations of the prices. Arbitrage in agiotage is therefore a way to generate profits in the foreign exchange market. Arbitrage with hedging is the means to make such profits without taking any risk. Here we attempt to design a structure within which we show how an investor can employ arbitrage in agiotage with hedging to make and then compound his profits. Arbitrage and hedging have, however, been exposed in the existing literature for a long time, and Keynes's work (1923) must be cited in this context as probably the formal beginning. Later Aliber (1973), Deardorff (1979), and Frenkel and Levich (1975, 1977), revived the issue and revitalized arbitrage and hedging in the currency market. Next, Blenman (1992), and Rhee and Chang (1992), among others, brought the literature to the limelight once more. In a recent work (1997a), Ghosh has taken arbitrage in currency markets to a new height. Subsequently, he extends his analytical structure in many directions (1997c, 1998, 1999), and, more recently, Ghosh and Prakash (2001) speculate about arbitrage with hedging. The results are important and very useful for both academics and practitioners, and yet a serious reflection on all of these works warrants further extensions and/ or modifications and particularly for an investor exposed to wide foreign exchange swings and currency crisis like the one that came into being in Asia in 1997–1998. The objective of this work is to move the already es- tablished results to one step forward for the sake of nicety as well as for more completeness. However, before we begin to do that, it is instructive that we sketch the basic structure of the analytical framework, and in that context we refer back to the existing literature relevant to this study.

ARBITRAGE WITH HEDGING BY FORWARD CONTRACT

Let us revisit the paradigm, as envisaged by Ghosh (1997a, 1997b), in which an investor, under condition of the market situations admitting of deviation from interest rate parity, makes profits from the currency market with hedging by forward contract by exploiting the market misalignment and compounding that initial profit by iterative arbitrage with and without leverage and transaction costs with full use of current cybertechnology. In the absence of transaction costs, it is shown that if the investor starts off with \$M, he can generate the following amount of total net profit (π_1) where:

$$\pi_1 = \frac{M}{S}(1 + r^*)F - M(1 + r) = M\left[(1 + r^*)\frac{F}{S} - (1 + r)\right] \quad (1.1)$$

Here M = initial investment amount (in U.S. dollars), S = current spot rate of exchange (\$/1 French franc), F = 1-year forward rate of exchange, r = domestic (U.S.) rate of interest, and r^* = foreign (French in this case) rate of interest.

This is the amount of profit out of arbitrage with forward contract hedging, and this measure has been noted in the literature for a long time. Ghosh extends that result and shows how much more profits can be generated by covered arbitrage. In the Ghosh model, the investor should not, however, stop after one round of arbitrage. Since the present value of π_1—defined by $\pi_1/(1 + r)$ and denoted by $\pi_{1(0)}$,—is the money the investor has now (made *instantly*),—that is, a millisecond later after he executes his strategy of exchanging his dollars (home currency) into French francs (foreign currency), he can put his $\pi_{1(0)}$ and play the same covered arbitrage he played in the first instant. Obviously,

$$\pi_{1(0)} = \frac{M}{(1 + r)}\left[\frac{F}{S}(1 + r^*) - (1 + r)\right] = M\rho \quad (1.2)$$

where

$$\rho = \frac{1}{(1 + r)}\left[\frac{F}{S}(1 + r^*) - (1 + r)\right]$$

is the discounted value of the rate of profit per dollar. In the *second* round of covered trade *via* forward sale of foreign currency (French francs), he can generate profits readily again the present value of which is:

$$\pi_{2(0)} = M\rho(1 + \rho) \tag{1.3}$$

This result is different since here we have included $(M + \pi_{1(0)})$—not just $\pi_{1(0)}$—in the second round of covered arbitrage as done in Ghosh (1997a, 1997b). That is, here we have the following:

$$\pi_2 = \left(\frac{M + \pi_{1(0)}}{S}\right)\left[\frac{F}{S}(1 + r^*) - (1 + r)\right]$$

unlike Ghosh (1997a, 1997b) where

$$\pi_2 = \left(\frac{\pi_{1(0)}}{S}\right)\left[\frac{F}{S}(1 + r^*) - (1 + r)\right]$$

By the same procedure, one gets:

$$\pi_3 = \left(\frac{M + \pi_{2(0)}}{S}\right)\left[\frac{F}{S}(1 + r^*) - (1 + r)\right]$$

and hence

$$\pi_{3(0)} = M\rho(1 + \rho + \rho^2), \text{ and}$$
$$\pi_{n(0)} = M\rho(1 + \rho + \rho^2 + .. + \rho^{n-1})$$

It is then recognized that that it is not the first round of arbitrage alone that the investor should engage in; he should instantly get into several iterations of the same arbitrage activity with hedging as long as the market data remain unchanged and the trader can execute millions of trade with current technology. Therefore, the cumulative profit in the consecutive n rounds (π_0^*) is defined by:

$$\pi_0^* = \sum_{i=1}^{n} \pi_{i(0)} = M\rho\sum_{k=0}^{n} (n - k) \rho^k \tag{n*}$$

The result is exceedingly useful, and yet there is further potential for higher profits out of this market environment, not captured earlier. In this model enunciated thus far, the trader in the *second* round enters into covered arbitrage by using initial amount ($\$M$) and the present value of the generated profits in the *first* round (i.e., $\$[M + \pi_{1(0)}]$), and in the *third* round the investor uses $\$[M + \pi_{2(0)})]$, and so on. One must wonder now why the trader would not use $\$[M + \pi_{1(0)}] + [\pi_{2(0)}]$ in this *third* round in place of $\$[M + \pi_{2(0)}]$. If we recognize that the arbitrageur can use the discounted value of the profits in all of the previous rounds, then in this modified scenario, his nth round begets the following amount of profit ($\tilde{\pi}_{n(0)}$10):

$$\tilde{\pi}_{n(0)}^* = M\rho(1 + \rho)^{n-1} \tag{$\tilde{n}$}$$

and hence the cumulative amount for the first n consecutive rounds of arbitrage operation ($\tilde{\pi}^*$) is:

$$\tilde{\pi}^* = \sum_{i=1}^{\infty} \tilde{\pi}_{i(0)} = M[(1 + \alpha)^n - 1] \qquad (\tilde{n}^*)$$

and thus for infinite rounds the cumulative profit is unlimited.

Note that we have thus far differed from the framework developed by Ghosh (1997a, 1997b) by the exclusion of the leverage parameter, which is certainly a useful and important ingredient in the age of margin trading most often practiced by investors. It is therefore instructive to bring the leverage parameter, θ, the proportion of funds borrowed by the investor against his equity position.

ARBITRAGE WITH HEDGING BY FORWARD CONTRACT AND LEVERAGE

Assume that the investor with his initial \$M can borrow \$$\theta M$ and arbitrage \$$M(1 + \theta)$ by hedging with forward contract exactly in the same way as has been done in the previous section. The profit out of the first round of covered arbitrage in this case is:

$$\begin{aligned}
\pi_1 &= \frac{M(1 + \theta)}{S}(1 + r^*)F - \$M(1 + \theta)(1 + r) \\
&= M(1 + \theta)\left\{(1 + r^*)\frac{F}{S} - (1 + r)\right\}
\end{aligned} \qquad (1)$$

and

$$\pi_{1(0)} = \frac{M(1 + \theta)}{(1 + r)}\left[(1 + r^*)\frac{F}{S} - (1 + r)\right] \qquad (1^*)$$

Here

$$\pi_2 = \left[\frac{M(1 + \theta) + \pi_{1(0)}(1 + \theta)}{S}\right](1 + r^*)\frac{F}{S} \\
- [M(1 + \theta) + \pi_{1(0)}(1 + \theta)](1 + r)$$

whence

$$\pi_{2(0)} = M(1 + \theta)\rho[1 + (1 + \theta)\rho]$$

and similarly,

$$\pi_{3(0)} = M(1 + \theta)\rho\{[1 + (1 + \theta)\rho]^2\}$$

and

$$\pi_{n(0)} = M(1 + \theta)\rho[(1 + (1 + \theta)\rho)^{n - 1}]$$

The summation of all these profits then yields the following amount $(\tilde{\pi}^*_0)$:

$$\pi_{n(0)} \Big/ \sum_{i=1}^{n} \tilde{\pi}_{i(0)} = M(1 + \theta) \rho \sum_{i=1}^{n}$$

$$[(1 + (1 + \theta)\rho)^{i-1}] = M[(1 + (1 + \theta)\rho)^n - 1]$$

ASIAN FINANCIAL CRISIS: A SYNOPTIC VIEW

Asia has been on focus for its recent records of financial distress and its spillover effects throughout the global village. From 1997 onward, stock markets almost went on a free fall, currency markets collapsed, banking sectors underwent severe hemorrhage, and the corporate sectors went nearly numb. It appeared as a domino effect, one market infecting and destroying other markets in the region. All these happened significantly for the banking and financial sectors' overextension of credits and not linking them to real economic growth. Debt problems in the 1970s and 1980s in Latin America were the creation of greedy American banks, and, in this case, it is the Asian financial institutions that engendered the economic problem to crisis proportions. Corruption, economic myopia, and lack of coordination must also be the culprits for this catastrophic condition. When all this macroeconomic radioactive fallout was crippling Asia in general, microeconomic agents were being swiftly swept away and simply became powerless to the force of financial avalanche. Yet, the question must be asked: could an investor overtake the storm and stay ahead even under this financial downswing? In this chapter, we make an effort to prove that with calculated moves an individual Asian investor still could beat the contagion and stay healthy economically. Before we attempt to do so, we must bring out the picture of Asia in this crisis-ridden period.

Asia is a continent, but for a real financial study it has become extraterritorial by including Australia in its fold, and yet ignoring India often enough. Here Asia refers to the eastern world consisting mainly of Japan, Thailand, Indonesia, South Korea, Malaysia, Philippines, Hong Kong, Singapore, China, and Taiwan. For the past few years of the last century, the world has witnessed the financial distress and economic disaster of this region, and the world community has got involved in the rescue mission in some form or another. It appears that although all these countries are cured enough and breathing better, they are badly bruised and very weak. Let us look at some of these economies briefly—particularly their situations in the recent past.

Japan

Japan came into turmoil after the failure of a few of its credit unions and banks in 1995–1996. Nissan Life—a life insurance company—was liquidated in May of 1997, Hokkaido Takushoku—a large bank in the country—went bust in October, and Yamaichi securities fell in November. The growth rate of gross domestic product continued dropping from 2.4 percent in 1995 to 1.7 percent in 1996 to 0.9 percent in 1997, and −2.9 percent in 1998. The massive flotation of bonds in the wake of liberalization created a bubble in the economy, and finally it burst. The stock market and currency market both fell significantly. Its impact finally spread through the rest of Asia in varying degrees.

Thailand

Thailand is a case of 21-month-old banking and debt disaster. Thailand experienced a negative growth rate (−0.4%) in 1997, and then it became (−8.0%) in 1998. The stock market plummeted by 35.4 percent and the baht dropped by nearly 52 percent. Nonperforming loans rose from 18 percent at the end of 1997 to 35 percent by the end of 1998. The International Monetary Fund (IMF) put in a $17.2 billion rescue package in August of 1997, which called for running a budget deficit of 6 percent of the gross domestic product (GDP)—1 percent higher than the last revision. The Financial Restructuring Authority (FRA) implemented the second auction of assets from 56 bust companies. Sixty-five banks and finance companies (half of them foreign firms) agreed to a new set of streamlined procedures for negotiating with corporate debtors.

Indonesia

The contagion spread quickly. Following the fall of the baht in Thailand, Indonesia's rupiah registered a drop of 39.8 percent against the dollar, and finally the collapse of the currency was marked by a drop of 69.3 percent, and the equity lost its value by 44.7 percent. Most of the banks became fatally ill last year. On March 13, 1998 the government brought out 45 banks of which 38 got burial order, and the remaining 7 were held separate for postmortem. The IMF cheered that decision of the government. Out of its $45 billion rescue package, the IMF injected $11 billion cash. Still Indonesia has been bleeding, and the pain may persist for a long time.

South Korea

From the mid-1970s South Korea maintained a controlled effective exchange rate to a basket of unspecified currencies, and from the early 1980s it allowed liberal foreign investment rules. The decade of the 1980s was one of liberalization, and the early 1990s saw the continuation of liberalization. The South Korean government relaxed foreign ownership restrictions slowly but steadily. Soon the trade deficits and attack on the won forced South Korea to abandon its defense of the won. The GDP growth rate turned negative (–5.8%) in 1998 from its positive rate of 5.5 percent of 1997. The stock market plunged (–33.3%) and the currency lost its value by 44.7 percent during the Asian crisis. As in Indonesia, banks in South Korea underwent radical surgery. Of the 29 life insurance companies, 10 were deemed nonsustainable by the *Financial Supervisory Service (FSS)*. IMF provided a $55 billion bailout package.

Malaysia

With its mission to become a member of the developed country club—enshrined in its VISION 2020—Malaysia moved ahead with huge construction and growth in infrastructure. In 1991 the government introduced the Outline Perspective Plan with its embedded emphasis on economic growth and encouragement of private investment, both domestic and foreign. First American Depository Receipt (ADR) was announced in 1992. Soon the cabinet approved the formation of the Securities Exchange Commission and the opening of Kuala Lumpur Options and Financial Futures Exchange, which indeed opened on January 15, 1995. The Asian flu after the Thai baht cut loose from the fixed exchange system infected the Malaysian economy. Foreign capital was moved out of the Malaysian jurisdiction, and the market in Malaysia began its free fall. The GDP growth rate of 7.8 percent in 1997 hit –7.5 percent in 1998. When the baht fell on July 2, 1997, Bank Negara Malaysia held ringgit firmly through for 12 days through market intervention, but on July 14 it yielded to the market pressure by letting the currency float. Roughly within seven months (by January 7, 1998) the ringgit's value reached RM 8.88 to a U.S. dollar—that is, about 50 percent depreciation of ringgit against the dollar. The Malaysian government imposed capital controls and pegged ringgit to the dollar at RM 3.80 = $1.

Philippines

Philippines also came under the weather when Asian flu started sweeping the region. The peso fell by 5 percent in October 1997, and it further dropped its value by 1.9 percent over a three-day period when the South Korean won's value slid. The Philippines' GDP declined by 0.5 percent in 1998. Following the yen's depreciation the Philippine peso lost 6.6 percent against the dollar.

Hong Kong and Singapore had some shock, but less severe by comparison. Hong Kong experienced a negative growth rate in 1998 (–5.1%), loss in equity value by close to 43 percent, and a current account deficit by 2.5 percent of its GDP. Singapore had the anemic growth rate of 1.5 percent in 1998 compared to 7.8 percent a year before, or 8.6 percent two years before, and 9.5 percent three years preceding. Three economies are vaunted as survivors of Asia's financial hurricane. Australia (which recently stopped pretending to be Asian), China (which, as the perception in the west goes, cooks its books), and Taiwan are these three countries. Taiwan, one of the Asian Tiger nations, has fared better than the rest. While South Korea and Southeast Asia are struggling, Taiwan has escaped with a small currency devaluation and a relatively modest decline in stock prices. Taiwan's financial system is about to fall prey to Asian-style contagion. Normally, Taiwan's exports account for 40 percent of GDP, but in 1998 exports dropped by 9 percent. Its stock market declined by 7 percent since October, and its currency, the New Taiwan dollar, was off by 12.5 percent against the U.S. dollar.

COULD AGIOTAGE AND ARBITRAGE WORK UNDER ASIAN CRISIS?

Against the backdrop of these realities, one may ask the question: could agiotage and arbitrage work for an investor under the Asian financial crisis? Could a prudent investor stay ahead even in the macroeconomic chaos in the financial and currency markets Asian economies were in? In this work, an effort is made to show that under a rational strategy of covered iterative arbitrage an investor could beat the down syndrome and stay ahead in the game of fall and fall-out of the past Asian contagion. In this section we explore and explain how the investment strategy of no-risk or covered risk position by hedging in the currency market could put an investor gain at his microeconomic environment. It should be noted that after the financial distress emerged in Asia, some governments put currency controls and many restrictive conditions on the conversion and movements of monetary assets. Yet, it cannot be ignored that leakage was possible by currency swaps, and before currency controls came into being (as in Malaysia), investors could, and indeed did, convert a given Asian currency or a basket of Asian currencies. Let us begin with that possibility and see how an investor could fare under the ongoing currency depreciation in Asia.

Consider an investor who could convert his, say, Malaysian ringgits (RM 25,000,0000 into the U.S dollars at RM 2.5 = $1) that existed in the precrisis period. With the converted amount of $10,000,000 he could enter into the iterative agiotage and arbitrage with forward cover with and without leverage, outlined in the previous two sections. Here we visualize the investor converting his dollars now into French francs, and going through the arbitrage hedged by forward contracts. Table 1.1 exhibits the profits made at each round of iterative covered arbitrage. Here the U.S. interest rate = 5.12 percent, French interest rate $r^* = 4.94$ percent, spot rate of exchange of a French franc in terms of the U.S dollar is $0.1388, and the 1-year forward rate is $0.1432, and the initial investment in agiotage

Table 1.1
Iterative Covered Arbitrage Profits

i	P	$[(1 +)^i - 1]$	$M[(1 + \_)^i - 1]$	$M[(1 + (1 + \theta)\rho)^n - 1]$
1	0.0299	0.0299	$373,750.00	$10,374,000.00
2	0.0299	0.060694	761,468.91	10,761,987.60
3	0.0299	0.092409	1,163,678.81	11,164,485.94
4	0.0299	0.125072	1,580,921.30	11,582,037.71
5	0.0299	0.158711	2,013,758.24	12,015,205.92
6	0.0299	0.193357	2,462,772.45	12,464,574.62
7	0.0299	0.229038	2,928,568.57	12,930,749.71
8	0.0299	0.265787	3,411,773.82	13,414,359.75
9	0.0299	0.203634	**3,913,038.87**	**13,916,056.81**
10	**0.0299**	**0.342612**	**4,433,038.70**	**14,436,517.33**
11	0.0299	0.382756	4,972,473.52	14,976,443.08
12	0.0299	0.424101	5,532,069.71	14,536,562.05
13	0.0299	0.466681	6,112,580.82	16,117,629.47
14	0.0299	0.510535	6,714,788.53	16,720,428.81
15	0.0299	0.555700	7,339,503.75	17,345,772.85
16	0.0299	0.602216	7,987,567.70	17,994,504.76
17	0.0299	0.650122	8,659,853.04	18,667,499.23
18	0.0299	0.699460	9,357,265.05	19,365,663.71
19	0.0299	0.750274	10,080,742.83	20,089,939.53
20	0.0299	0.802607	10,831,260.60	20,841,303.27
21	0.0299	0.856505	11,609,828.96	21,620,768.01
22	0.0299	0.912015	12417496.32	22,429,384.73
23	0.0299	0.969184	13,255,350.24	23,268,243.72
24	0.0299	1.028063	14,124,518.96	24,138,476.04
25	0.0299	1.088702	15,026,172.85	25,041,255.04

$M = \$10,000,000, S = 0.1388, F = 0.1432, r = 0.0512, r^* = 0.0494$

is M = $10,000,000. With these data (real time at a different point) for illustrative purpose, one can get the profit amounts from column 4 and column 5 in Table 1.1 at different iterations (i = 1, 2, 3, ... 25). If the investor could play well under the strategies described in the previous two sections, he could generate $4,443,038.70 with no leverage, and $14,436,517.33 with a borrowed amount of 25 percent against his equity on the tenth round of covered arbitrage. Other values are given in the table, and it is easy to see what the investor could do under different iterations. Note that $4,443,038.70 is equal to RM 11,107,596.75. That means he makes a return of 44.43 percent, and $14,436,517.33 is equal to RM 36,091,293.33, which is a return of 144 percent on the investment of his initial RM 25,000,000. Had the investor made 25 iterations, which could be done in the age of cybernetic engineering in a few seconds, he could have generated profits in the tune of $15,026,172.85 (=RM 37,565,432.13, which is a return of 150%) or (with 25% leverage) $25,041,255.04 = RM 62,603,137.60, which signifies a return of 250 percent. Note that all these could be earned in a short slice of time, and note that RM depreciated from RM 2.50 to RM 4.76, which is way below the rate of return a smart investor could earn. One may compute similar results in all these Asian economies where the national currencies lost exchange value in almost similar magnitudes. So, our conclusion is unmistakably clear that a rational investor could easily weather the turbulence in the Asian economy as a microeconomic agent. At the macro level, if every investor tried to play the same game, arbitrage opportunity could evaporate, and the opportunity of staying ahead of the storm could have possibly failed.

REFERENCES

Aliber, R. G. (1973). "The Interest Rate Parity Theorem: A Reinterpretation," *Journal of Political Economy*, 81 (November/December), pp. 1451–1459.

Blenman, L. P. (1992). "A Model of Covered Interest Arbitrage under Market Segmentation," *Journal of Money, Credit, and Banking*, 23, no. 4 (November).

Dalal, A. J. (1979). "Decision Rules for an Investor in Forward Exchange Markets," *Journal of International Economics*, 9 (December), pp. 539–558.

Deardorff, A. V. (1979). "One-Way Arbitrage and Its Implications for the Foreign Exchange Markets," *Journal of Political Economy*, 87 (April).

Frenkel, J. A., and R. M. Levich. (1975). "Covered Interest Arbitrage: Unexploited Profits?" *Journal of Political Economy*, 83 (April).

————. (1977). "Transaction Costs and Interest Arbitrage: Tranquil versus Turbulent Periods," *Journal of Political Economy*, 85 (December).

Ghosh, D. K. (1997a). "Profit Multiplier in Covered Currency Trading with Leverage," *Financial Review*, 32 (May), pp. 391–409.

————. (1997b). "Arbitrage with Hedging by Forward Contracts: Exploited and Exploitable Profits," *European Journal of Finance*, 3 (November), pp. 349–361.

———. (1997c). "Risk Free Profits with Forward Contracts in Exchange Rates and Interest Rates," *Journal of Multinational Financial Management*, Vol. 7 (December).

———. (1998). "Covered Arbitrage in the Foreign Exchange Market with Forward Forward Contracts in Interest Rates," *Journal of Futures Markets*, 18 (February).

———. (1999). "Covered Arbitrage in the Foreign Exchange Market with Forward Forward Contracts in Interest Rates: Reply," *Journal of Futures Markets*, 19, no. 1 (February).

Ghosh, D. K., and A. J. Prakash. (2001). "Strategic Rules on Speculation in the Foreign Exchange Market," *Journal of Financial Research*, 24, pp. 15–26.

Kenen, P. B. (1965). "Trade, Speculation, and the Forward Exchange Rate." In R. E. Baldwin et al. (Eds.), *Trade, Growth, and the Balance of Payments, Essays in Honor of Gottfried Haberler* (pp. 248–262). Amsterdam: North-Holland Publishing Company.

Keynes, J. M. (1923). *A Tract on Monetary Reform*. London: Macmillan.

Neihans, J. (1984). *International Monetary Economics*. Baltimore, MD: Johns Hopkins University Press.

Rhee, G. S., and R. P. Chang. (1992). "Intra-Day Arbitrage Opportunities in Foreign Exchange and Eurocurrency Markets," *The Journal of Finance*, XLVII, no. 1 (March).

Surajaras, P., and R. Sweenney. (1992). *Profit-Making Speculation in Foreign Exchange Market*. Boulder, CO: Westview Press.

Sweeney, R. J. (1986). "Beating the Foreign Exchange Market," *Journal of Finance*, 41 (March), pp. 163–183.

———. (1991). "Technical Speculation in Foreign Exchange Markets: An Interim Report," *Recent Developments in Banking and Finance*, 3 (August), pp. 236–270.

Tsiang, S-C. (1959). "The Theory of Forward Exchange and Effects of Government Intervention on the Forward Exchange Market," *International Monetary Fund Staff Papers*, 7 (April), pp. 75–106.

———. (1973). "Spot Speculation, Forward Speculation and Arbitrage: A Clarification and Reply," *American Economic Review*, 63 (December), pp. 999–1002.

CHAPTER 2

Financial Liberalization, Emerging Stock Market Efficiency, and Currency Crises

Vincent Dropsy

INTRODUCTION

Following the world debt crisis of the 1980s, many developing countries turned to capital markets for their borrowing needs. More specifically, a dozen nations from Latin America and Southeast Asia liberalized their stock markets, allowing foreign capital to flow almost freely and finance their development. As a result, most of these countries experienced huge capital inflows in the first half of the 1990s. Table 2.1 illustrates the tremendous growth of stock market capitalization from the official date of financial liberalization to 1999 for 12 nations selected for this study. Yet, most of these countries became victims of financial and economic crises in the second half of the 1990s.

The objective of this chapter is to examine the relationship between financial liberalization, emerging stock market (ESM) efficiency, and currency crises. Financial theory postulates that equity markets should become more integrated with world financial markets following liberalization. In this case, the initial capital inflows and the subsequent crises would have simply reflected rational hopes dashed by macroeconomic mismanagement. On the other hand, it is also possible that these emerging markets suffered from inefficiencies and allowed speculative bubbles to develop and ultimately burst. In any case, the liberalizations of emerging stock markets appear to have played an important role. Consistent with financial theory, Bekaert and Harvey (2000) and Henry (2000b) find that these liberalizations reduce the cost of capital. Henry (2000a) and Bekaert, Harvey, and Lundblad (2001) also conclude that these financial liberaliations boost

Table 2.1
Stock Market Capitalization and Gross Domestic Product

	Argentina		Brazil		Chile		Colombia		Mexico		Venezuela	
	1989	1999	1990	1999	1991	1999	1990	1999	1988	1999	1989	1999
Market cap. (bn$)	4.2	228.0	16.4	228.0	28.0	68.2	1.4	11.6	13.8	154.0	1.5	7.5
Change of Mkt. cap.		5,296%		1,294%		1,44%		719%		1,018%		408%
GDP (bn$)	69.0	283.2	465.0	751.5	34.6	67.5	46.9	86.6	174.2	483.7	38.5	102.2
Change of GDP		310%		62%		95%		85%		178%		166%
Mkt. cap./GDP (%)	6%	81%	4%	30%	81%	101%	3%	13%	8%	32%	4%	7%

	Indonesia		Korea		Malaysia		Philippines		Taiwan		Thailand	
	1988	1999	1991	1999	1988	1999	1990	1999	1990	1999	1986	1999
Market cap. (bn$)	0.3	64.1	96.4	305.5	23.3	145.4	5.9	48.1	100.7	376.0	2.9	58.4
Change of mkt. cap.		25,231%		217%		524%		712%		273%		1,928%
GDP (bn$)	84.3	142.5	295.2	406.9	34.8	79.0	44.3	76.6	160.2	275.0	41.7	124.4
Change of GDP		69%		38%		127%		73%		72%		199%
Mkt. cap./GDP (%)	0.3%	45%	33%	75%	67%	184%	13%	63%	63%	137%	7%	47%

The first date corresponds to the year before the official financial liberalization.

investment and economic growth. On the other hand, Kawakatsu and Morey (1999) conclude that stock markets have not become more efficient following their liberalization. Bacchetta and Van Wincoop (1998) also show that financial liberalization leads to an initial period of asset price overshooting, before a crisis occurs.

The first stage of this study is to test the weak efficiency of these Latin American and East Asian emerging stock markets before and after their official liberalization to examine its effect. The analysis is then refined by introducing the contemporaneous effect of world stock markets and currency crises on excess stock returns to take into account potential market integration. Finally, this study examines whether emerging stock markets provide a warning signal of impeding currency crises or vice versa.

METHODOLOGY

The Efficient Market Hypothesis (EMH) states that market prices always fully reflect available information. Its weak version is based on an information set that includes only the history of prices themselves. It also implies that stock returns should not be forecastable based only on their past values. Campbell, Lo, and MacKinlay (1997) suggest a series of econometric procedures to ascertain the predictability of asset returns based on their past values (as well as on other variables in other EMH versions, as we will discuss later). To test weak efficiency, we apply Breusch-Godfrey maximum likelihood (ML) serial correlation tests and Wald tests for autocorrelation to excess stock returns excess return (ER), which are defined as the monthly percentage change in stock prices, denominated in U.S. dollars, minus the world interest rate (one-month London Inter Bank Offered Rate or LIBOR):

$$ER_t = \alpha_0 + \alpha_1 ER_{t-1} + \alpha_2 ER_{t-2} + \alpha_3 ER_{t-3} \qquad (2.1)$$

Weak efficiency tests are easy to implement, but they do not take into account risk exposure. The International Capital Asset Pricing Model (CAPM) provides a measure, known as "beta," of the risk of a portfolio relative to the risk of a diversified portfolio (i.e., the world portfolio). We can also interpret the value and statistical significance of the world market beta as a measure and test of stock market integration. If ESMs are integrated, we can again apply serial correlation tests to evaluate the degree of efficiency of these markets.

The international CAPM also needs to include a measure of foreign exchange risk, unless purchasing power parity holds. The two-factor model states that local excess stock returns ER are proportional to world excess returns, ER^W, and on a crisis index, CRISIS, defined in Cartapanis, Dropsy, and Mametz (2001) as an average of real currency appreciation rates (against the U.S. dollar) and percentage changes in foreign exchange reserves, respectively weighted by their inverse standard deviation. A currency crisis is therefore characterized by a large negative crisis index, which is expected to correlate positively with local excess stock returns. We also use Wald tests (with three lags) to investigate the significance of past world excess returns and currency crises on current local excess returns and test efficiency:

$$\begin{aligned} ER_t = {}& \alpha_0 + \alpha_1 ER_{t-1} + \alpha_2 ER_{t-2} + \alpha_3 ER_{t-3} \qquad (2.2) \\ & + \beta_0{}^* ER^W{}_t + \beta_1{}^* ER^W{}_{t-1} + \beta_2{}^* ER^W{}_{t-2} + \beta_3{}^* ER^W{}_{t-3} \\ & + \delta_0{}^* CRISIS_t + \delta_1{}^* CRISIS_{t-1} + \delta_2{}^* CRISIS_{t-3} + \delta_3{}^* CRISIS_{t-3} \end{aligned}$$

Lastly, we use Granger causality tests to investigate the significance of past ESM excess returns on current crises:

$$\begin{aligned} CRISIS_t = {}& \delta_0 + \delta_1{}^* CRISIS_{t-1} + \delta_2{}^* CRISIS_{t-3} + \delta_3{}^* CRISIS_{t-3} \qquad (2.3) \\ & + \alpha_1 ER_{t-1} + \alpha_2 ER_{t-2} + \alpha_3 ER_{t-3} \end{aligned}$$

Given that stock prices in an efficient market should be equal to the present discounted values of expected future cash flows based on all information available, they could produce signals about currency overvaluation or the imminence of currency crises.

EMPIRICAL RESULTS

The empirical study is conducted on a panel of 12 ESMs (Argentina, Brazil, Chile, Colombia, Mexico, and Venezuela for Latin America, and Indonesia, Korea, Malaysia, Philippines, Taiwan, and Thailand for Asia), and on two subsamples: from January 1976 (or first date available) to the month prior to the official liberalization date (cf. Bekaert and Harvey [2000] and table 2.1), and from the liberalization date to June 2000.

The data on emerging stock dollar-denominated price indices (IFCG) is obtained from Standard & Poor's *Emerging Stock Markets Factbook*, while the world stock (gross) price index is extracted from Morgan Stanley Capital International. The crisis index is calculated using data from the International Monetary Fund's *International Financial Statistics*. Preliminary unit root tests indicate that all variables are stationary.

Weak efficiency test results, presented in Table 2.2, surprisingly reveal

Table 2.2
Weak Efficiency Tests

	Argentina		Brazil		Chile		Colombia		Mexico		Venezuela	
Sample begins:	76.01	89.11	76.01	91.05	76.01	92.01	85.01	91.02	76.01	89.05	85.01	90.01
Sample ends:	89.10	00.06	91.04	00.06	91.12	00.06	91.01	00.06	89.04	00.06	90.00	00.06
Wald test: Prob. (Lag1 = Lag2 = Lag3 = 0)	22.8%	4.9% *	85.2%	55.9%	0.1% *	30.5%	1.7% *	0.1% *	7.4%	48.5%	50.8%	25.4%
Breusch-Godfrey LM test Prob. (no serial correlation)	12.2%	79.7%	75.1%	3.3% *	15.4%	86.4%	99.2%	39.2%	62.4%	37.0%	37.8%	98.0%

	Indonesia		Korea		Malaysia		Philippines		Taiwan		Thailand	
Sample begins:	76.01	89.09	76.01	92.01	85.01	88.12	85.01	91.06	85.01	91.01	76.01	87.09
Sample ends:	89.08	00.06	91.12	00.06	88.11	00.06	91.05	00.06	90.12	00.06	87.08	00.06
Wald test: Prob. (Lag1 = Lag2 = Lag3 = 0)	#N/A	19.2%	94.3%	91.9%	73.3%	3.2% *	0.0% *	0.9% *	89.6%	50.4%	0.1% *	8.4%
Breusch-Godfrey LM test Prob. (no serial correlation)	#N/A	70.5%	84.2%	80.0%	54.6%	9.9%	97.0%	63.9%	99.9%	4.9% *	95.6%	4.7% *

The left column corresponds to the subsample until the official financial liberalization.
The right column corresponds to the subsample from the official financial liberalization.
An asterisk means that the null hypothesis is rejected at a 5 percent significance level.

that none of ESMs, except for Chile, did not become more efficient after their liberalization: on the contrary, four stock markets (Argentina, Brazil, Malaysia, Taiwan) lost their efficiency after their liberalization, while three other stock markets stayed weakly inefficient before and after their liberalization (Colombia, Philippines, Thailand). When the contemporaneous effect of world stock markets and currency crises are included, the empirical results, shown in Table 2.3a and 2.3b, lead to similar conclusions. The stock market in Brazil now appears to be efficient after its liberalization, but the Indonesian stock market is not efficient anymore, because of the Asia crisis. In addition, 10 of the 12 countries appear to have integrated ESMs after their liberalization (measured by the significance of the world beta), of which only 2 countries were integrated before liberalization. Currency crises also significantly (and contemporaneously) affect excess returns in 8 of the 12 nations after financial liberalization, whereas this was only the case twice before liberalization. Finally, only three ESMs seem to provide some predictive power in terms of currency crises, as shown in Table 2.4.

Table 2.3a
International CAPM and Financial Liberalization

	Argentina		Brazil		Chile		Colombia		Mexico		Venezuela	
Sample begins:	78.01	89.11	83.01	91.05	78.01	92.01	85.01	91.02	78.01	89.05	85.01	90.01
Sample ends:	89.10	00.06	91.04	00.06	91.12	00.06	91.01	00.06	89.04	00.06	90.00	00.06
World excess returns	-0.17	0.84	0.59	1.38	0.19	0.71	0.18	0.28	0.57	0.80	-0.08	0.05
	(0.36)	(2.47)	(1.22)	(4.23)	(0.98)	(2.52)	(1.31)	(1.11)	(1.57)	(4.00)	(0.26)	(0.12)
Crisis index	0.012	-0.006	0.043	0.037	0.007	0.010	0.004	0.007	0.018	0.020	-0.012	-0.002
	(0.89)	(0.56)	(2.31)	(4.53)	(1.46)	(2.44)	(0.67)	(1.22)	(1.84)	(3.11)	(1.09)	(0.16)
R2	4.2%	11.3%	11.9%	34.5%	16.8%	23.1%	21.5%	30.4%	26.3%	34.2%	11.6%	6.0%
Pr (no serial correlation)	29.9%	63.8%	44.6%	1.9% *	67.0%	52.8%	67.5%	86.9%	37.2%	34.1%	21.4%	17.1%
Pr (Lag1 = Lag2 = Lag3 = 0):												
Excess stock returns	74.6%	0.3% *	70.6%	95.9%	0.2% *	46.1%	0.4% *	1.5% *	9.4%	55.8%	60.0%	65.7%
World excess returns	29.3%	26.5%	38.9%	46.6%	8.5%	98.3%	24.7%	5.2%	5.1%	26.0%	75.0%	73.7%
Crisis index	77.5%	78.6%	82.6%	19.5%	6.8%	38.9%	34.4%	82.4%	40.4%	35.2%	49.8%	7.8%
Lags of all variables	85.3%	1.1% *	39.3%	43.5%	0.1% *	37.5%	1.4% *	0.3% *	9.7%	49.1%	74.0%	5.4%

The left column corresponds to the subsample until the official financial liberalization.
The right column corresponds to the subsample from the official financial liberalization.
An asterisk means that the null hypothesis is rejected at a 5 percent significance level.

Table 2.3b
International CAPM and Financial Liberalization

	Indonesia		Korea		Malaysia		Philippines		Taiwan		Thailand	
Sample begins:	78.01	89.11	83.01	91.05	78.01	92.01	85.01	91.02	78.01	89.05	85.01	90.01
Sample ends:	89.10	00.06	91.04	00.06	91.12	00.06	91.01	00.06	89.04	00.06	90.00	00.06
World Excess Returns	#N/A	1.43	0.54	1.03	0.64	0.88	0.94	1.02	0.41	0.77	-0.09	1.36
	#N/A	(5.10)	(3.17)	(3.02)	(1.64)	(4.26)	(3.09)	(4.05)	(0.58)	(2.86)	(0.68)	(5.60)
Crisis index	#N/A	0.031	0.001	0.033	0.011	0.022	-0.006	0.030	0.009	0.013	0.011	-0.002
	#N/A	(4.78)	(0.22)	(3.21)	(1.08)	(2.68)	(0.90)	(5.27)	(0.50)	(2.11)	(2.39)	(0.34)
R2	#N/A	44.1%	7.2%	39.4%	23.7%	39.1%	31.0%	47.6%	28.7%	22.4%	27.8%	28.3%
Pr (no serial correlation)	#N/A	99.9%	69.7%	89.7%	46.2%	4.5% *	27.8%	81.5%	3.6% *	10.2%	67.1%	22.0%
Pr (Lag1 = Lag2 = Lag3 = 0):												
Excess stock returns	#N/A	0.8% *	88.2%	82.0%	62.2%	8.7%	0.4% *	56.7%	72.3%	65.5%	0.1% *	11.6%
World excess returns	#N/A	75.7%	84.9%	23.6%	90.6%	21.3%	5.2%	0.8% *	97.5%	57.3%	34.8%	20.1%
Crisis index	#N/A	0.5% *	92.0%	5.8%	52.1%	5.3%	35.6%	1.7% *	4.6% *	7.8%	20.7%	39.4%
Lags of all variables	#N/A	12.3%	98.3%	22.1%	93.8%	0.1% *	0.1% *	0.1% *	33.9%	1.9% *	0.1% *	4.5% *

The left column corresponds to the subsample until the official financial liberalization.
The right column corresponds to the subsample from the official financial liberalization.
An asterisk means that the null hypothesis is rejected at a 5 percent significance level.

CONCLUSIONS

The main goal of this study was to investigate the relationship between financial liberalization, emerging stock market efficiency and currency crises. More specifically, empirical results first revealed that financial liberalization did not improve the efficiency (in its weak form) of Latin American and East Asian emerging stock markets following their liberalization. When the analysis is refined to take into account contemporaneous effects of world stock markets and currency crises, the empirical results confirm the robustness of the previous conclusions, but also point out to increasing market integration. Finally, Granger causality tests show that most emerging stock markets do not provide warning signals of impeding currency crises. Therefore, it appears that the hypothesis of financial market overshooting is consistent with a loss of efficiency following liberalization.

Table 2.4
Predictive Power of Emerging Stock Markets in Terms of Currency Crises

	Argentina		Brazil		Chile		Colombia		Mexico		Venezuela	
Sample begins:	78.01	89.11	83.01	91.05	78.01	92.01	85.01	91.02	78.01	89.05	85.01	90.01
Sample ends:	89.10	00.06	91.04	00.06	91.12	00.06	91.01	00.06	89.04	00.06	90.00	00.06
Granger Causality test (3 lags): Currency crises	7.6%	23.4%	5.3%	0.4%*	4.5%*	13.1%	58.5%	5.8%	32.1%	11.0%	71.2%	0.1%*

	Indonesia		Korea		Malaysia		Philippines		Taiwan		Thailand	
Sample begins:	78.01	89.09	78.01	92.01	85.01	88.12	85.01	91.06	85.01	91.01	78.01	87.09
Sample ends:	89.08	00.06	91.12	00.06	88.11	00.06	91.05	00.06	91.00	00.06	87.08	00.06
Granger causality test (3 lags): Currency crises	#N/A	51.8%	12.7%	69.7%	34.4%	57.5%	19.5%	2.4%*	22.8%	18.6%	13.5%	47.9%

The left column corresponds to the subsample until the official financial liberalization.
The right column corresponds to the subsample from the official financial liberalization.
An asterisk means that the null hypothesis is rejected at a 5 percent significance level.

REFERENCES

Bacchetta, P., and E. Van Wincoop. (1998). "Capital Flows to Emerging Markets: Liberalization, Overshooting and Volatility." CEPR discussion paper no. 1889 (May). MIT Press: Massachusetts.

Bekaert, G., and C. Harvey. (2000). "Foreign Speculators and Emerging Equity Markets," *Journal of Finance*, 55 (April), pp. 565–613.

Bekaert, G., C. Harvey, and C. Lundblad. (2001). "Does Financial Liberalization Spur Growth?" NBER working paper no. W8245 (April). MIT Press: Massachusetts.

Campbell, J., A. Lo, and C. MacKinlay. (1997). *The Econometrics of Financial Markets*. Princeton, NJ: Princeton University Press.

Cartapanis, A., V. Dropsy, and S. Mametz. (2001). "The Asian Currency Crises: Vulnerability, Contagion or Unsustainability?" *Review of International Economics*, 5, no. 2.

Henry, P. B. (2002a). "Do Stock Market Liberalizations Cause Investment Booms?" *Journal of Financial Economics*, 55 (January), pp. 301–334.

———. (2000b). "Stock Market Liberalization, Economic Reform and Emerging Market Equity Prices," *Journal of Finance*, 55 (April), pp. 529–564.

Kawakatsu, H., and M. Morey. (1999). "Financial Liberalization and Stock Market Efficiency: An Empirical Examination of Nine Emerging Market Countries," *Journal of Multinational Financial Management*, 9 (November), pp. 353–371.

CHAPTER 3

Political Risk in Taiwan: Valuing the Doubly Stochastic China Factor

Ephraim Clark and Radu Tunaru

INTRODUCTION

Taiwan is an island of 21 million inhabitants, 99 percent of whom are ethnic Chinese. It is considered a Chinese province and is a major economic and political success story in its own right. It has evolved from a postwar, one-party dictatorship into a flourishing democracy. By 1994 Taiwan had a per capita gross domestic product (GDP) of $13,000 and its annual growth rate between 1980 and 1995 was close to 8 percent. It is characterized by economic liberalism and minimal state intervention.[1] China demands that Taiwan reunite with the mainland and Taiwan claims it seeks eventual reunification, in spite of rumors of independence and the democratic presidential elections of 1996 and 2000.[2] China's adamant and increasingly aggressive behavior toward Taiwan, however, has raised the stakes and changed the rules. This has complicated the situation with increased uncertainty for foreign companies with an ongoing activity in Taiwan or contemplating an eventual presence there.

The immediate problem is not integration with mainland China and the associated increase in political risk that this implies. The immediate problem is how China's behavior toward Taiwan will impact on the business climate and economic activity up to the time that reunification takes place, if it ever does. Thus, foreign firms with an ongoing or projected presence in Taiwan are faced with analyzing the consequences of the political process surrounding the reunification dispute. To this end they must attempt to come up with adequate answers to a number of thorny questions: (1) What measures will the mainland take to press its claims? (2) How will Taiwan react? (3) What are the consequences of the political give and take for corporate operations?

The question addressed in this chapter is how to model the randomness of political events when the randomness is itself random. These are called doubly stochastic processes. More specifically, we develop a model for quantifying doubly stochastic political risk in Taiwan that incorporates a Bayesian methodology whereby parameters can be updated in an endogenous evolutionary process that takes advantage of new information. Using standard techniques in stochastic calculus and the existing literature, we model political risk as an index of exposure to loss (Brewer, 1991; Clark, 1991; Clark & Tunaru, 2001; Mahajan, 1990; Robock & Simmonds, 1973; Root, 1973; Sethi & Luther, 1986; Shapiro, 1978; Stonehill & Nathanson, 1968; Wilmott, 1998). We adopt the very broad definition of political risk as the probability of politically motivated change that affects the outcome of foreign direct investment and make a distinction between explicit events and ongoing change. Explicit events take the form of legislation or decrees such as price controls, taxes, devaluations, etc. The nature of explicit events is that they arrive intermittently at discrete intervals and that they generate an actual loss. Explicit events can be represented by a Poisson jump process. Ongoing change takes the form of continuous activity such as macroeconomic management and monetary policy, legislation, or social and political evolution that affects some or all aspects of the foreign direct investment's (FDI) overall environment. Thus, in our model, ongoing change impacts on the level of what can be lost in the case of an explicit event and can be represented by geometric Brownian motion. With these distinctions in mind, the effects of political risk on the outcome of an FDI can be measured as the value of an insurance policy that reimburses all losses resulting from the political event or events in question.

The chapter is organized as follows. The section entitled "The Real Options Model of Heterogeneous Political Risk" uses standard techniques of stochastic calculus to develop a general model for measuring the cost of political risk generated by a doubly stochastic Poisson process. The section entitled "The Bayesian Updating Process" presents the Bayesian updating process. The section entitled "Real Options Pricing of Political Risk for FDI Decisions" shows how the model can be implemented in the case of Taiwan and the section "Conclusion" ends the chapter.

THE REAL OPTIONS MODEL OF HETEROGENEOUS POLITICAL RISK

In this section, we develop a model for quantifying political risk when the risk emanates from multiple sources of mutually dependent political events. Following Clark (1997) we measure the effects of political risk on the outcome of a foreign direct investment as the value of an insurance policy that reimburses all losses resulting from the political event or events in question. We define political risk as the probability of politically motivated change that affects the outcome of foreign direct investment and distinguish between explicit events and ongoing change.

Explicit events take the form of legislation or decrees such as expropriations, nationalizations, devaluations, and so forth or the form of direct actions such as strikes, boycotts, terrorist acts, and the like. The nature of explicit events is that they arrive intermittently at discrete intervals and that they generate an actual loss. The arrival of loss-causing events can be represented by a stochastic process like the Poisson jump process. Ongoing change takes the form of continuous activity such as macroeconomic management and monetary policy, legislation, or social and political evolution that affects some or all aspects of the FDI's overall environment. Thus, in our model, ongoing change impacts on the level of what can be lost in the case of an explicit event and can be represented by a geometric Brownian motion.

The continuous change is modeled with a geometric Brownian motion $x(t)$ and represents the exposure to loss in the case of an explicit political event

$$dx(t) = \alpha x(t)dt + \sigma x(t)dz(t) \tag{3.1}$$

where α is the rate of growth of the investment, $dz(t)$ is a Wiener process with zero mean and variance equal to dt, and σ^2 is the variance of $dx(t)/x(t)$ due to political risk.

Denote by V the value of an insurance policy covering the investment against losses arising from political events. When such events occur the losses are reimbursed by the insurance. Given the nature of the typical direct investment, we consider the insurance policy V as a perpetual claim whose value does not depend explicitly on time.[3] This means that $V = V(x(t))$ so applying Ito's formula to equation (3.1) and taking the expectation of this return (recalling that $dz(t)$ is a Wiener process with zero mean), gives:

$$E(dV) = \alpha x(t)\frac{dV}{dx} dt + \frac{1}{2} \sigma^2 x(t)^2 \frac{d^2V}{dx^2} dt \tag{3.2}$$

The Doubly Stochastic Process

We now develop the framework that incorporates multiple sources of mutually dependent political events. Following Clark and Tunaru (2001), the jump process we propose evolves through time and does not have independent increments. This approach generalizes the known results of valuing political risk based on a Poisson process for the arrival of loss causing events and it provides practitioners with a better tool for measuring the effects of multiple types of political events that are interrelated in time.

The modeling of the arrival of loss causing political events is very important. Any discrepancy from reality may lead to over- or underestimation of political costs. There are three main reasons for concern. First, the political conditions evolve in time so the model should be dynamic and not static. To solve this problem we consider a learning process in a Bayesian framework, updating the estimates and the solution in time. Second, the arrival process is not time independent; we expect some events to trigger others in a type of chain reaction. Therefore a solution is needed to allow heterogeneity in time. Third, the number of possible sources generating political events can be quite large and new sources may appear over time due to new political and environmental factors.

To solve all those problems let $\{N(t), t \geq 0\}$ be the jump process (counting process) and Λ be a positive random variable. Then, the process $\{N(t), t \geq 0\}$ is called a *conditional Poisson process* if, given that $\Lambda = \lambda$, $\{N(t), t \geq 0\}$ is a Poisson process with rate λ. It has to be noted once again that $\{N(t), t \geq 0\}$ itself is not a Poisson process since it has stationary increments, but it does not have independent increments. In addition, Λ can take an infinite number of possible positive values.

Because the model should be dynamic, we need to know how the past information influences the current solution. Knowing that there were exactly n events prior to time t_0, it can be shown, applying Bayes's formula, that

$$P(N(t_0 + dt) - N(t_0) = k \mid N(t_0) = n)$$
$$= \begin{cases} E(\Lambda \mid \{N(t_0) = n\})dt + o(dt), k = 1 \\ o(dt), k \geq 2 \\ 1 - E(\Lambda \mid \{N(t_0) = n\})dt + o(dt), k = 0 \end{cases} \qquad (3.3)$$

One way of interpreting this relationship is that, knowing that up to time t_0 there were n losses, the probability that a loss causing political event will actually occur over the time interval dt is $E(\Lambda \mid \{N(t_0) = n\})$. Thus the expected loss is $E(\Lambda \mid \{N(t_0) = n\}) \kappa(x, t)$. It would be very useful to know $E(\Lambda \mid \{N(t_0) = n\})$ and this is possible for the case when the random variable Λ is distributed according to a gamma distribution $G(w, z)$. The parameterization used in this paper for the gamma density function is

$$p(\lambda \mid w, z) = \frac{z^w}{\Gamma(z)} \lambda^{w-1} e^{-z\lambda} \qquad (3.4)$$

so it follows that the mean of this distribution is w/z and the variance is w/z^2.

Basic probability formulas (Ross, 1983) imply that

$$P(\Lambda = \lambda \,|\, \{N(t_0) = n\}) = \frac{P(N(t_0) = n\,|\,\Lambda = \lambda)P(\Lambda = \lambda)}{P(N(t_0) = n)} \tag{3.5}$$

$$= \frac{(z + t_0)^{w+n}}{\Lambda(w + n)}\lambda^{w+n-1}e^{-\lambda(t+z)} \tag{3.6}$$

which is exactly the density of the gamma distribution $G(w + n, t_0 + z)$. The mean of this distribution is equal to $(w + n)/(t_0 + z)$. Therefore the expected loss when a Poisson event occurs, knowing that at time t there were n events recorded, is $[(w + n)/(t_0 + z)]x(t)$.

The expected total return on the insurance policy is equal to $E(dV)$ plus the expected cash flow generated by the explicit event, that is, $[(w + n)/(t_0 + z)]\,\kappa(x, t)dt$. Under the assumption that the world economy is risk neutral and that the risk free interest rate is constant at r, the riskless rate obtained on the insurance policy V is

$$rdVdt = \alpha x \frac{dV}{dx} dt + \frac{1}{2}\sigma^2 x^2 \frac{d^2V}{dx^2} dt + \frac{w + n}{t_0 + z} \kappa(x,t) dt. \tag{3.7}$$

This differential equation can be simplified and rewritten as

$$\frac{1}{2}\sigma^2 x^2 \frac{d^2V}{dx^2} + \alpha x \frac{dV}{dx} - rV + \frac{w + n}{t_0 + z} \kappa(x,t) = 0. \tag{3.8}$$

For a policy concerned with a series of losses, it is obvious that $\kappa(x,(t), t) = x(t)$. Making the assumption that $r > \alpha$, the solution to the differential equation is

$$V(x(t)) = \frac{(w + n)x(t)}{(t_0 + z)[r - \alpha]} + A_1 x(t)^{\gamma_1} + A_2 x(t)^{\gamma_2} \tag{3.9}$$

where $\gamma_1 > 1$ and $\gamma_2 < 0$ are the roots of the quadratic equation in γ:

$$\frac{\sigma^2}{2}\gamma^2 + \left(\alpha - \frac{\sigma^2}{2}\right)\gamma - r = 0. \tag{3.10}$$

which are

$$\gamma_1, \gamma_2 = \frac{-\left(\alpha - \dfrac{\sigma^2}{2}\right) \pm \sqrt{\left(\alpha - \dfrac{\sigma^2}{2}\right) + 2\sigma^2 r}}{\sigma^2} \tag{3.11}$$

The constants A_1 and A_2 are determined from the following boundary conditions.

It is obvious that $V(0) = 0$, which implies that $A_2 = 0$. The next condition is based on the idea that an increase in the value of the insurance policy due to a small increase in the value of exposure should always be finite, which rules out speculative bubbles. Mathematically this is equivalent to $V'(\infty) < \infty$ which leads to $A_1 = 0$. The explicit solution for the quantification of political risk is given in this case by the following formula

$$V(x(t)) = \frac{(w + n)x(t)}{(t_0 + z)(r - \alpha)} \tag{3.12}$$

THE BAYESIAN UPDATING PROCESS

One can make the assumption that the time scale is partitioned by the time points $\{t_m\}$, where m is any positive integer. This can be due to business cycles in the economy or political elections or similar recurrent events that affect the overall business environment. The political risk for the future period (t_m, t_{m+1}) can be calculated at the end of the period (t_{m-1}, t_m) during which n_m events, say, are recorded. The probability distribution $G(w,z)$ attached to the political risk parameter Λ is changing dynamically in time as new information is collected from the arrival of new events.

Let $p^{(m)} = p(\lambda \mid w^{(m)}, z^{(m)})$ be the probability density function updated at the time point t_m and used for deriving the solution $V^{(m)}$ for the next period of time (t_m, t_{m+1}). In Figure 3.1 the initial quantities are $t_0 = 0$ and $p^{(0)} = p(\lambda \mid w, z)$ given in equation (3.3) above.

Figure 3.1
Bayesian evolution of quantified political risk when the number of events are changing in time.

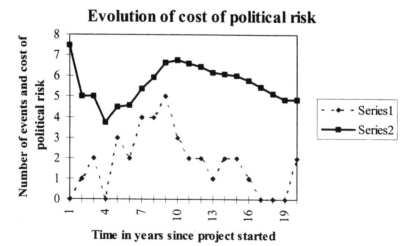

Series 1 = the number of events (to be read on the vertical axis); Series 2 = the value of the insurance policy

The advantage of taking a Bayesian approach is that the solution can be updated when new information is available. In a Bayesian framework, the posterior distribution resulting from the combination of a Poisson likelihood for the arrival of events with a gamma distribution for the rate of the Poisson distribution is again a gamma distribution. Thus, all $p^{(m)}$ are densities of gamma type. With this in mind, the evolution equations regarding the gamma distribution parameters are

$$w^{(m)} = w^{(m-1)} + n_m \tag{3.13}$$

$$z^{(m)} = z^{(m-1)} + t_m - t_{m-1} \tag{3.14}$$

so the distribution for next period of time $(t_m, t_{m+1}]$ is $G(w^{(m)}, z^{(m)})$. The system of recurrent equations can be solved analytically giving the solution

$$w^{(m)} = w^{(0)} + \sum_{i=1}^{i=m} n_i \tag{3.15}$$

$$z^{(m)} = z^{(0)} + t_m - t_0 \tag{3.16}$$

Therefore, the number of events changes the shape parameter of the gamma distribution and the time points determine the scale parameter of the gamma distribution. Thus, the only quantities needed for modeling the discrete part of the real options model, that is the arrival process, are the number of events and the time points providing the partition.

The value of the covering policy at the end of the period, calculated as described before, is given by

$$V^{(m)}(x(t)) = \frac{w^{(m)} x(t)}{z^{(m)}(r - \alpha)} \tag{3.17}$$

It is clear that the same boundary conditions are used for each time period. In other words the boundary conditions described above are homogeneous in time. Other types of boundary conditions that would not be homogeneous in time are described in Clark (1997). For that type of solution the domain of the solutions is changing dynamically as well as the structural form of the mathematical solution of political risk.

REAL OPTIONS PRICING OF POLITICAL RISK FOR FDI DECISIONS

In this section we use a simulated scenario to show how the technique introduced above can be applied to foreign direct investment in Taiwan, knowing that there are many possible political risks due to China's foreign affairs policy.

Consider a U.S. company making a one-off $5 million investment. All the profits are repatriated so the expected rate of net investment is zero.

This means that $\alpha = 0$. If there is no political risk involved, in other words if there is no China factor, the certainty equivalent net cash flow is estimated at $1 million. Suppose that the riskless rate is 8 percent. The investment in this case is worth $12.5 million

$$\left(\int_0^\infty \$1 e^{-0.08} dt = \$12.5 \right)$$

and its net present value (NPV) is $7.5 million ($12.5 − $5).

Now suppose that the exposure to political risk at the outset is estimated to be the full value of the net cash flow of $1 million ($x(0) = \$1$ million). The NPV of the overall portfolio is equal to the NPV of the FDI ($7.5 million) minus the value of the insurance policy. To estimate the value of the insurance policy, we need only two extra parameters, namely, w and z the parameters of the gamma distribution. Based on an analysis of the China/Taiwan situation over the last five years, we estimate that loss causing events are very likely to come at a rate of 0.6 and that it would be very uncommon to have an arrival rate higher than 1.5.[4] In fact, this is the only information we need to know. This subjective opinion can easily be quantified by a gamma distribution with $w = 3$ and $z = 5$ because the mean of this specific gamma distribution is 0.6 and 97.5 percent of the mass of the probability density function lies below 1.44 (in other words there is only a 2.5 percent chance that the arrival rate is larger than 1.44). In practice, risk managers have to give two opinions about the arrival rate in order to identify two parameters for a gamma distribution that corresponds to the forecast.

Suppose now that the time partition is given by a five-year cycle period. We do not have any events at the beginning of the budgeting process and assume that there are 1, 2, 0, and 3 events respectively, in each of the next four of five-year periods, so for a total time horizon of 20 years. The details are summarized in Table 3.1.

Table 3.1
Evolution of Insurance Solution in Time and Depending on the Number of Events Occurred

$x(t)$	R	alpha	w	Z	T_m	n_m	$V(x(t))$
1	0.08	0	3	5	0	0	7.5
1	0.08	0	4	10	5	1	5
1	0.08	0	6	15	10	2	5
1	0.08	0	6	20	15	0	3.75
1	0.08	0	9	25	20	3	4.5

We can see that in Taiwan's current situation quantified political risk is $7.5 million or 7.5 times the amount of the exposure to loss. Based on our ad hoc forecasts of political events over the next 20 years, we can also see that quantified political risk varies considerably over the period—falling, staying constant, and rising—as the parameters of the gamma distribution after the first period are updated with the new information according to formulas (3.9) and (3.10). In Figure 3.1 we can see that there is an obvious correlation between the number of events and the quantified political risk but the relationship is not linear. For example, the number of political events jumps up and down. The quantified political risk follows these fluctuations but the evolution is much smoother.

Figure 3.2 shows the difference between the solution proposed in this paper and a simple solution in Clark (1997, 1998) where the political risk parameter λ is not stochastic but has a fixed value over each time window. Then, the constant rate of arrival λ can be estimated (for the next window) as the number of events divided by the size of the window. Because λ must be positive, we add 0.005 to the number of events in order to avoid problems of zero estimates.

It is clear from Figure 3.2 that the solution proposed in this chapter has a much smoother evolution over time, thereby showing that not taking the stochastic character of the arrival rate into consideration may lead to serious over- or underestimation of the cost of political risk.

Figure 3.2
Comparison between the solution proposed in this Chapter and Clark's.

Series 1 = Doubly stochastic solution; Series 2 = Solution with nonstochastic Poisson process

CONCLUSION

The question addressed in this chapter is how to quantify the political risk in Taiwan, given the numerous possibilities at the disposal of mainland China for making trouble. The problem can be defined as modeling the randomness of political events when the randomness is itself random. Processes such as these are called doubly stochastic. More specifically, we develop a model for quantifying doubly stochastic political risk in Taiwan that incorporates a Bayesian methodology whereby parameters can be updated in an endogenous evolutionary process that takes advantage of new information. We show that the model is easy to implement, requiring only an initial estimate of two straightforward parameters that can be expressed in nontechnical terms as very likely and very unlikely.

The subsequent parameter updates are effected from observed data, that is, the number of realized political events over the specified period. We estimate that the current cost of political risk in Taiwan is 7.5 times the current exposure to loss. We show that this cost can rise, fall, or remain constant as the number of actual political events varies through time. The evolution of the cost of political risk is much smoother than the evolution of the number of political events. It is also much smoother than the evolution of political risk calculated with a nonstochastic Poisson process.

NOTES

1. A recent study of 102 countries from 1975 to 1995 finds Hong Kong 1st and Taiwan 16th in overall economic freedom. See James Gwartney, Robert Lawson, and Walter Block, *Economic Freedom of the World: 1975–1995* (Vancouver: Fraser Institute, 1996).

2. Hong Kong reverted to mainland control on July 1, 1997.

3. The typical direct investment involves setting up a subsidiary in the host country or purchasing all or part of an already existing company in the host country. Legislation in most countries is such that either there is no specified life span for a company or when the life span is specified, such as in France, it can be renewed indefinitely. Consequently, the typical direct investment can be viewed as a perpetual claim. Many direct investments, of course, do have a specified contractual life span. When this is the case, V is a function of time as well as of the exposure to losses arising from political risk. The consequences of this on the value of the insurance policy depend on the particular conditions for terminating the investment on the specified date.

4. In practice, this opinion could be obtained from an expert consultant, an analyst or a specialized agency.

REFERENCES

Brewer, T. L. (1991). "Integrating Political Variables into Foreign Investment Theory: An Analytical Framework." Paper presented at the 1991 Association of International Business meeting in Miami.

Clark, E. (1991). *Cross Border Investment Risk.* London: Euromoney Publications.

———. (1997). "Valuing Political Risk," *Journal of International Money and Finance,* 16, pp. 477–490.

———. (1998). "Political Risk in Hong Kong and Taiwan: Pricing the China Factor," *Journal of Economic Integration,* 13, no. 2 (June), pp. 276–291.

Clark, E., and R. Tunaru. (2001). "Modelling Political Risk with a Doubly Stochastic Poisson Process." Eastern Finance Association Annual Meeting.

Mahajan, A. (1990). "Pricing Expropriation Risk," *Financial Management, 19* (Winter), pp. 77–86.

Robock, S. H., and K. Simmonds. (1973). *International Business and Multinational Enterprise.* Homewood, IL: R. Irwin.

Root, F. (1973). "Analysing Political Risks in International Business." In A. Kapoor and P. D. Grub (Eds.), *Multinational Enterprise in Transition.* Princeton, NJ: Darwin Press.

Ross, S. (1983). *Stochastic Processes.* London: Wiley.

Sethi, P. S., and K. N. Luther. (1986). "Political Risk Analyses and Direct Foreign Investment: Some Problems of Definition and Measurement," *California Management Review,* 28, pp. 57–68.

Shapiro, A. C. (1978). "Capital Budgeting for the Multinational Corporation," *Financial Management,* 7 (Spring), pp. 7–16.

Stonehill, A., and L. Nathanson. (1968). "Capital Budgeting and the Multinational Corporation," *California Management Review,* 4 (Summer), pp. 39–54.

Wilmott, P. (1998). *Derivatives: The Theory and Practice of Financial Engineering.* London: Wiley.

CHAPTER 4

Foreign Exchange Rate Exposure during a Financial Crisis: The Case of Malaysian Multinationals

Bala Ramasamy

INTRODUCTION

Exchange rate variability that results from the floating exchange rate system is a major source of macroeconomic uncertainty affecting firms in an open economy. This is because exchange rates are found to be ten times more volatile than interest rates and four times more volatile than inflation (Jorion, 1990).

Exchange rate variability is found to affect operating cash flows and firm value through translation, transaction, and operating effects of exchange risk exposure (Loudon, 1993). This variability is found not only to affect firms with foreign operation but also firms whose operations are entirely domestic (Adler & Dumas, 1984). Thus, it is not surprising why measuring foreign exchange exposure has been a central issue in international financial management since the advent of the flexible exchange rate system (Choi & Prasad, 1995).

Exposure to exchange rate variability is also a major concern in Malaysia. Since the introduction of the flexible exchange rate in 1973, the exchange rate has shown itself to be volatile (Bank Negara Malaysia, 1994). Being a small, open economy, exchange rate volatility, no doubt is a major source of uncertainty for Malaysian firms that are operating both in the domestic and international markets. This problem was magnified when the currency crisis hit the Southeast Asian Region in mid-1997. During this period, the exchange rate was highly unstable and had shown considerable effects on firm values (Bank Negara Malaysia, 1998). Thus, to overcome the problems related to exchange rate variability, the Malaysian government reintroduced the fixed exchange rate system on September 1, 1998 (*New Straits Times*, September 2, 1998), pegging the ringgit to the U.S. dollar at RM 3.80.

But the real question remains. Are Malaysian firms, especially multi-national corporations (MNCs), really exposed to currency variability? Do Malaysian MNCs engage in risk management strategies that reduce their exposure to exchange rate variability? Such practices are common among MNCs in developed countries as literature shows that multinational firms engage significantly in hedging activities that reduce exposure to ex-change rate risk (Malindretos & Tsanacas, 1995; Sucher and Carter, 1996). Further, does conventional wisdom still apply during periods of severe volatility in the exchange rate movements? In other words, during a drastic depreciation of the ringgit, do Malaysian MNCs still benefit in terms of an increased cash flow and wider markets as a result of cheaper exports?

Although the impact of exchange rate variability is considerably larger on the Malaysian economy, compared to other factors such as interest rates and inflation, research done on exchange rate variability and its impact on firm value is scant. This gap will be addressed in this study by using Malaysian MNCs as a sample.

This study will determine whether Malaysian MNCs are exposed to exchange rate variability. This assessment in turn will be evidence for firms to evaluate and undertake risk management strategies to curtail exposure to exchange rate variability. Based on the above, the specific research objectives of this study are: (1) to determine whether Malaysian MNCs are exposed to exchange rate variability and (2) to determine whether exchange-rate exposure is related to the degree of foreign in-volvement as well as firm size.

LITERATURE REVIEW

There has been extensive literature examining the definition of ex-change rate exposure, the relationship between exchange rate exposure and firm value, the measurement of exchange rate exposure, and the de-terminants of exchange rate exposure.

Adler and Dumas (1984) defined exchange rate exposure as the regres-sion coefficient of the real value of the firm on exchange rate across states of nature while Jorion (1990) defined exchange rate exposure as the sen-sitivity of firm value to exchange rate variability. These two definitions can be said to be in line with Shapiro's early findings where he states that accounting techniques cannot truly account for a devaluation's effect on the value of a firm (Shapiro, 1975).

Literature shows that the sensitivity of firm value to foreign exchange variability differs across studies with some showing a strong relationship while others show a weak one. Studies done by Choi and Prasad (1995) and Miller and Reuer (1998) on U.S. multinationals found strong sensitivity of firm value to exchange exposure. In a recent study on foreign exchange exposure on Japanese multinationals, it was found that 25 percent of sample firms showed economically significant positive exposure effects (He and Ng, 1998). Frennberg (1994) and Donnely and Sheely (1996), who studied Swedish and U.K. firms, respectively, also found significant relationship between firm value and foreign exchange exposure.

Conversely, Jorion (1990), Bodnar and Gentry (1993), and Loudon (1993) found weak sensitivity on firm value to exchange rate variability in their studies. Jorion (1990) emphasized that, although weak, the size of the exposure was found to be positively correlated with the degree of foreign involvement.

The mixed results obtained by previous research may be attributed to several factors, most of which relate to the methodology that had been used. First, several researchers have used a single proxy for foreign exchange movements (Booth & Rotenberg, 1990) while others have employed weighted indices of exchange rates (Amihud, 1994; Bartov & Bordnar, 1994; Donnely & Sheely, 1996; Jorion, 1990). Yet, others have used multiple exchange rates to capture the exposure (Miller & Reuer, 1998). Second, several researchers have focused on firm as their unit of analysis (Miller & Reuer, 1998) while others (Amihud, 1994; Donnely & Sheely, 1996) have focused on industries or portfolios of firms.

The different level of sensitivity of firm value to exchange rate exposure can be attributed to the difficulty of deriving an operational measure of exposure, given the complexity of the determinants (Bartov & Bodnar, 1994; Loudon, 1993) and the hedging activities undertaken by the firms to minimize exposure risk (Jorion, 1990). Hedging activities of the firm are found to be impounded into the share price of the firm thus affecting the measure of exposure. This was evidenced by Jorion (1990), who attributed the low level of sensitivity of his results to the multinational's hedging activities.

Literature suggests that the foreign exchange exposure experienced by firms can be attributed to risk inherent in the form of translation, transaction, and operating risk (Jorion, 1990). Rodriguez (1979) states that multinationals have high transaction and translation risk. However, he states that firms will not be exposed if they undertake sufficient hedging policies to minimize the effects of these risks. Both UK and U.S. firms have high transaction and translation risks, but U.S. firms are found to be less exposed due to their hedging policies (Collier et al., 1992). This further explains the weak relationship found between foreign exchange exposure and firm value for U.S. multinationals identified above.

The question of what contributes to the degree of foreign exchange exposure has also been a subject of interest in previous literature. Among others, the magnitude of a firm's exchange rate exposure can be attributed to the degree of foreign involvement. The degree of foreign involvement can be measured by a variety of factors. Jorion (1990) found that the sensitivity of firm value to exchange rate exposure of U.S. multinationals was positively related to the degree of foreign operations, using the ratio of foreign sales to total sales as a proxy for foreign involvement. This was later confirmed by Harris, Wayne, and Spivey (1991) for commercial banks. Shapiro (1975) posits that the volume of foreign sales is also a prime determinant of export firm exposure. A few scholars, when considering the determinants of exchange sensitivity of U.S. multinationals, found that foreign sales, foreign profits, foreign assets, and variable costs influence the exchange risk exposure of multinationals.

Chow, Lee, and Solt (1997) found that larger firms are less exposed to foreign exchange volatility because of the ability to enjoy economies of scales in hedging activities. Miller and Reuer (1998), on the other hand, regressed foreign exchange rate exposure with the firm's export intensity, the level of FDI by the firm, the level of differentiation and the ratio of foreign sales to total sales and found that exposure is reduced significantly through FDI. Martin (1999) confirms the positive relationship between export intensity and exposure for U.S. MNCs operating in Europe and suggested that firms operationally hedge their exposure by balancing their exports and imports.

Although there has been extensive literature on various aspects of foreign exchange exposure and its impact on firm value, these studies are all based on samples from developed nations. To date, no study has been carried out to investigate the exchange rate exposure using a sample of firms either from Newly Industrialized Economies (NIEs) or developing nations. The only Asian country that has been used for studies in this area is Japan (Bodnar & Gentry, 1993; He & Ng, 1998). Thus, this study will also be undertaken to fill this gap. This analysis should be warranted to reflect the growing importance of the NIEs and developing nations in the world economy.

METHODOLOGY

Exchange rate exposure, defined as the effect of exchange rate changes on the value of a firm, does not imply any causal relationship between exchange rate fluctuations and changes in firm value. Both stock prices and firm value are assumed to be endogenously determined. This means that stock prices and exchange rates depend on the nature of the shock affecting the economy (Jorion, 1990). But for the purpose of this analysis, as in previous studies, it is assumed that the exchange rates are exogenous to the value of the firm.

The exchange rate exposure of MNCs will be measured using a two factor model, where (R_{it}) the return on company i's stock at time t, is a linear function of the return of the market (R_{mt}) and the exchange risk factor (e_i) as stated below:

$$R_{it} = \alpha_i + \beta_i R_{mt} + \gamma_i e_i + E_{it} \qquad (4.1)$$

The coefficient β_i is the measure of market risk while the γ_i measures the exchange rate sensitivity of the firm. E_{it} is the idiosyncratic error term. The constant α incorporates the effect of the correlation between market movements and the exchange rate.

This model, developed by Jorion (1990), based on an earlier model by Adler and Dumas (1984), demonstrates that the exchange rate exposure can be viewed as a regression coefficient. The model posits firm value as a function of market return and exchange rate exposure. Thus, γ, the slope of the model that represents the exchange rate exposure measure, describes the sensitivity of stock returns to the variability in exchange rate. Although this model does not take into account other risk factors such as interest rates and inflation explicitly, Khoo (1994) posits that these factors will be automatically incorporated into the market factor, R_{mt}.

The exchange rate coefficient, γ, based on previous literature, is expected to be positive when the currency depreciates. The positive coefficient suggests that a depreciation of the ringgit against the U.S. dollar will improve an MNC's competitiveness. Conventional wisdom will attest that when the currency depreciates, (1) the MNC's cash flow will increase due to the translation foreign currency to the ringgit (more ringgits will be obtained from every U.S. dollar) and (2) the MNC may be able to increase market share as its goods will become less expensive to foreigners. As both these factors work in the same direction, the depreciation of the ringgit should have a positive impact on firm value (Khoo, 1994). This implies that MNCs benefit (are hurt) when the ringgit depreciates (appreciates) against the USD. However, during periods of extreme volatility, does this conventional wisdom still hold true? This question needs to be answered based on the statistical results of equation 4.1.

For the purpose of the second objective, the hypotheses will be tested using the following cross-sectional regression:

$$\gamma_i = \alpha + \phi_i A + \eta \qquad (4.2)$$

where γ_i, the exchange rate sensitivity, is a linear function using firm specific variables (represented by A) as proxies for degree of foreign involvement and firm size. For the former, the ratios of foreign assets to total assets, foreign sales to total sales and foreign profits to total profits were tested while for firm size, the natural logarithm of the firm's market capitalization was used, as suggested by Chow, Lee, and Solt (1997).

In assessing the exchange rate exposure of Malaysian MNCs, the following hypothesis is tested.

H_1: Malaysian MNCs exhibit significant exposure to foreign exchange variability.

Choi and Prasad (1995) suggest that a firm level study is necessary to understand the factors contributing to the exposure. Jorion (1990) states that the level of foreign involvement contributes toward varying degrees of exchange rate exposure among firms. Based on literature discussed in the section on the literature review, foreign assets, foreign profits, and foreign sales are determined as factors that are strongly related to the degree of foreign involvement. These factors will be used as proxies for the degree of foreign involvement in order to determine whether the varying level of exchange risk sensitivity among Malaysian MNCs is related to the degree of foreign involvement. Chow, Lee, and Solt (1997) found that there was an inverse relationship between firm size and the exchange rate sensitivity. This is attributed to the hedging activities of large firms. In other words, the larger the firm, the lesser the exposure because large firms tend to engage in hedging activities and thus reduce their exposure. These determinants of foreign exchange exposure were tested using the hypotheses below:

H_2: The level of foreign assets is significantly related to the degree of foreign exchange exposure.

H_3: The level of foreign sales is significantly related to the degree of foreign exchange exposure.

H_4: The level of foreign profits is significantly related to the degree of foreign exchange exposure.

H_5: Firm size is significantly related to the degree of foreign exchange exposure.

Data for this study was collected for the period of 36 months from January 1996 to December 1998. This time period is selected to incorporate both an 18-month period prior to the crisis (defined as June 1997) as well as a similar period during the crisis period. Time period of study used in previous research varies. Jorion (1990), for example, uses a 17-year time period, while others use a 6-year period. Our study is much closer to Frennberg's (1994), which uses an event-based study, that is, "to concentrate the analysis exclusively on large exchange rate movements" (Frennberg, 1994: 128).

Malaysian MNCs that have complete price information for the period are included in the study. Sample of firms that will be used for the study are MNCs that have a minimum of two active foreign subsidiaries. An active foreign subsidiary is defined as one in which the parent company has at least 20 percent equity and control assets. Monthly time-series of stock returns for the MNCs and the monthly market returns were obtained from the Kuala Lumpur Stock Exchange (KLSE) database for the period of January 1996 through December 1998. The monthly change of the ringgit's exchange rate against the U.S. dollar was collected from the Bank Negara database. The data for the determinant factors was obtained from the Annual Companies Handbook and the KLSE database.

For model 1, the dependent variable, which is the firm value, is proxied by the monthly return of the firm's stock. This is consistent with literature, where a firm's stock price is used as a proxy of firm value when measuring the sensitivity of firm value to the exchange rate exposure (Donnely & Sheely, 1996; He & Ng, 1998; Jorion, 1990; Loudon, 1993; Prasad & Choi, 1995). This measurement is based on the assumptions of the efficient market hypothesis that capital markets react instantaneously to changes in the exchange rates.

The independent variables are the market return and the exchange rate variable. The monthly return on the Kuala Lumpur Stock Exchange Composite Index (KLSE-CI) was used as a proxy market returns as it contains stock indexes for 100 major companies listed on the Main Board of the KLSE. The exchange rate variable was the nominal monthly exchange rate change of the ringgit against the U.S. dollar. The currency exchange of the ringgit was measured against the U.S. dollar as most foreign transactions in Malaysia are quoted in U.S. dollars. The nominal instead of the real rate was used as studies have found no significant difference in the results using either rates (Khoo, 1994). Furthermore, the nominal rate was chosen because the results can be interpreted in the context of the market model.

In this chapter, the value of the firm's stock, the KLSE-CI, and the exchange rate were averaged between the highest and lowest values recorded in the month.

For model 2, the dependent variable, γ_i, was obtained from model 1. The absolute value of exposure was employed to indicate its magnitude (Choi & Prasad, 1995). Data for the independent variables (the ratio of foreign assets to total assets, the ratio of foreign sales to total sales, the ratio of total foreign profits to total profits and firm size) was obtained from the annual reports and averaged over the years 1996–1998.

RESULTS OF ANALYSIS AND DISCUSSION

The qualitative analysis of companies listed in the main board of the KLSE resulted in the identification of 207 companies that fulfilled our requirement of an MNC. Among the leading companies that were included in the list are Sime Darby, Amsteel, Petronas, Genting, and United Engineers of Malaysia (UEM). Of these 207 companies, complete data was available for 146 companies. The remaining companies were either listed or suspended during the period under study or data for several months was missing. Thus 146 companies formed our final sample for model 1. The results of the foreign exchange exposure are shown in Table 4.1.

From the 146 firms that were tested, 56 (or 38%) exhibited significant exposure, after correcting for autocorrelation. This is far higher than the value arrived at by previous research. Choi and Prasad (1995), for example, found significant exposure for only about 15 percent of the firms in their study (at the 0.01 level) while Jorion (1990) found significant exposure for only 5 percent of the firms under study (at the 0.005 level). Hence, our study seems to have produced firmer results. Based on these results, H_1 is accepted. It is very interesting to note that of the 56 companies showing significant exposure, only two had positive exposures, while the rest experienced negative effects.

Table 4.2 shows the distribution of the exposure coefficients. It is also evident from Table 4.2 that the magnitude of the negative exposures far outweighs the positive effects (–5.27 compared to 1.19).

This means that for most Malaysian companies, the depreciating ringgit had an adverse effect on the value of the firm. Based on the large number of firms that showed this adverse effect, we need to question the conventional wisdom that a depreciating ringgit will benefit the multinationals. In fact, during times of a currency crisis, it seems that a depreciating domesitic

Table 4.1
Exchange Risk Exposures of Malaysian Multinationals

Total Firms	Significant Exposure[*] (% of total firms)	Positive Exposures (% Significant)	Negative Exposures (% Significant)
146	56 (38.36%)	11 (7.53%)	135 (92.47%)

[*] Significant at the 0.01 level.

Table 4.2
Exchange Rate Exposures Based on Nominal Data for the January 1996–December 1998 Period

	Mean	Standard Deviation	Minimum	Maximum
All 56 Firms with significant exposures*	-1.0213	1.0826	-5.27	1.19
First quartile	-2.4899	1.0920	-1.40	-5.27
Second quartile	-0.9677	0.2285	-1.35	-0.74
Third quartile	-0.5127	0.1165	-0.71	-0.35
Fourth quartile	-0.0845	0.4620	-0.34	1.19

* Significant at the 0.01 level.

currency can pose a debilitating effect on the firm. The large number of firms showing negative exposure may also indicate the lack of hedging activities among Malaysian multinationals. Our results further imply that the move to peg the ringgit to the U.S. dollar by the government of Malaysia was a good one as this might have saved these multinational firms from sinking further into the crisis.

Equation 4.2 was used to test the determining factors of foreign exchange exposure. From the 56 firms that exhibited significant exposures (Table 4.1), data on foreign profits, assets, and sales was available for only 22 firms. Twenty-six firms reported insignificant foreign involvement, that is, segmented geographical data was not reported in the annual reports due to very small foreign activity. Data was not available for eight firms. Hence, equation 4.2 was tested based on firm level data of the 22 firms. Since the sample size for equation 4.2 is moderate, and no prior knowledge about the distribution of data was evident, nonparametric correlation analysis was employed. The analysis involved ranking the data and measuring the correlation between the ranked data. Table 4.3 shows both the Kendall's tau and Sperman's rho statistics for the correlation between foreign exchange exposures and the various firm level variables.

Table 4.3 indicates that the degree of foreign involvement significantly explains the extent of foreign exchange exposure for two of the three variables used. Only the proportion of foreign assets does not show significant correlation. The signs of the relationship are, however, consistent with theory in that the larger the degree of foreign involvement, the smaller the absolute magnitude of exposure. For example, the larger the ratio of foreign profits to total profit, the smaller the exposure to foreign exchange rate volatility. An explanation that can be forwarded is that foreign activity indirectly acts as a form of hedging, in that by diversifying into other regions, the firm can rely on its foreign subsidiaries to counter the negative effect of the financial crisis on its parent company.

Table 4.3.
Determinants of Foreign Exchange Exposure

	Proportion of Foreign Sales	Proportion of Foreign Profit	Proportion of Foreign Assets	Size of Firm
Kendall's tau	-0.2641**	-0.2105*	-0.1002	0.2381*
	(0.0427)	(0.0972)	(0.2629)	(0.0655)
Sperman's rho	-0.3574*	-0.3083*	-0.1656	0.3623*
	(0.0512)	(0.0930)	(0.2365)	(0.0532)

Values in parentheses are p-values of the corresponding statistics.
** Significant at the 0.05 level.
* Significant at the 0.1 level.

As for the size of the firm, the coefficient is significant at the 0.1 level. Statistical results indicate positive relationship, showing that a larger firm is more exposed to foreign exchange rate volatility. This result contradicts earlier studies (e.g., Nance, Smith, and Smithson, 1993) that larger companies are more likely to engage in hedging activities. This indicates that Malaysian multinationals do not actively participate in hedging activities *per se*, which may account for significant negative foreign exchange exposures. It further implies that the financial crisis came unexpectedly and these companies were unable to make corrective actions soon enough.

Based on the statistical results obtained, we can accept hypothesis H_1, H_3, and H_4 but H_5 needs to be rejected.

CONCLUSION

The objective of this chapter is to examine whether there exists any relationship between stock returns and fluctuation in the exchange rates among Malaysian multinationals. The chapter differs from other research in this area in two ways. First, no previous research has examined such relationship among firms from a developing country. Second, the study focuses during a time period of financial crisis, specifically the recent Asian financial crisis. We find that for the period January 1996 to December 1998, 38 percent of the 146 Malaysian multinationals have significant exposure to foreign exchange rate volatility. Our results are markedly better than previous research findings. Of the 56 firms with significant exposure, only two had positive exposure. The large number of firms that show negative exposure indicates the severity of the crisis and the idea that our results are merely based on chance needs to be rejected. This finding contrasts with previous research findings indicating that under a severe financial crisis, a depreciating currency can have a debilitating effect on firm value. Thus, the decision of the government of Malaysia to peg the ringgit to the U.S. dollar is justified.

That foreign exchange exposure is determined by the level of foreign activity to a large extent can be confirmed by this study as our results are significant to the required level. Furthermore, there is a significant reason to believe that firm size contributes positively to the absolute magnitude of the exposure.

When the Malaysian government introduced drastic measures to combat the financial crisis in September 1998, there were many objections from inside and outside of the country. As we pass the fourth anniversary of the crisis, it is evident that these drastic measures may have produced the much-needed stability. The decision to peg the ringgit is still enforced and as this study shows, it was a step in the right direction. Whether Malaysia should return to the foreign exchange open market, however, is outside the scope of this study.

REFERENCES

Adler, M., and B. Dumas. (1984). "Exposure to Currency Risk: Definition and Measurement," *Financial Management*, 29 (Summer), pp. 41–50.

Amihud, Y. (1994). "Evidence on Exchange Rates and Valuation of Equity Shares." In Y. Amihud and R. M. Levich (Eds.), *Exchange Rates and Corporate Performance*. New York: Irwin Professional Publishing.

Bank Negara Malaysia. (1994). *Money and Banking in Malaysia–35th Anniversary Edition 1959–1994*, 4th ed. Kuala Lumpur: Bank Negara Malaysia.

———. (1998). *Bank Negara Malaysia: Annual Report 1997*. Kuala Lumpur: Bank Negara Malaysia.

Bartov, E., and G. Bodnar. (1994). "Firm Valuation, Earnings Expectation and the Exchange Exposure Effect," *Journal of Finance*, 64, no. 5, pp. 1755–1785.

Bodnar, G. M., and W. M. Gentry. (1993). "Exchange Rate Exposure and Industry Characteristics: Evidence from Canada, Japan and the USA," *Journal of International Money and Finance*, 12, pp. 29–45.

Booth, L., and W. Rotenberg. (1990). "Assessing Foreign Exposure: Theory and Application Using Canadian Firms," *Journal of International Financial Management and Accounting*, 2, no. 1, pp. 1–21.

Choi, J. J., and A. M. Prasad. (1995). "Exchange Risk Sensitivity and Its Determinants: A Firm and Industry Analysis of US Multinationals," *Financial Management*, 24, no. 3, pp. 77–88.

Chow, E. H., W. Y. Lee, and M. E. Solt. (1997). "The Economic Exposure of US Multinational Firms," *Journal of Financial Research*, 20, pp. 191–210.

Collier, P., E. W. Davis, J. B. Coates, and S. G. Longden. (1992). "Policies Employed in the Management of Currency Risk: A Case," *Managerial Finance*, 18, nos. 3 and 4, pp. 41–53.

Donnely, R., and E. Sheely. (1996). "The Share Price Reaction of UK Exporters to Exchange Rate Movements: An Empirical Study," *Journal of International Business Studies*, 27, pp. 157–165.

Frennberg, P. (1994). "Stock Prices and Large Exchange Rate Adjustments: Some Swedish Experience," *Journal of International Financial Markets, Institutions & Money*, 4, nos. 3 and 4, pp. 127–148.

Harris, J. M., M. M. Wayne, and M. F. Spivey. (1991). "Exchange Rate Movements and the Stock Returns of US Commercial Banks," *Journal of Business Research*, 22.

He, J., and L. K. Ng. (1998). "The Foreign Exchange Exposure of Japanese Multinational Corporations," *Journal of Finance*, LIII, no. 2, pp. 733–753.

Jorion, P. (1990). "The Exchange Rate Exposure of US Multinationals," *Journal of Business*, 63, no. 3, pp. 331–345.

Khoo, A. (1994). "Estimation of Foreign Exchange Exposure: An Application to Mining Companies in Australia," *Journal of International Money and Finance*, 13, no. 3, pp. 342–363.

Loudon, G. (1993). "The Foreign Exchange Operating Exposure of Australian Stocks," *Accounting and Finance*, 23 (May), pp. 19–32.

Malindretos, J., and D. Tsanacas. (1995). "Hedging Preferences and Foreign Exchange Exposure Management," *Multinational Business Review*, 3, no. 2, pp. 56–63.

Martin, A. D. (1999). "Economic Exchange Rate Exposure of US based MNCs Operating in Europe," *Financial Review*, 34, no. 2, pp. 21–37.

Miller, K. D., and J. J. Reuer. (1998). "Firm Strategy and Economic Exposure to Foreign Exchange Rate Movements," *Journal of International Business Studies*, 29, no. 3, pp. 493–514.

Nance, D. R., C. W. Smith Jr., and C. W. Smithson. (1993). "On the Determinants of Corporate Hedging," *Journal of Finance*, 48, pp. 391–405.

Rodriguez, R. (1979). "Measuring and Controlling Multinationals' Exchange Risk," *Financial Analysts Journal*, 35, no. 6.

Shapiro, A. (1975). "Exchange Rate Changes, Inflation, and the Value of the Multinational Corporation," *Journal of Finance*, 30, no. 2, pp. 485–501.

Sucher, P., and J. Carter. (1996). "Foreign Exchange Exposure Management Advice for the Medium Sized Enterprise," *Management Accounting*, 74, no. 3, pp. 59–65.

CHAPTER 5

Impact of Globalization on Capital Markets: The Egyptian Case

Shahira Abdel Shahid

INTRODUCTION

This chapter attempts to address the impact of globalization on capital markets in general with special reference to the Egyptian market. The first section of the chapter starts by giving an overview of globalization and how it has affected nations, businesses, and individuals. Then it discusses the effects of globalization on capital markets and its impact on the future role and activities undertaken by stock exchanges worldwide. To effectively present our study we have examined extensively the existing literature (for instance, Cairo & Alexandria Stock Exchange, 2000a, 2000b, 2001; Huband, 1999; National Association of Securities Dealers, 1998; New York Stock Exchange, 1998; Ruggiero, 1996, 1998; U.S. Securities and Exchange Commission, 1995).

The second section of the chapter focuses on the Egyptian case. It gives an overview of the Egyptian economy, Egypt's regional agreements, privatization program, and capital markets. The chapter also explains why Egypt is poised to be the leading financial center in the Middle East North Africa (MENA) Region. It concludes by highlighting the modernization plan implemented by the Egyptian Exchange to assume this leading role as well as ensures its readiness to globalization.

AN OVERVIEW OF GLOBALIZATION

The end of the twentieth century has witnessed the rising importance of globalization with the formation of economic blocks like NAFTA, European Union (EU), FTAA, MERCOSURE, and so on.

However, the globalized world is about much more than trade or capital flows. Countries are increasingly linked together by travel, communications, and culture, as well as by trade, services, and investment. Television, mobile phones, and the Internet are erasing the barriers, not just between economies, but between people as well. The unavoidable transformation of international relations and world economies as a result of globalization requires that we all adapt.

As globalization is affecting everyone—from nations to businesses, communities, and individuals alike—the winners will be those that are prepared to benefit from it, not to disregard it.

EFFECTS OF GLOBALIZATION ON CAPITAL MARKETS

The stock exchange is no exception. In reaction to the global technological advancements in business, the world's stock exchanges are being forced to update, consolidate, and expand their activities. While globalization is widening the range of opportunities for developed countries, it is also opening the door for emerging markets that were previously unable to compete. Particularly for this latter group, knowledge of how to navigate these changes in the world stock markets is an essential key for success. Globalization has affected capital markets in the following:

Deregulation of markets includes eliminating foreign exchange controls, reducing taxes imposed on foreign investors, relaxing restrictions on the purchase of domestic securities by foreign investors, the issuance of bonds by foreign borrowers, and the involvement of foreign investment banks in underwriting bonds and stocks in domestic stock markets.

Technological advancements in telecommunications help in connecting dealers all over the world so that orders can be promptly executed. It transmits real life information on prices, which allows investors to monitor global markets and assess the impact the information will have on the risk/return profile of their investments. Due to heavy investment by markets and the financial services sector in the latest technology, money has become enormously mobile with the touch of a computer, irrespective of national borders.

Maximizing investment return has become a global pursuit. The biggest increase in cross-border activity has been in equities. Cross-border equity flows have increased almost tenfold in the past 20 years.

Capital raising has also become a global endeavor. Major exchanges have experienced this trend as large number of foreign companies listed on exchanges with the primary purpose of raising capital. It is expected that more companies will tap world markets, motivated by the need to raise capital, as well as the desire to obtain higher valuations, increase their shareholder base, and raise their company's profile via listing on international world exchanges.

Equity markets have become more global. Though the U.S. markets remain dominant, their market share is declining. In 1985, the United States accounted for 50 percent of the world's equity market capitalization. In 1995, it accounted for 39 percent. It is projected that by the year 2005, it will account for less than 30 percent. In other words, other markets will demonstrate a higher rate of growth compared to the United States.

Markets are becoming more dominated by financial institutions such as mutual funds, pension funds, insurance companies, and so on. Globalization is accompanied by institutionalization. Today, giant institutions control huge sums of money, which they move continuously. In European and Japanese markets, institutions dominate virtually all trading. In the United States, retail investors still remain active participants. It is worth noting that ownership of foreign shares of the largest 200 pension funds grew by roughly 34 percent to more than U.S. $225 billion over the past two years.

THE MAIN ACTIVITIES OF A STOCK EXCHANGE

Listing, trading, and regulation are the three fundamental activities of any stock exchange. The exchange provides the place for large and small companies to raise capital and to have their shares publicly traded. In addition, the exchange provides comprehensive trading and information services to the listed companies and investors respectively. Finally, the exchange regulates both capital raising and trading markets, issuers and members, assessing applications of companies wishing to join the main market, monitoring listed companies' ongoing compliance with any rule breaches. It is also responsible for the conduct of its member firms that deal on its market in order to ensure that market operations are orderly conducted and thus ensure proper protection to investors.

THE FUTURE OF STOCK EXCHANGES

Globalization Has Changed the Traditional Role Played by Stock Exchanges

Sweeping changes are happening in the world of investing due to globalization. An explosion of Internet and computer-based trading is revolutionizing investing and shattering geographic boundaries.

Contemporary investors, from the smallest individual shareholder to the largest institutions, are demanding and increasingly getting instant access to information and immediate execution of trades. The economy now is global and interconnected and the markets are evolving to meet capital formation needs worldwide.

Accordingly, stock markets have to change to meet these needs. The next generation of stock markets must provide worldwide and instantaneous price discovery, allow for trade executions in a fair, orderly, and low-cost environment without time zone limitations. Regulations, which allow this phenomenon, must adapt accordingly.

Stock exchanges have to be internationally competitive and to live with falling costs for their services. In order to maintain their cash flow, exchanges must be able to enhance the services they provide, to deliver additional value-added, linking into payment and stock transfer facilities and provide a wide range of online information and communication services.

Technology

The Internet is the major technology trend of the decade, perhaps the century. It is not only opening up new avenues for trading, but also bringing information to the general public, which was once the exclusive privilege of professional investors. In case of trading, it is technology that is enabling investors to execute transactions through order-driven and quote-driving trading systems with ever-greater efficiency, and at increasingly lower cost-to-trade ratios.

As part of such dramatic changes to the existing market system, exchanges are studying the possibility of extending trading hours thus providing investors with a wider time window and, consequently, deepen liquidity and narrow spreads. In short, markets must rely on and make continual investment in technology if they are to survive and adequately serve market users.

Electronic Communication Networks (ECNs)

Markets are no longer monopolistic. Most countries have or are well on their way toward abolishing monopolistic protection and competition now typifies the securities industry. It is not so much the competition between the established markets but the competition between the established markets and other forms such as Electronic Communication Networks (ECNs) for order flow. ECNs are electronic boards registering interest to sell/buy, constantly searching for better-interrelated, more efficient, and more reliable markets and prices. A few large ECNs dominated 90 percent of Internet trading in 1999 in the United States. Namely, Instinet and Island succeeded in capturing 30 percent of Nasdaq orders in 1999.

Island filed with the Securities Exchange Commission (SEC) to register as an exchange. The same occurred in the UK where both tradepoint and Jiway applied to the Financial Securities Advisory (FSA) in order to be exchanges. With increased competition in the market, better execution, cheaper transactions, and more efficiency will take place. The liquidity provided by ECNs is now threatening established exchanges like New York, London, and so on.

Due to the competition from ECNs, it is expected that the number of exchanges in the United States will be reduced. This trend has already started when in mid-March 2000, Archipelago, an active ECN, merged with Pacific Exchange to create the first national electronic exchange in the United States that trades both listed and over the counter (OTC) companies listed on New York, Nasdaq, and American Stock Exchanges.

Hence in the future, one can expect to find few surviving markets in Europe, Latin America, Asia, and Africa.

Demutualization of Exchanges

A lot of exchanges across the globe are either implementing or studying demutualization after being employed by the Australia, Singapore, and Sweden exchanges. Demutualization means restructuring the stock exchange and changing it from a nonprofit organization owned by its members into a profitable one owned by the public at large. The shares of the exchange can then be distributed among members, financial institutions, and the public at large. Done properly, a change in the status of the exchange could provide the needed capital to build the marketplace, lower costs to members, and better serve investors.

In other words, exchanges will no longer be run exclusively by their members but by the new shareholders comprising public, financial institutions, and so forth. Accordingly, the exchanges' profitability and survival will depend on the value (price) of their traded shares, the same as any other listed company. This will end the current ownership monopoly of member firms and their reluctance sometimes in taking decisions that may benefit the market and issuers, since those decisions may be conflict with their own vested interests.

Thus the management of demutualized exchanges will be compelled to take decisions that are geared toward the well-being and profitability of the exchanges. Otherwise, management will be fired by shareholders like any other organization and exchanges will face the threats of takeovers or price decline.

Consolidations and Alliances between Exchanges

Markets, like the financial services industry itself, will consolidate. It is expected that stock markets will merge, acquire each other, or form partnerships, creating few truly global giants. The efficiencies created by these economies of scale will be passed on to investors and issuers alike.

Exchanges will be continuing to explore acquisitions and alliances with other stock markets, both domestically and internationally. This will help expose foreign investors outside the home country to listed companies at home and expose local investors to listed companies from abroad.

The initial integration talks between London and Frankfurt exchanges in 1998 attracted six other European exchanges to seriously evaluate the technicalities of having one Pan European Exchange. The Pan European Exchange project faced difficulties in the beginnings due to nationalistic issues, for example, which trading platform, legislation, clearing, and settlement systems are to be employed, and so on.

These conflicts delayed the implementation of a Pan European Market. Nevertheless, the fierce competition in the market resulted in several more alliances in 1999 and 2000 including Benelux, Easdaq, EuroNext, EuroNM. In early May 2000, the London and Frankfurt exchanges announced that they would merge into iX. The merger failed when Swedish OM Gruppen tried through an unsuccessful bid to take over the London Stock Exchange. A much more successful merger was launched later in September 2000—EuroNext, comprising the Paris, Brussels, and Amsterdam exchanges.

From another perspective, Nasdaq already has a presence in Europe through the Brussels-based electronic exchange, Easdaq, but it is seen as a disappointment since listings have fallen well below expectations. Nasdaq announced in 1999 that it was setting up Nasdaq Europe, a pan-European electronic stock market that was to be based in London and was due to open in the fourth quarter of 2000. Nasdaq is ambitious and wants to link to other markets around the world, creating a global, real-time trading platform, 24 hours per day, that is, Nasdaq Hong Kong, Nasdaq Australia, Nasdaq Middle East, and so on. This will enable Microsoft shares, for instance, to trade around the clock. Microsoft shares, which currently trades 25 million shares eight hours a day in the United States, will trade 60 million shares, 24 hours a day, through the facilities of Nasdaq alliances globally.

In a counter-reaction, on June 7, 2000, the New York Stock Exchange (NYSE) joined another 10 international exchanges in a merger. The plan is to link NYSE with the Tokyo Stock Exchange, the Australian Stock Exchange, and bourses in Paris, Brussels, Amsterdam, Toronto, Hong Kong, Mexico, and São Paolo. The idea is to set up a 24-hour, $20 trillion global market controlling 60 percent of the world equity market. The ambitious global equity market (GEM) project would be a direct competitor to Nasdaq-alliances.

The future of these ambitious alliances is still unclear and faces various challenges including harmonization of listing and trading rules, legislation as well as clearing, settlement, and payment systems.

In conclusion, the world is not likely to move to a single consolidated market, but rather a group of few markets, such as the two groupings mentioned above, that is, bigger players comprising various markets with a global reach. This will not cancel the existence of domestic regional markets focusing on local small cap companies.

Trading Systems: The Future of Order-Driven versus Quote-Driven Systems

Order-driven markets tend to be strongest when executing comparatively small orders. They perform especially well for more liquid securities, where they are cheap and quick, because there is no need for intermediation.

Large orders, on the other hand, take longer to execute but are often done at a competitive price. Quote-driven markets, by contrast, seem to do well in the execution of large professional trades. All orders can typically be executed quickly and there is no need for any trading halts.

Order-driven systems may be most appropriate for retail businesses and quote driven ones for professional businesses.

Currently, neither the order-driven auction structure nor the quote-driven dealer market is suited to the rigors of modern-day trading and investing.

The auction market has not changed fundamentally since the 1890s. Specialists still control order flow at the exchanges the same way they have for more than two hundred years. Also market makers still compete with one another on various exchanges in fundamentally the same way competing dealers have operated for hundreds of years. The issue is not whether the markets have done a great job of serving investors and companies. They have and continue to do so. The issue is how they can do an even better job in the future.

The Securities Traders Association's Institutional Committee in the United States did a survey on what most institutions found desirable with respect to trading systems. Topping the list was order anonymity and a fully integrated system of price discovery, execution, and transaction reporting. The problem is that no stock market offers all those services.

It is no wonder investors started seeking nontraditional trading systems such as ECNs and that these systems began to flourish. But while that trend responded to institutional investors' needs, it was less responsive to individual investors. Trading systems like Instinet, Posit, and Jiway offer institutional investors liquidity and price improvement, but individual investors had no access to those prices.

In conclusion, it is expected that there will be multiple marketplaces in the future, that is, auction markets, dealer markets, crossing systems, or hybrids of all of these, in order to ensure both retail and institutional investors that they have different services available to them to meet their specific trading needs.

Listing and Information Disclosure

With the increasing internationalization of the markets, there are a number of new factors that will affect the operation of the stock exchanges. It is expected that listing rules will be harmonized and that information disclosure standards will be uniform across the globe.

The way companies present their annual and semiannual statements is moving toward a set of harmonized international standards [International Accounting Standards (IAS)]. Some multinational enterprises are raising new capital on several stock markets simultaneously.

This requires coordination between exchanges. It is increasingly being realized that the home country of a company that has shareholders around the world has a responsibility for ensuring that price-sensitive information is available to all shareholders and not just to those in the home country.

Thus international regulatory initiatives, particularly those aimed at standardizing accounting and other disclosure requirements, will be enforced vigorously. These changes will further empower investors, giving them more control over trading in these global markets and access to company information that is formatted to a global standard.

In the future, one expects listing rules to be harmonized and that information disclosure standards will be uniform across global exchanges.

Regulation

Regulation of trading in the new global market will be enhanced by new Internet technology including advanced electronic surveillance systems to ensure continued investor confidence, which remains a cornerstone of a successful market.

Markets must be well regulated. They must put the investor first. The ability to protect investors adequately and inspire investor confidence will be a necessary and integral part of competing effectively as globalization marches on.

Investors

The global investor of tomorrow will be able to execute trades more efficiently, that is, in a less costly manner than ever before. The combination of better technology and heightened competition will essentially push trading costs to a very small amount if not to zero, with investors benefiting directly. Large and small investors are being empowered through information and regulation.

The Internet has been a tremendous leveler of the information playing field—putting individual and institutional investors on a more equal footing. The Internet is, however, a double-edged weapon in that it also puts the public at risk of receiving fraudulent information. At the same time, investors have never enjoyed a better, fairer trading environment since all market players, stock markets, banks, brokerages, are trying to find the best way to serve the investor, as competitive service is the key to survival.

Markets must accommodate both the needs of the sophisticated, the institutional investor and the individual investor. This means that markets must reach a market structure that accommodates investors of all sizes.

Core Functions of Tomorrow's Stock Market

The combination of institutionalization, automation, and globalization will lead to more market liquidity, greater volatility, and lower trading costs.

Technology will allow for an unlimited number of liquidity providers. At the same time, the more linked economies and markets become, and the more money is controlled by institutions, all chasing a limited number of investment options, the more volatility. Price volatility is a fact of life and it will remain so for quite some time. While it impacts the active trader, it has virtually no impact on the long-term investor, whose success depends on patience and the ability to spot superior companies with long-term growth potential.

Spotting such companies, evaluating their potential, and investing in them should all improve in the coming years. Microsoft, for instance, has its financial reports translated into six languages and makes them accessible on its Web site. This is the wave of the future.

Equity markets face the challenge of accommodating these investors through efficient systems and market structures and to protect those same investors through sound regulation.

In light of these trends, tomorrow's stock market must be able to perform four core functions:

1. *It must serve as a consolidator of information.* Until recently, this meant informing investors about the price at which market professionals were willing to buy and sell. The Securities Exchange Commission's recent rules necessitate that brokers publish prices that include the limit orders that their customers took. This is a step further. In the future, a market will have an information system that pulls together all buy and sell quotes in its stocks anywhere in the world.

2. *It must provide a facility for institutional and retail limit orders to meet and interact.*

That, most effectively, can occur through an electronic limit-order book where investors' orders of all sizes can be routed, displayed, and executed.

3. *It must provide an electronic link to all pools of liquidity.* That is, it must provide the means for investors, institutional and retail alike, to access bid and ask quotes for market makers, the limit-order book, private trading systems, and even other competitive exchanges throughout the world.

4. *A market must be a standard bearer and enforcer of integrity.* Self-regulation is a cornerstone of building the investor confidence necessary to support any modern marketplace. To be truly successful, a market must do all of these things, and do them right, at a very low cost. In an age where communication costs are approaching zero and market and regulatory technology are becoming more and more efficient, the successful market of the future must provide a fast, fair, and low-cost means for investors to receive and act on that information.

In conclusion, one can say that globalization will bring major benefits to many different groups. The public will benefit from more efficient markets, which allow a broader range of companies to raise capital at attractive costs. This capital will be used to create jobs, finance growth, and cycle back to the public in the form of attractive investment opportunities. Companies should see their institutional support grow, their investor base expand, spreads narrowed even further, and liquidity in their stock enhanced. In the long run, the financial community will benefit as the market continues to grow in size and range and opportunities are created worldwide. But no group will benefit more than the retail investors, who will obtain lower transaction costs, direct access, improved transparency, and additional opportunities to obtain the best execution.

After discussing the impact of globalization on capital markets in general, the chapter will shed light on the Egyptian market and its role in the Middle East North Africa (MENA) region and its readiness to globalization.

EGYPTIAN ECONOMY

The Egyptian government remains firmly committed to the macroeconomic adjustment policies launched in 1991, which have been successful. Overall, the strength of the Egyptian economy is reflected in the following indicators:

- Real gross domestic produce (GDP) growth in Egypt was 6.0 percent in 2000. According to International Monetary Fund (IMF) estimates,

- Egypt's real GDP growth rate is expected to be 5 percent in year 2000, which is the highest in the MENA region.

- Average annual inflation was 2.5 percent in December 2000.

- The current account deficit was 3.7 percent of GDP in December 2000.
- Foreign exchange reserves reached $14 billion in December 2000, which covers seven months of imports.
- Foreign debt was reduced from $50 billion to $26.7 billion and the debt service ratio was 7.6 percent of GDP as of December 2000.

EGYPT AND REGIONAL COOPERATION

The free trade agreement with the EU, which Egypt has been negotiating since 1992, was signed in November 2000. Noting that the EU is Egypt's main trading partner, representing approximately 40 percent of its total foreign trade, this agreement is expected to boost Egyptian exports.

In addition, being a member of the Common Market of Eastern and Southern African Countries (COMESA), Egypt benefits from a 90 percent customs exemption in trade with 21 African states on the establishment of COMESA Free Trade Area by the end of October 2000.

The possibility of having blue chip companies in COMESA countries list on the Egyptian Exchange by virtue of its being the largest and most modern exchange in the region was one of the key themes discussed in "COMESA 2000: the Emerging African Market," the first international conference held in Cairo at the end of February 2000.

Egypt has also signed free trade agreements with some Arab countries including Lebanon, Morocco, and Jordan, which will gradually abolish custom duties to reach zero percent by the year 2008.

EGYPTIAN PRIVATIZATION PROGRAM VIA THE STOCK MARKET

The Egyptian government is undertaking steps to accelerate the privatization process by encouraging the participation of the private sector and foreign investors in many areas. The recent acquisitions of large multinationals to Egyptian companies in the cement, banking and financial services sectors confirm this move. To date there are 53 public companies that were privatized via the stock market with sales proceeds amounting to LE 7 billion, approximately 50 percent of the total proceeds earned by the government from its privatization program. The remaining 50 percent proceeds were realized from privatization of public enterprises using other privatization methods such as sale to anchor investors, Employee Share Ownership Plans, asset sales, leasing, and liquidation.

Privatization of utility firms that were previously owned by the government is expected to improve the efficiency of these sectors as well as increase the market capitalization (currently at around 34 percent of GDP) and the depth of the stock market.

CAIRO & ALEXANDRIA STOCK EXCHANGES (CASE)

Overview

CASE is both the engine of Egypt's capital market growth, as well as being the most technologically advanced institution within the capital markets in the region and consequently a model that exchanges are likely to follow.

Egypt's Stock Exchange has two locations: Cairo and Alexandria. The same chairman and board of directors govern both. The Alexandria Stock Exchange was officially established in 1888 followed by Cairo in 1903. The two exchanges were very active in the 1940s and the Egyptian Stock Exchange ranked fifth in the world. Nevertheless, the central planning and socialist policies adopted in the mid-1950s led to demise of activity on the stock exchange, which remained dormant between 1961 and 1992.

In 1991, the Egyptian government started an economic reform and restructuring program. The move toward a free-market economy has been remarkably swift and the process of deregulation and privatization has stimulated the stock market activity. Between 1992 and 1996, the Capital Market Authority (CMA) played an instrumental role in initiating and leading the effort for the revival of the Egyptian stock market. Capital Market Law 95/1992 laid the regulatory framework within which financial intermediaries such as brokers, venture capital firms, underwriters, and fund managers can operate.

The principal method utilized to activate the stock market was through public offerings of state-owned enterprises and which provided around LE 15 billion as sales proceeds to the Treasury. Nevertheless, beginning of 1997, large family private sector companies in Egypt started tapping the stock market as a venue of raising capital and were able to raise LE 4 billion since then, which reflects the increasingly important role played by the stock market in the Egyptian economy.

Main Market Indicators

By the end of December 2000, 1,076 companies were listed on the stock exchange with a market capitalization of LE 121 billion (US$1 = 3.85 LE). The top 100 listed companies accounted for 90 percent of the value and volume traded in 2000. Furthermore, the annual traded value increased sharply from LE 233.9 million in 1991 to LE 54 billion in 2000, of which foreign participants represented 20 percent.

From Table 5.1, it can be viewed that the volume of securities traded increased slightly by 3 percent, from 1.07 billion shares in 1999 to 1.10 billion shares in 2000. Furthermore, the total value of shares traded rose

Table 5.1
Main Market Indicators for the Egyptian Market over the Period 1991–2000

Main Indicators	1991	1992	1993	1994	1995	1996	1997	1998	1999	2000
Volume of listed securities	19.2	20.7	13.7	29.3	43.7	170.5	286.7	440.3	841.1	1,029.3
Volume of unlisted securities	3.5	8.9	4.0	30.5	28.5	37.2	85.8	130.5	233.0	78.7
Total volume of listed & unlisted securities (million)	**22.7**	**29.6**	**17.7**	**59.8**	**72.2**	**207.7**	**372.5**	**570.8**	**1,074.0**	**1,108.0**
Value traded (listed securities)	233.9	371.4	274.9	1,214.0	2,294.2	8,769.2	20,282.4	18,500.6	32,851.0	45,789.10
Value traded (unlisted securities)	193.9	225.3	293.7	1,343.2	1,555.2	2,198.3	3,937.4	4,863.4	6,235.1	8,223.31
Total value traded (LE million)	**427.8**	**596.7**	**568.6**	**2,557.2**	**3,849.4**	**10,967.5**	**24,219.8**	**23,364.0**	**39,086.1**	**54,012.4**
Average monthly value traded (listed securities)	19.5	30.9	22.9	101.2	191.2	730.8	1,690.2	1,541.7	2,737.6	3,815.8
Average monthly value traded (unlisted securities)	16.1	18.8	24.5	111.9	129.6	183.2	328.1	405.3	519.6	685.3
Total (LE million)	**35.6**	**49.7**	**47.4**	**213.1**	**320.8**	**914.0**	**2,018.3**	**1,947.0**	**3,257.2**	**4,501.0**
Number of transactions (Listed securities)	9,626	11,648	11,184	51,862	260,964	2,279,521	1,142,510	672,649	892,291	1,276,209
Number of transactions (unlisted securities)	679	855	750	42,880	208,651	36,843	82,841	14,564	12,909	10,102
Total number of transactions	**10,305**	**12,503**	**11,934**	**94,742**	**469,615**	**2,316,364**	**1,225,351**	**687,213**	**905,200**	**1,286,311**
Number of listed companies	627	656	674	700	746	649	654	870	1033	1076
Number of traded companies	218	239	264	300	352	354	416	551	663	659
Average monthly traded companies	79	78	84	91	113	129	168	218	243	232
Market capitalization end of year (LE million)	**8,845**	**10,845**	**12,807**	**14,480**	**27,420**	**48,086**	**70,873**	**82,232**	**112,331**	**120,982**
Turnover Ratio(%)	**2.64**	**3.42**	**2.15**	**8.38**	**8.37**	**18.24**	**28.62**	**22.50**	**29.24**	**37.85**

* Securities include stocks, bonds, and mutual funds listed on the Exchange.

Market Capitalization = number of listed shares × market price end of year.

Turnover Ratio = Traded Value of Listed Securities / End of Year Market Capitalization.

by 38 percent, from LE 39 billion in 1998 to LE 54 billion in 2000. The number of transactions also increased by 42 percent from 905,200 in 1999 to 1,286,311 in 2000. Comparing the main indicators of the Egyptian market over the period 1997–2000, one can view the notable surge in all indicators.

Market Instruments

In Egypt, the main instruments traded on the exchange comprise common stocks (1,076), preferred stock (15), government bonds (27), corporate bonds (32), and two close-ended funds as of end of December 2000.

Egypt versus Emerging Markets

As of the end of December 2000, Egypt had very attractive equity valuations. With a very low price/earnings (P/E) multiple of 6.8 times and a very high dividend yield of 19 percent, Egypt ranked first compared to other emerging markets tracked by the IFC such as Greece, Morocco, Mexico, Poland, China, and so on. Hence the Egyptian market stands out as a very good opportunity for equity investments.

Table 5.2 presents the yield on 91-days Egyptian treasury bills as of the end of December 2000, which was 9.09 percent. Compared to an earnings yield of 14.62 percent for the Egyptian market on the same date, results in a positive yield gap of 5.53 percent, which ranks second, when compared to a selected group of 17 emerging markets.

Market Participants

Currently, 149 brokerage firms are operating in Cairo and Alexandria. In addition, 21 local funds (19 open-ended and 2 closed-ended) are currently operating in Egypt and 10 Egyptian offshore funds. Other institutions also flourished. Thirty portfolio management firms, 28 underwriters, 10 venture capital firms, and 6 rating companies are currently operating in Egypt.

Trading System

The trading system in the Cairo & Alexandria Stock Exchanges (the exchange) witnessed a gradual evolution from an open outcry system prior to 1992 to an automated order-driven system. As a result of the growth in business volume, the exchange has procured the second phase of automation, a tried, proven, and scalable system conforming to international standards and state-of-the-art technology. The signing of the contract with the

Table 5.2
The Yield Gap for a Selected Group of Emerging Markets (End of December 2000)

Rank	Emerging Markets	91 day TB rate % End of December 2000	Earnings Yield % End of December 2000	Yield Gap % End of December 2000
1	Mexico	1.67	7.69	6.02
2	Egypt*	9.09	14.62	5.53
3	Morocco	5.70	8.38	2.68
4	South Africa	7.08	9.35	2.27
5	Bahrain	6.38	7.73	1.35
6	SriLanka	17.78	19.08	1.30
7	Russia	27.59	26.53	-1.06
8	India	8.77	5.96	-2.81
9	Oman	4.94	0.68	-4.26
10	Nigeria	13.22	8.86	-4.36
11	Hungary	11.67	7.02	-4.65
12	Phillipines	12.88	3.82	-9.06
13	Argentina	10.00	-0.11	-10.11
14	Czech Republic	5.40	-6.11	-11.51
15	Poland	16.75	5.17	-11.58
16	Malaysia	13.70	1.09	-12.61
17	Thailand	2.33	-14.53	-16.86
18	Slovakia	7.80	-20.70	-28.50

Earnings yield is the reciprocal of the P/E ratio.
* Earnings Yield is based on the 100 most active companies only.
The 91 day TB rate is the interest earned on the 91 day treasury bill. A positive yield gap means that earnings on stocks is higher than interest earned on TB. A negative yield gap means that earnings on stocks is less than interest earned on TB.

Canadian Software Company, EFA, in May 1998, provides the exchange with a new trading, clearing, and settlement system. The trading component was fully operational by mid May 2001.

Clearing, Settlement, and Central Depository

Miser Clearing, Settlement, and Depository (MCSD) is a private company that handles the clearing and settlement operations in Egypt. The company's main shareholders include Cairo & Alexandria Stock Exchanges—35 percent, brokers—15 percent, and banks—15 percent. Since MCSD was established, the securities market in Egypt has been moving toward a dematerialized environment, with stocks transferred directly between the accounts of member firms of the depository. Shares traded in the Egyptian market can either be physical or in scripless form. Settlement for physical shares is T + 4 and for the dematerialized shares is T + 3. A guarantee fund was established by MCSD and started operations on January 2000. Since its operation, the number of unsettled transactions was negligible.

Market Surveillance and Investor Protection

The exchange undertook serious steps in order to enhance investor's protection in the market. The development of an advanced surveillance system has been completed, which will avail the exchange with real-time online functionality equipped with a complete range of alerts and freezes on the order level as well as information from listed companies for offline surveillance.

In addition, the exchange established an information dissemination company, which will ensure that news on stock prices is reflected in a rapid and efficient manner. The company, which was established in August 1999, is expected to start dissemination by the end of 2001.

Capital Market Outlook

Despite the fact that Egypt, similar to many developed and emerging markets has been negatively affected by some of the global and local adverse macroeconomic factors in 1998, the economic outlook remains positive. In July 2000, Morgan Stanley announced that Egypt will be included in its MSCI free indices as of the end of May 2001.

Also the United Kingdom has identified Egypt as one of the top 10 emerging markets, thus encouraging investors to invest in the Egyptian market. Many investment and brokerage houses are operating now in Egypt, such as HSBC–James Capel, Morgan Stanley, Citibank, Fleming, and lately, ABN-AMRO, which acquired a local brokerage firm. These international investment banks have recommended that their investors should increase their investment in Egypt, reflecting their positive outlook for the future of the Egyptian market.

It is expected that the performance of the stock market in Egypt will be enhanced given the strong economic fundamentals, the increase in foreign flow of funds, the increase in mergers and acquisitions, the planned listings of more Egyptian GDRs abroad, and the upcoming privatization of utilities, all of which will have a favorable impact on the market.

EGYPT IS POISED TO BE THE LEADING FINANCIAL CENTER IN THE MENA REGION

The Middle East and Africa do not have a viable international financial center. Though Bahrain and Lebanon are trying hard to be financial centers, in reality their success is doubtful. The developments that occurred in the 1990s such as the Gulf War, the waning influence of the Organization for Petroleum Exporting Countries (OPEC), the staggering peace process between Israel and the remaining Middle Eastern countries, besides the recent and continuous modernization efforts in the Egyptian Exchange, all set Egypt to be the leading financial center in the MENA.

Fundamentally, both the timing of the reforms and the size of the domestic market have advantaged Egypt, and its stock market has been able to activate as a means of perpetuating those reforms.

Meanwhile, other markets in the region have failed to match Egypt's pace, breadth, and dynamism. This is due to Egypt's strategic location, with Cairo being at the center of the Middle East and North Africa, besides its demographics and market volume.

Egypt is the largest country in the region in terms of population (66 million) and market capitalization as of the end of December 2000 stood at US$31.4 billion. The companies listed on the exchange include diversified range of industries including telecoms, financials, cement, food, building, tourism, pharmaceuticals, and so on. Egypt has no restrictions on foreign investment and no taxes on capital gains, dividends, or repatriation of earnings. Foreign investors enjoy full market access and suffer no restrictions on capital mobility or convertibility and a steady inflow of Foreign Direct Investment (FDI) is expected to continue in forthcoming years, as Egypt was included in the Morgan Stanley Free Indices Series as of the end of May 2001.

Steps Undertaken by the Cairo & Alexandria Stock Exchange That Reflect Its Readiness to Undertake Globalization

When the exchange started its modernization program in June 1997, it defined its mission and objectives clearly, set its priorities carefully, and then proceeded to accomplish them in a systematic and methodical manner. As of today, the exchange has successfully achieved many of its set goals and is coming closer to accomplishing others.

Technology

A modern and robust technology infrastructure is being implemented at the exchange to complement the advanced market solution acquired by the exchange. This includes the installation of a state-of-the-art telecommunications and networking infrastructure covering local and wide area networks and linking all market entities to the exchange.

This solution allows for the expansion of the number of remote trading terminals ensuring wide coverage and accessibility of the trading system for information broadcast as well as for trading accessibility. This network represents the backbone for the spread of trading to other locations all over Egypt. The exchange has also started the implementation of institutionwide information systems, to equip the exchange with intelligent decision support and strategic planning tools and information.

The exchange embarked on, and successfully completed, an ambitious project to restore and renovate the building housing the Cairo Stock Exchange, furnishing it with the latest technology trading floor, which was inaugurated mid-May 2001.

Trading System

Perhaps the most important achievement of the exchange was the acquisition and modification of the new automated trading system, EFA. The revision of the trading rules have been finalized, the testing of the trading system is close to completion, and it went live in mid-May 2001.

Recognizing the importance of the role of the Egyptian market in the region, EFA has decided to establish a support office in Cairo to service the exchange in Egypt, as well as the regional markets, Saudi Arabia, Bahrain, and Kuwait, using the same EFA system. This presence will not only guarantee support for the system being implemented, but it will also ensure a complete and sustained transfer of know-how and technology to the Egyptian market and will also enhance the opportunities for regional cooperation.

Investor Protection

One of the exchange's main objectives and priorities is protecting its investors. The exchange has approached this objective along two axes: a monitoring and regulatory axis and an information dissemination axis. On the monitoring and regulatory side, an advanced surveillance system has been developed. This integrated, open, and expandable system uses the latest data warehousing technologies that provide for real-time online surveillance functionality and furnish a wealth of information for offline surveillance. To further protect investors' interests, the guarantee fund that ensures timely settlement of transactions was recently implemented. Finally, the exchange has recently started developing an alternative dispute resolution (ADR) system to solve disputes involving investors and brokerage firms in a swift and less costly manner than traditional courts.

Investor Education and Creating an Investment Culture

To increase the awareness of the general public and the media of the significant role that a stock market plays and the different products on the market, the exchange has undertaken a few programs and has planned several more to be implemented next year. Last year, the exchange offered training programs and seminars to members of the press and management of listed companies. The leadership of the exchange also participated in local and international seminars, conferences, and television programs addressing the same issues. In addition, the exchange started publishing its educational leaflets explaining in simple terms the fundamentals of investment in the stock market.

The exchange undertook a large market study of the retail investors to have a better understanding of their needs and started responding to them. The exchange is also focusing on the next generation by designing programs for schools and colleges to educate students on the role of the stock market using instructional guides such as simulation games and videos.

Information Disclosure

With respect to information dissemination, the exchange has established a firm devoted to this purpose. It is expected to start transmitting information via satellite-based systems and television broadcasting by the end of 2001. In the first phase of the project, the exchange will focus on disseminating financial, economic, and company information in Egypt and will expand the range of dissemination in the second phase to the MENA region. Other achievements that demonstrate the exchange's serious commitment to information dissemination are the setting up of a Web site in December 1998 and the establishment of an investors' club (in May 1999) supplied with the latest market research and the continuous stream of publications produced by the Research and Market Development Department at the exchange. A second investors' club will be inaugurated in Alexandria by the end of 2000.

In parallel, in October 1997, the Ministry of Economy published the Egyptian Accounting Standards, similar to International Accounting Standards (IAS), requiring joint-stock companies to prepare their future accounts based on IAS, a move that will enhance the quality of information issued by listed companies.

Listing and Membership Rules

Over the past few months, the exchange has been devoting more time to the development of new listing rules. The rules are being formulated to ensure the lack of ambiguity in requirements for listing in the different schedules. This will help listed firms meet the requirements and, more importantly, will provide investors with an understanding of the difference in perceived risks and returns associated with each of the schedules. High standards have been set for the listing rules in certain schedules to provide blue chip companies the option of cross-listing in other leading stock exchanges. The market regulator is currently reviewing the new listing rules. Also, the exchange, with the assistance of international experts, has drafted a set of membership rules to ensure that they conform to international standards.

Regional Integration

As it is becoming more and more evident that stock exchanges will require some form of integration to enhance efficiency, liquidity, and to remain competitive, the chairman of the Cairo & Alexandria Stock Exchange has discussed avenues for cooperation with exchange leaders in the Persian Gulf area and Saudi Arabia.

This campaign will continue throughout the MENA region and CO-MESA countries. Equipped with an EFA trading system and its powerful market solution that is shared by several markets in the region, the exchange in Egypt is in a favorable position to play a leading regional role in the medium term. In the short term, the exchange will encourage listings of blue chip global issuers whether located in the United States or Arab and African countries on the Cairo & Alexandria Stock Exchange.

International Advisory Committee

To ensure that the Cairo & Alexandria Stock Exchanges remain abreast of all new development practices, policies, and ideas relating to capital markets, an international advisory committee was established in early 1999. The committee is made up of internationally renowned investment bankers, economists, financiers, and investors. It provides continuous guidance to the management of the exchange and feedback on its policies. It also sheds light on problems perceived by the international community and discusses possible solutions.

CONCLUSION

The chapter discussed the recent changes in the globalization of capital markets. It realized that the traditional role and activities of world exchanges must change in order to compete in the era of globalization. Exchanges that will survive in the twenty-first century are those that are committed to investing more in technology, providing liquidity for both institutional and retail investors in a fast, fair, well-regulated manner and at the lowest possible costs. Reviewing the Egyptian market, it was shown that Egypt's economic reform as well as privatization programs had a positive impact on the growth of its capital market. Furthermore, the Egyptian Stock Exchange has embarked on an aggressive modernization plan, which not only sets Egypt as a leading market in the Middle East North Africa region but also prepares the exchange for the globalization era.

NOTE

This paper was submitted for presentation at the First International Conference on Banking and Finance, Kuala Lumpur, Malaysia, August 2000. It was also submitted for presentation at the eighth Global Finance Conference, Los Angeles, California, in April 2001. The author would appreciate that the copyright of this conference chapter be respected and that no part of it is cited without the author's permission. The author presented the chapter in both conferences. The views and findings expressed in this chapter are those of the author and do not reflect the opinion of Cairo & Alexandria Stock Exchanges. The author retains all responsibility for content. Any error is her own.

REFERENCES

Cairo & Alexandria Stock Exchanges. (2000a). *Annual Factbook* (September). Cairo & Alexandria, Egypt.
———. (2000b). *Financial Securities* (December).
———. (2001). *Statistical Highlights* (January).
Huband, M. (1999). *Egypt Leading the Way: Institution Building and Stability in the Financial System.* Euromoney Publications. New York.
National Association for Securities Dealers. (1998). *The Market of Markets.* Annual report.
New York Stock Exchange. (1998). *The Technology of Leadership.* Annual report. New York.
Ruggiero, R. (1996). *Managing a World of Free Trade and Deep Interdependence.* Buenos Aires: Argentinean Council on Foreign Affairs.
———. (1998). *A Global System for the Next Fifty Years.* London: Royal Institute of International Affairs at Chatham House.
United States Securities and Exchange Commission, Fifth Annual International Institute for Securities Market Development. (1995). *Securities Market Development for Policy Makers.* Washington, D.C.: IFC.

INTERVIEWS

The author conducted two interviews with regard to the future of stock exchanges with:
William Zima, Director, Nasdaq International, December 1, 1999.
George Sofianos, Vice President, International & Research, New York Stock Exchange, December 2, 1999.

CHAPTER 6

Optimization, Temporary Inefficiencies, and Profitability of Technical Trading Rules in Currency Markets

Dennis Olson

INTRODUCTION

Beginning with Meese and Rogoff (1983), several studies have shown that the random walk forecasts exchange rate movements about as well as structural forecasting models. Further evidence by Meese and Rose (1990) and Brooks (1997) suggests that more complicated nonlinear statistical models do not improve upon point forecasts or the directional accuracy of the random walk model. A conflicting strand of literature starting with Sweeney (1986) has shown that technical trading rules can be used to earn abnormal returns and "beat the foreign exchange market." Subsequent work by Levich and Thomas (1993), Neely (1997), and LeBaron (1999) suggests that technical trading rules may provide abnormal returns of 5 percent to 10 percent annually, even after transaction costs. One reason for the apparently contradictory results is that studies supporting the random walk and market efficiency have generally focused upon point forecasts, whereas studies finding abnormal returns to technical trading rules are based on less restrictive up-down forecasts. Nevertheless, even within the group of studies using technical trading rules there is considerable discrepancy between results. In contrast to rather large forecasting profits reported by Sweeney (1986) and other authors, Lee and Mathur (1996) report that no significant trading rule profits are available in European spot cross-rate currencies.

Differences in the reported profitability of trading rules between studies arise from alternative periods considered, different currencies tested, and choice of trading rule. Another possible source of abnormal returns may be a form of optimization. By testing enough trading rules for a limited number of currencies and reporting results in-sample or for a short out-of-sample period, some rules may randomly yield large abnormal returns over any given data set. To limit the impact of optimization and the possibility of generalizing from small samples, this chapter tests the profitability of technical trading rules over a broader range of currencies (28) for a longer time period (30 years) than considered in previous work. Specifically, moving average technical trading rules are optimized in-sample using data prior to 1990 for daily U.S. dollar exchange rates for 28 foreign currencies. Then, profitability is examined out of sample for the decade of the 1990s. If trading rule profits were as high in the 1990s as in previous years, market inefficiency would be suggested. Instead, out-of-sample profitability of the best in-sample rules declines and this chapter further examines the reasons for this result. The assumption is that if there exist other moving average trading rules in the 1990s that yield profits similar to those found by optimizing trading rule profits on the pre-1990 data, then optimization may have contributed to the apparent success of trading rule strategies in the past. Instead, if all trading rules yield lower profit in the 1990s, then the smaller returns from the best in-sample rules may be attributable to improved efficiency in the foreign exchange markets.

LITERATURE REVIEW

For many years, dealers and traders in the foreign exchange markets have extensively used technical analysis to help predict the future. For example, Lui and Mole (1998) report that 85 percent of Hong Kong foreign exchange dealers rely on both technical and fundamental analysis to forecast exchange rate movements. They tend to prefer technical to fundamental analysis for short-run forecasts of exchange rate movements, and moving averages and other trend following systems are the most popular technical analysis techniques. Since technical analysis is so important to finance practitioners, a substantial body of literature has evolved showing both the successes and failures of various technical trading rules. If exchange rates follow a random walk, technical analysis has no value. Also, even if exchange rates move nonrandomly, and if currency markets are perfectly efficient, technical analysis will not be of value. However, if there is some degree of predictability, technical analysis may work and it may be possible to earn abnormal returns. That is, it may be possible to "beat the market." In exchange rate forecasting this means achieving returns above 0 percent.

Market Efficiency Group of Authors

In one of the first articles testing for predictability in exchange rate, Meese and Rogoff (1983) report that structural exchange rate models forecast no better than the random walk. Subsequent work by Meese and Rose (1990) and Brooks (1997) shows that nonlinear models do not improve forecast accuracy for point forecasts, although they suggest that nonlinear models may be useful for variance or kurtosis forecasting. Similarly, Dacco and Satchell (1999) show that regime-switching models generally underperform the random walk in out-of-sample tests based upon the mean square error criterion. They suggest that a possible reason for poor performance over long horizons is that structural changes occur unpredictably approximately every three to five years.

Risk Explanation Group of Authors

Cheung and Wong (1997) test filter rules on four Asian currencies and find that technical traders could earn profits of up to 10 percent annually, before transaction costs. They argue that transaction costs and adjustments for risk reduce these profits to a statistically insignificant level. Similarly, Kho (1996) examines weekly data for three currency futures contracts for the U.S. dollar relative to the British pound, the German mark, and the Japanese yen from 1980 to 1991. In the absence of transaction costs or risk adjustments, moving average trading rule profits for buys and sells range from 5.8 percent to 13.6 percent annually. Such profits are generally higher than those found in other studies. However, after adding transaction costs and using a bootstrap methodology plus a Generalized Auto Regressive Conditional Heteroscedasticity-Modified (GARCH-M) model to obtain a risk premium, Kho (1996) concludes that most of the apparent abnormal returns can be explained as a premium for bearing time varying risk. He shows that periods of higher returns are associated with periods of greater volatility and that any profits remaining after adjusting for risk are statistically insignificant.

Abnormal Profits and/or Market Inefficiency Group of Authors

Dooley and Shafer (1983) provided the first rigorous empirical evidence that technical analysis could be profitably used to trade currencies. They used filter rules ranging from 1 percent to 25 percent for nine different currencies during the period from 1973 to 1981. For this rule, an investor or trader buys the foreign currency if it rises by some specified amount, say 1 percent, from a previous low. They sell the foreign currency if drops by some specified percentage from a previous high. Filters of 1 percent to 5 percent were the most successful, with annual percentage gains reaching as high as 17.28 percent for the Japanese yen during the second half of their data period. Sweeney (1986) confirmed the profitability of filter rules for 10 currencies for 1973–1980. Unlike most other studies, Sweeney (1986) only took long positions and no short positions in the foreign currency. Again the smaller filters, from 0.5 percent to 2 percent were the most profitable and profits were significantly different from zero in about one-third of the cases considered. Since successful filter rule strategies would trade quite frequently, profits would be sensitive to transaction costs. To see whether the inclusion of transaction costs substantially reduces profitability of technical trading rules, one can refer to work by Levich and Thomas (1993). Their results for five currencies over the period 1976–1990 suggest a level of trading activity that would incur transaction costs of 1.62 percent to 2.60 percent per year. After inclusion of transaction costs, trading rule profits exist for both filter rules and moving average crossover rules of about 4 percent to 7 percent annually for trading the British pound, Japanese yen, German mark, and the Swiss franc. Profits for moving average rules were about one percentage point higher than for filter rules; however, the inclusion of transaction costs essentially eliminated the possibility of successfully trading the Canadian dollar. By using bootstrapping methods they also showed that the trading rule profits generated for five of the six currencies were unusual or significantly different from what would be produced randomly. Similarly, Neely (1997) obtains abnormal profits of up to 6.4 percent with filter rules and 7.5 percent with a 50-day moving average rule trading the deutsche mark over a 23-year period.

A potential problem with studies reporting large abnormal returns to trading rules is that sometimes the tests are conducted over an entire sample, rather than choosing the best rule for some initial period and then testing that rule out-of-sample. To address this problem, Neely, Weller, and Dittmar (1997) use genetic algorithms to select from among a large set of possible technical trading rules (with moving average techniques playing a leading role in the successful choice set of rules) for six different exchange rate series. The period of 1974–1980 is used to train and select the optimal trading rules, while 1981–1995 is used as an out-of-sample test period. Out-of-sample mean abnormal returns range from 1.02 percent for trading the pound versus the Swiss franc rate, up to 6.05 percent for the U.S. dollar/deutsche mark exchange rate. They find that these abnormal returns cannot be attributed to bearing systematic risk. Similarly, Neely and Weller (1998) find significant excess profit for trading three of four European Monetary System currencies over the period 1986–1996. Again there is no evidence that abnormal returns of 0.06 percent up to 2.75 percent annually are attributable to bearing systematic risk. These two studies indicate that trading rules may be more profitably applied to U.S. dollar exchange rates than to Japanese or European cross-rates.

Lee and Mathur (1996) argue that technical analysis generally provides better forecasts of future exchange rates than economic or fundamental models. Nevertheless, they find that moving average trading rules are only marginally profitable for six European spot cross-rates during the period 1988–1993. In fact, even within sample these profits are not statistically different from zero. Such results conflict with Szakmary and Mathur (1997), who used the same moving average trading rule on tests of profitability between the U.S. dollar and the British pound, the Japanese yen, the German mark, and the Swiss franc. Hence, there appear to be trading rule profitability opportunities between the dollar and the European currencies, but not among the European currencies.

LeBaron (1999) obtains trading rule abnormal profits of 7 percent to 10 percent before transaction costs for the Japanese yen and the deutsche mark, 1979–1992 (1.5–2% less after transaction costs). Some previous studies have been criticized for ignoring interest rate differentials between countries, but his work shows that inclusion of these differentials slightly increases the profitability of trading rules. Furthermore, LeBaron (1999) shows that risk is not a major issue in explaining abnormal returns because the Sharpe ratio is larger for the trading rule strategy than for buying and holding stocks.

Summarizing the different strands of literature, the random walk generally outperforms more sophisticated point forecasting models, while technical trading rules involving filters and moving averages have been shown to earn abnormal returns in some studies. Success of trading rules depends upon the currency selected, the time period chosen, and in a few instances it arises from optimizing rules over an entire data set without using a holdout sample. The next two sections use in-sample optimization and an out-of-sample hold out period to address the potential impact of optimization versus increased efficiency on trading rule profits.

DATA AND METHODOLOGY

Daily exchange rates for 28 currencies with the U.S. dollar are obtained from the U.S. Federal Reserve Web site for the period January 4, 1971, to December 31, 1999. The data includes all freely floating exchange rates available electronically at this Web site that have more than 10 years of daily data. Hence, currencies tied to the U.S. dollar (e.g., the Hong Kong dollar) and currencies that have been replaced with a new version of the same currency (e.g., the Mexican peso) are not included in the sample. The exchange rate series represent indirect rates from a U.S. investor's viewpoint, and show the number of U.S. dollars that are needed to purchase one unit of the foreign currency. The mean daily percentage return (Ret$_t$) for any currency is 100 times the log difference of daily currency prices, or

$$\text{Ret}_t = 100 * \ln (P_t - P_{t-1}), \tag{6.1}$$

where P_t and P_{t-1} denote today's and yesterday's daily spot price for the exchange rate series. For each currency, the in-sample period for optimizing moving average trading rules extends from the beginning of the data series until December 31, 1989. The out-of-sample testing period is the ten years from 1990–1999, which consists of 2,516 daily observations.

Descriptive Statistics

Panels A, B, and C of Table 6.1 provide descriptive statistics for the in-sample period and represent the information that an investor would have

Table 6.1a
Description of Data—*Panel A: Independent Floating Currencies*

	AD	CD	DK	GD	JY	NK	NZD	SAR	SK	SF	UKP
Data period	1975– 1999	1971– 1999	1971– 1999	1981– 1999	1971– 1999	1971– 1999	1971– 1999	1979 – 1999	1971– 1999	1971– 1999	1971– 1999
Sample size	6,274	7,277	7,277	4,704	7,267	7,271	7,256	5,044	7,271	7,272	7,272
Mean (in %)	— 0.0138	— 0.0029	0.0021	— 0.0496	0.0192	0.0016	— 0.0133	— 0.0442	0.0039	0.0217	— 0.0083
Std. Dev. (in %)	0.640	0.227	0.661	0.837	0.597	0.553	0.752	1.065	0.572	0.740	0.596
ρ_1	0.030	0.069	-0.056	-0.037	0.043	-0.031	-0.009	-0.007	-0.41	0.026	0.060
ρ_2	-0.047	0.002	0.018	-0.007	0.017	-0.011	-0.038	0.011	-0.017	0.002	0.004
LBP	15.65	32.26	23.35	6.04	23.81	9.52	10.25	11.54	12.83	7.07	25.36

Note: In-sample summary statistics for the log of the first difference of the daily exchange rate between the country listed and the U.S. dollar. Rate is measured in U.S. dollars per unit of Australian dollar (AD), Canadian dollar (CD), Danish kroner (DK), Greek drachma (GD), Japanese yen (JY), Norwegian kroner (NK), New Zealand dollar (NZD), South African rand (SAR), Swedish kronor (SK), Swiss franc (SF), or U.K. pound (UKP).

Table 6.1b
Description of Data—*Panel B: Euroland Currencies*

	AS	BF	FM	FF	GM	IP	IL	NG	PE	SP
Data period	1971– 1998	1971– 1998	1971– 1998	1971– 1998	1971– 1998	1971– 1998	1971– 1998	1971– 1998	1971– 1998	1971– 1998
Sample size	7,012	7,020	6,313	7,020	7,020	7,020	7,019	7,020	6,517	6,869
Mean (in %)	0.0164	0.0070	— 0.0029	— 0.0009	0.0162	0.0091	0.0149	0.0133	— 0.0402	0.0118
Std. Dev. (in %)	.755	.626	.568	.625	.641	.695	.567	.619	.803	.701
ρ_1	-.130	.019	-.049	.029	.030	-.112	.048	.022	-.155	-.046
ρ_2	.010	-.010	-.025	.000	-.006	.000	.009	.004	.024	.005
LBP	81.94	11.23	22.76	9.44	14.68	65.52	20.85	10.64	109.17	18.22

Note: In-sample summary statistics for the log of the first difference of the daily exchange rate between the country listed and the U.S. dollar. Rate is measured in U.S. dollars per unit of Austrian schilling (AS), Belgian franc (BF), Finnish markka (FM), French franc (FF), German mark (GM), Irish punt (IP), Italian lira (IL), Netherlands guilder, (NG), Portuguese ecsudo (PE), or Spanish peseta (SP).

Table 6.1c
Description of Data—*Panel C: Managed Float Asian Currencies*

	IR	MR	SD	SLR	SKW	TD	TB
Data period	1/3/73–1 0/15/99	1/5/71–9 /4/98	1/3/81–1 0/15/99	8/7/84–1 0/15/99	4/14/81– 10/15/99	2/22/84– 10/15/99	1/3/85–1 0/15/99
Sample size	6,764	6,919	4,768	3,507	4,653	3,702	3,690
Mean (in %)	-0.0176	0.0028	0.0042	-0.0349	-0.0004	0.0325	0.0046
Std. Dev. (in %)	0.513	0.562	0.310	0.335	0.094	0.171	0.475
ρ_1	-0.150	-0.318	-0.118	-0.381	0.116	0.255	-0.431
ρ_2	-0.013	0.003	-0.037	0.073	0.137	0.072	0.078
LBP	104.84	479.66	40.83	206.80	227.40	161.75	246.05

Note: In-sample summary statistics for the log of the first difference of the daily exchange rate between the country listed and the U.S. dollar. Rate is measured in U.S. dollars per unit of Indian rupee (IR), Malaysian ringitt (MR), Singapore dollar (SD), Sri Lankan rupee (SLR), South Korean won (SKW), Taiwan dollar (TD), or Thai baht (TB).

available at the beginning of the testing period. Panel A for independent floating currencies shows the exchange rates between the U.S. dollar and the Australian dollar (AD), Canadian dollar (CD), Danish kroner (DK), Greek drachma (GD), Norwegian kroner (NK), New Zealand dollar (NZD), South African rand (SAR), Swedish kronor (SK), Swiss franc (SF), and the UK pound (UKP). Each of these series contains over 20 years of daily data and for 8 of the 11 currencies, data is available from January 5, 1971, to December 31, 1999. The maximum numbers of observations are 7,277 for the Canadian dollar and Danish kroner. Other data series are shorter due to national holidays, suspension of trading, or data availability on a particular day. For example, data is not available for the Greek drachma prior to 1981 or for the South African rand prior to 1979. Also, periods of quasi-fixed rates are excluded, so data for the Australian dollar begins in 1975, rather than in 1971. The out-of-sample data set is 2,516 observations for all currencies.

Panel B presents descriptive statistics for the 10 European currencies that formed the euro on January 1, 1999. Daily data for the Austrian schilling (AS), Belgian franc (BF), Finnish markka (FM), French franc (FF), German mark (GM), Irish punt (IP), Italian lira (IL), Netherlands guilder (NG), Portuguese ecsudo (PE), and the Spanish peseta (SP) begin on January 5, 1971, and extend to December 31, 1998. The sample size for the Euroland currencies ranges from 6,313 for the Finnish markka to 7,020 for major currencies such as the German mark. The out-of-sample data set is 2,264 observations for all currencies.

Panel C describes the data for seven "managed float" Asian currencies: the Indian rupee (IR), Malaysian ringgitt (MR), Singapore dollar (SD), Sri Lankan rupee (SLR), South Korean won (SKW), Taiwan dollar (TD), and the Thai baht (TB). These exchange rate series contain fewer observations than those in the previous panels because the currencies have experienced periods of fixed or quasi-fixed rates with the U.S. dollar or other currencies. For example, the Singapore government followed a policy of maintaining an indirect link with a basket of currencies (the foremost of which was the U.S. dollar) during the 1970s and early 1980s. The new Taiwan dollar, which began trading in 1984, was only allowed to float within a 2.25 percent band around the official exchange rate with the U.S. dollar until April of 1989. Also, Malaysia began imposing capital controls in 1994 that effectively reduced exchange rate movements from 1994 to 1998. A more detailed discussion of the institutional features of the Asian currencies is presented in Cheung and Wong (1997). Since the Asian currencies have been moving from a managed to float to a more freely floating status over time, profitable trading rules from earlier years do not work in later years. These exchange rate series may not provide a fair test for trading rule profits, but results are presented for comparison with the other currencies.

In Panel A, the mean daily return is near zero across all currencies. It ranges from –0.0496 percent for the German mark to 0.0217 percent for the Swiss franc. Standard deviations range from 0.227 percent for the Canadian dollar to 1.065 percent for the South African rand. For most currencies, standard deviation is near 0.6 percent. Many exchange rate return series exhibit negative skewness and all exhibit significant excess kurtosis. As a result, the Jarque-Bera test (not presented in Table 6.1) rejects normality at the 1 percent confidence level for all 28 currencies. The augmented Dickey-Fuller test (also not presented) rejects nonstationarity at the 1 percent confidence level for all 28 currencies. Thus, all of the return series change considerably over time, making forecasting difficult.

Autocorrelations for the previous five trading days (only ρ_1 and ρ_2 presented) are small but persistent for most currencies. The Ljung-Box-Pierce (LBP) statistic generally rejects (at the 5% significance level) the null hypothesis of no autocorrelations in the first five lags of most returns series in Panel A and for all of the currencies in Panels B and C. (Values for LBP above 12.33 and 9.83 represent rejections at the 1% and 5% significance levels.) Hence, autocorrelations are significant for most currencies and there exists the possibility that trading rules can be devised to take advantage of statistical patterns in past data. Nevertheless, as shown in the next section, high daily autocorrelations need not lead to profitability of trading rules out-of-sample. Perhaps the best candidate currencies with relatively large values for ρ_1 and ρ_2 are the Canadian dollar, the Japanese yen, the UK pound, and the Italian lira. Even larger values are found in Panel C for the Taiwan dollar and South Korean won, but as noted earlier, caution must be exercised because these currencies have been moving toward a more freely floating status. Similarly, the large negative values of p_1 for the Thai baht, Sri Lankan rupee, and Malaysian ringitt in Panel C, which reflect government actions to maintain a managed float and reverse price changes tending to move out of a narrow band, need not mean that antitrending short-term trading rules will be profitable out-of-sample.

Hurst Exponents

For technical analysis to be useful, past prices should influence current prices. This need not occur in a simple linear pattern that would be identified by examining lags of autocorrelations. The Hurst exponent is one possible technique for discovering a nonrandom, nonlinear long-memory process in exchange rates. The Hurst exponent (H) and rescaled range analysis represent a slight modification of the theory of Brownian motion. The range (R), or distance covered by a random particle undergoing collisions from all sides, is directly proportional to the square root of time (T), or:

$$R = k*T^{.5}. \tag{6.2}$$

For rescaled range analysis (R/S)

$$R/S = k*N^H, \tag{6.3}$$

where R/S = rescaled range or range between high and low divided by standard deviation, N = number of observations (or a time index), and k is a constant that varies between data series. If H = 0.5, the time series is Brownian motion, or white noise, and it follows a random walk. If H < 0.5, the series is antipersistent, or pink noise, and it will reverse itself often. This type of series is seldom found in nature, or in financial data. Finally, if H > 0.5, the series is persistent, or black noise, and a variable that increases in one period is more likely to increase in the next period. The larger the value for H, the greater is the trending behavior of the series, and presumably the more predictable is the variable. Unfortunately, there is no rule for judging when a deviation away from H = 0.5 becomes important for traders. Also, as conditions change over long periods of time, H may not be well defined and it may be preferable to calculate H for shorter periods—perhaps for 1,000 days.

Table 6.2 presents Hurst exponents calculated over the past 1000 observations at the end of the years 1979, 1984, 1989, 1994, and 1998. Values for H at the end of 1989 represent values that an investor could examine at the beginning of the testing period. Other years are presented to show that H often fluctuates considerably between years. That is, currencies display varying degrees of predictability over time. An examination of the independent floating currencies at the end of 1989 suggests that trad-

Table 6.2a
Hurst Exponents at End of Year—*Panel A: Independent Floating Currencies*

	Hurst Exponent at end of year				
	1979	1984	1989	1994	1998
Australian dollar	0.609	0.636	0.609	0.555	0.573
Canadian dollar	0.543	0.602	0.519	0.594	0.540
Danish kroner	0.566	0.568	0.589	0.626	0.583
Greek drachma	ND	0.569	0.552	0.606	0.559
Japanese yen	0.641	0.595	0.611	0.570	0.618
New Zealand dollar	0.567	0.540	0.596	0.516	0.523
Norwegian kroner	0.594	0.601	0.585	0.615	0.529
South African rand	ND	0.618	0.619	0.545	0.597
Swedish kronor	0.585	0.518	0.557	0.623	0.550
Swiss franc	0.597	0.541	0.582	0.609	0.574
U.K. pound	0.661	0.574	0.580	0.625	0.521
Group Averages	0.596	0.578	0.581	0.589	0.561

Note: ND signifies no data. Hurst exponents for 28 currencies at the end of the year listed. The exponent is calculated using the previous 1000 days of data. Values near H = 0.5 indicate a random walk, H > 0.5 indicates persistent or trending behavior, and H < 0.5 shows antitrending behavior. The larger the value of H, the greater the degree of trending behavior during the previous four years.

Table 6.2b
Hurst Exponent at End of Year—*Panel B: Euroland Currencies*

	Hurst Exponent at end of year				
	1979	1984	1989	1994	1998
Austrian schilling	0.569	0.556	0.570	0.602	0.575
Belgian franc	0.593	0.551	0.588	0.603	0.571
Finnish markka	0.596	0.557	0.565	0.598	0.599
French franc	0.603	0.563	0.587	0.609	0.579
German mark	0.586	0.577	0.629	0.603	0.583
Irish punt	0.583	0.547	0.571	0.632	0.562
Italian lira	0.595	0.551	0.583	0.640	0.582
Netherlands guilder	0.592	0.586	0.591	0.605	0.577
Portuguese escudo	0.564	0.515	0.550	0.626	0.576
Spanish peseta	0.616	0.523	0.608	0.650	0.600
Group averages	0.591	0.553	0.584	0.617	0.580

Note: Hurst exponents for 28 currencies at the end of the year listed. The exponent is calculated using the previous 1,000 days of data. Values near H = 0.5 indicate a random walk, H > 0.5 indicates persistent or trending behavior, and H < 0.5 shows antitrending behavior. The larger the value of H, the greater the degree of trending behavior during the previous four years.

Table 6.2c
Hurst Exponents at End of Year—*Panel C: Managed Float Asian Currencies*

	Hurst Exponent at end of year				
	1979	1984	1989	1994	1998
Indian rupee	0.545	0.561	0.509	0.605	0.637
Malaysian ringitt	0.583	0.520	0.587	0.654	0.641
Singapore dollar	ND	0.551	0.619	0.608	0.5556
South Korean won	ND	ND	0.822	0.530	0.599
Sri Lankan rupee	ND	ND	0.667	0.657	0.423
Taiwan dollar	ND	ND	0.792	0.652	0.624
Thai baht	ND	ND	0.492	0.540	0.608
Group averages	.564	.544	0.641	0.607	0.584

Note: ND signifies no data. Hurst exponents for 28 currencies at the end of the year listed. The exponent is calculated using the previous 1,000 days of data. Values near $H = 0.5$ indicate a random walk, $H > 0.5$ indicates persistent or trending behavior, and $H < 0.5$ shows antitrending behavior. The larger the value of H, the greater the degree of trending behavior during the previous four years.

ing rules might be most profitably employed for the Australian dollar, the Japanese yen, and the South African rand. Within the European currencies, the German mark and the Spanish peseta appear to offer the most hope for trading strategies. The high values for H among the Asian currencies and the value of $H < 0.5$ for the Thai baht may or may not suggest profitable opportunities. These values show the obvious—that a managed float is somewhat predictable. Nevertheless, even for the independent floating currencies, high values for H need not guarantee trading rule profits. The exact nature of the persistent relationship may be complicated, or relationships that once existed may change over time. To somewhat anticipate results in the next section, note that H fluctuates considerably for most currencies after 1989. Looking at group averages for the freely floating currencies, H tends to increase between 1989 and 1994 and then decrease thereafter. Such fluctuations are not encouraging for the ongoing success of previously discovered successful trading rules.

Methodology

To address the impact of optimization, this study selects from a variety of trading rules during the in-sample estimation period and examines the performance of the best rule(s) during an out-of-sample testing period. All data up to December 31, 1989, is used to derive the best moving average trading rule for each currency. Profits are obtained from both long and short positions in the foreign currency. A long position involves holding one of the 28 foreign currencies and a short position means selling the foreign currency and holding U.S. dollars. The investor is assumed to be fully invested at all times and holds either foreign currency or the U.S. dollar. Interest earned on holding either currency is ignored. This creates a potential bias if interest rates are significantly different between countries, but Sweeney (1986) and LeBaron (1999) report that omission of interest rate differentials between countries has only a negligible impact on profitability of currency trading strategies. Since there are innumerable possible trading strategies, most chapters have focused upon a limited number of trading rules: primarily moving average crossover and filter rules. Among these rules, Levich and Thomas (1993) have concluded that moving average rules are generally more profitable. This study is therefore limited to an examination of various moving average crossover rules. To make the analysis manageable, only fixed-length simple moving averages are used, even though some traders may employ exponentially smoothed, triangular, or variable-length moving averages with trading bands to prevent whipsaw effects from entering and closing positions within a few days. For simplicity, this analysis assumes that a buy signal is generated if the short-term moving average of prices (SMA$_t$) is greater than or equal to the long-term moving average LMA$_t$. More formally, the investor is long and holds the foreign currency whenever

$$\text{SMA}_t = (1/S) \sum_{i=1}^{S} P_{t-i} \geq \text{LMA}_t = (1/L) \sum_{i=1}^{L} P_{t-j} \tag{6.4}$$

An investor will hold U.S. dollars during sell signals, or whenever SMA$_t$ < LMA$_t$. This could lead to frequent trading, but in practice, signals are generally in place for several days or weeks. Buying and selling is assumed to occur at the closing price on the day when the signal is observed. In other studies, delaying the purchase or sale of a currency by one day after the signal has been received has not had a major impact on results.

The number of possible short-term and long-term moving averages must be limited to a manageable size. For SMA$_t$, all lengths from 1 to 10 days are examined. For LMA$_t$, 23 different periods are considered. These include lengths of 5, 10, 15, 20, and 25 days as well as all possible 10-day increments from 30 to 200 days. Since the length of the long-term moving average must exceed the length of the short-term moving average, this requires the examination of trading rule profits for 223 possible strategies (4 for the 5-day LMA, 9 for the 10-day LMA, and 210 for remaining 21 LMAs). For each currency, the best moving average crossover rule is selected within sample and then applied to the testing period. Since all traders face some transaction costs, this study follows LeBaron (1999) and assumes 0.1 percent roundturn costs for buying and selling the foreign currency. The in-sample strategies are optimized based upon this 0.1 percent transaction fee. In most instances, the same trading rule would be chosen for transaction costs of 0 to 0.125 percent, as employed in other studies. Finally; with only a few exceptions, short- and long-term moving averages near the same duration as the optimal rule chosen lead to similar in-sample profits.

RESULTS

Table 6.3 shows the profitability of the best in-sample trading rule for each of 28 currencies. As expected this pure optimization exercise generates substantial trading rule profits ranging from 1.86 percent annual return on the Canadian dollar up to 15.29 percent for the Belgian franc. The group averages are 8.75 percent annualized returns for the independent floating currencies and 11.34 percent for the Euroland currencies. On average, the in-sample trading rule abnormal returns are significantly different from zero at the 1 percent level for both groups of currencies. Even for the managed float Asian currencies, annualized optimal trading rule returns average 4.47 percent, which is significantly different from zero at the 1 percent level. In-sample annual abnormal returns for these seven currencies range from a low of .08 percent for the Thai baht up to 9.82 percent for the South Korean won.

There is a wide range of optimal lengths of moving averages for the best crossover rules among the various currencies. Focusing on the in-

Table 6.3a
Profitability of Trading Rules—*Panel A: Independent Floating Currencies*

	Best Rule in Sample	% Return in Sample	% Return out of Sample	Best Rule 1990s	% Return Best Rule 1990s
Australian dollar	(10,40)	5.54**	-2.76	(20,180)	2.47
Canadian dollar	(7,25)	1.86	-0.64	(2,15)	0.73
Danish kroner	(5,25)	11.62***	1.50	(10,50)	3.65
Greek drachma	(5,25)	5.21	-2.04	(10,60)	4.03
Japanese yen	(3,15)	12.89***	0.12	(10,60)	10.55***
New Zealand dollar	(10,200)	7.62	2.82	(20,200)	3.94
Norwegian kroner	(5,30)	8.39**	-0.58	(5,50)	2.33
South African rand	(10,90)	12.81**	4.44	(5,50)	6.37
Swedish kronor	(5,30)	8.36***	-1.60	(10,40)	4.99
Swiss franc	(1,20)	11.37***	-0.42	(10,50)	5.14
U.K. pound	(1,20)	10.58***	-2.04	(3,10)	1.57
Group averages		8.75***	-0.11		4.16

***, **, and * denote significance at the 1 percent, 5 percent, or 10 percent levels, respectively.

Note: Profits are obtained from both long and short positions. The holding period for a trade can vary between one day and the entire estimation period. Returns presented are annualized mean compound returns from trading the listed currency. Transaction costs are 0.1 percent roundturn for buying and selling the currency, as used by LeBaron (1999).

Global Financial Markets

Table 6.3b
Profitability of Trading Rules—*Panel B: Euroland Currencies*

	Best Rule in Sample	% Return in Sample	% Return out of Sample	Best Rule 1990s	% Return Best Rule 1990s
Austrian schilling	(5,20)	12.32***	0.73	(1,200)	4.66
Belgian franc	(6,20)	15.29***	1.51	(1,200)	7.46**
Finnish markka	(4,20)	7.06***	-0.45	(20,200)	6.25
French franc	(6,20)	12.65***	2.16	(1,20)	5.77*
German mark	(4,20)	12.74***	1.01	(1,20)	5.19
Irish punt	(6,25)	9.55***	1.70	(10,200)	5.92*
Italian lira	(1,20)	9.68***	5.74*	(6,30)	8.11**
Netherlands guilder	(6,20)	14.53***	-1.95	(5,50)	4.87
Portuguese escudo	(4,25)	9.68***	-1.11	(20,200)	5.73*
Spanish peseta	(7,25)	9.90***	5.50	(1,100)	5.65*
Group Averages		11.34***	1.48		5.96*

***, **, and * denote significance at the 1 percent, 5 percent, or 10 percent levels, respectively.

Note: Profits are obtained from both long and short positions. The holding period for a trade can vary between one day and the entire estimation period. Returns presented are annualized mean compound returns from trading the listed currency. Transaction costs are .1 percent roundturn for buying and selling the currency, as used by LeBaron (1999).

Table 6.3c
Profitability of Trading Rules—*Panel C: Managed Float Asian Currencies*

	Best Rule in Sample	% Return in Sample	% Return Out of Sample	Best Rule 1990s	% Return Best Rule 1990s
Indian rupee	(10,100)	3.46*	5.24**	(8,100)	5.59**
Malaysian ringitt	(10,50)	2.93	4.91	(10,40)	6.44*
Singapore dollar	(6,20)	2.17	3.47*	(5,50)	5.12***
South Korean won	(10,60)	9.82***	7.32	(10,60)	7.32
Sri Lankan rupee	(1,120)	4.45	3.45	(5,100)	5.01**
Taiwan dollar	(1,120)	8.37***	-0.64	(5,20)	5.70**
Thai baht	(10,180)	0.08	-0.41	(5,30)	7.00**
Group Averages		4.47*	3.33		6.03**

***, **, and * denote significance at the 1 percent, 5 percent, or 10 percent levels, respectively.

Note: Profits are obtained from both long and short positions. The holding period for a trade can vary between one day and the entire estimation period. Returns presented are annualized mean compound returns from trading the listed currency. Transaction costs are 0.1 percent roundturn for buying and selling the currency, as used by LeBaron (1999).

dependent floating and Euroland currencies, a typical rule might involve about a 5-day short-term moving average (SMA) and a 20- to 25-day long-term moving average (LMA). Trading frequency, though not reported in the table, can be examined for some representative currencies. For the UK pound, the crossover rule involving the 1- and 20-day moving averages requires 417 trades over a 20-year period. This involves about 21 trades per year, or a holding period for each short or long position of about 12 trading days. As another example, the 7-day and 25-day crossover rule for the Canadian dollar requires 185 total trades, or about 9 per year and a holding period of about 27 trading days. The optimal trading rule for the New Zealand dollar uses the longest-term LMA of any of the currencies (200 days) and requires only 25 total trades over 20 years. This strategy implies an average holding period of about 200 trading days or around 10 months.

The optimal length moving average crossover rule for each currency discovered by optimizing returns within sample can now be examined out-of-sample during the decade of the 1990s. The results in the third column of Table 6.3 show a rather abysmal performance with an average abnormal return of –0.11 percent for the independent floating currencies and 1.48 percent for the EuroLand currencies. With the sole exception of the Italian lira, such returns are not statistically different from zero at even the 10 percent level of significance. These results are dramatically different from the average in-sample annual abnormal returns of 8.75 percent and 11.34 percent for the same two groups of currencies.

To help distinguish between optimization and temporary inefficiencies as a source of trading rule profits, the fifth column of Table 6.3 indicates that the best rule produces average annual abnormal returns in the 1990s of 4.16 percent for the independent floating currencies and 5.96 percent for the EuroLand currencies. These returns are about one-half the magnitude of in-sample optimized returns reported for the 1970s and 1980s. For the independent floating currencies, even the best moving average trading rules provide statistically significant abnormal returns for only one currency—the Japanese yen. For the EuroLand currencies, the best rules obtained by optimization in the 1990s generate abnormal returns significantly different from zero at the 5 percent confidence level for 2 of 10 currencies. Such results indicate that currency markets have changed substantially over time. As an upper bound, up to one-half of in-sample profits may be due to optimization, while more than one-half of the in-sample abnormal returns represent temporary inefficiencies that the currency markets correct over time.

Although average trading rule profits are not very large out-of-sample, they vary between currencies. One might wonder whether they are larger for the more frequently or the less frequently traded currencies. Efficient market theory would suggest that temporary inefficiencies are more likely to exist for the less traded currencies. In contrast, Siddiqui (1998) argues that technical trading is a self-fulfilling prophecy, which might mean higher profits for the more heavily traded currencies. As shown in Table 6.3, the largest out-of-sample annual returns among currencies are 4.44 percent for the South African rand, 2.82 percent for the New Zealand dollar, 5.74 percent for the Italian lira, and 5.50 percent for the Spanish peseta. These are all among the lesser traded currencies. Out-of-sample abnormal trading rule returns for the more heavily traded Canadian dollar, Japanese yen, Swiss franc, and UK pound are all either negative or near zero. For all of the independent floating and Euroland currencies, the optimized rules for the 1990s show considerably smaller returns than the optimized rules for the 1970s and 1980s. This suggests that markets are becoming more efficient over time.

For the managed float Asian currencies, the out-of-sample annual abnormal return of 3.33 percent is not as noticeably different from the in-sample results. In fact, trading rule profits persist in the 1990s for the Indian rupee, Malaysian ringitt, Sri Lankan rupee, and South Korean won. In three cases, returns are larger in 1990s than during the in-sample period when trading rules were optimized. Such results appear to be an artifact of currencies becoming more freely floating over time. Further evidence supporting this view is that abnormal returns for the best out-of-sample rules are fairly close to those found for the other currencies in the 1990s. Hence, the success of trading rules for the Asian currencies may have persisted in the 1990s due to the movement toward less managed rates, but following the example of other currencies, such abnormal returns may soon disappear.

One can now compare actual results with those predicted when looking at autocorrelations, standard deviations, and Hurst exponents as presented in Tables 6.1 and 6.2 at the end of the in-sample period. Based upon autocorrelations, one might expect the highest trading rule profits the Canadian dollar (although it has a low standard deviation of returns), the Japanese yen, the UK pound, and the Italian lira. Among these only the Italian lira produces significant abnormal returns out-of-sample. Based upon the size of Hurst exponents, one might expect the highest abnormal returns for Australian dollar, New Zealand dollar, Japanese yen, South African rand, German mark, and Spanish peseta. Noticeable, although not statistically significant, abnormal returns have already been mentioned for the South African rand, New Zealand dollar, and Spanish peseta. Even the German mark has slight positive out-of-sample abnormal returns of 1.01 percent annually, as shown in Table 6.3. Although not a perfect indicator, high values for Hurst exponents appear to have some value in predicting which currencies are likely to generate higher out-of-sample abnormal returns for trend following trading rules. This may be an interesting area for further research.

Although not shown in Table 6.3, one could examine whether trading rule profits come primarily from the long or short side of the trading strategies. Perhaps most noteworthy is that all of the abnormal return for the South African rand comes from the short side while the trader is holding U.S. dollars and watching the rand depreciate in value. Without futures markets, such returns are not readily available to foreign investors, even though they are meaningful for South African investors. Similarly, the apparent large returns on the Indian rupee, Malaysian ringitt, South Korean won, and the Sri Lankan rupee in the 1990s come primarily from the short side and may not be available to foreign investors. Such results support market efficiency and suggest that it is now difficult to earn abnormal returns in any of the currency markets.

CONCLUSIONS

This study has investigated the out-of-sample profitability of simple moving average technical trading rules. It has shown that profitability, or apparent abnormal returns, disappear for most currencies out-of-sample in the 1990s. The exception is for a few of the lesser-traded currencies such as the South African rand, New Zealand dollar, Italian lira, and the Spanish peseta. However, among these currencies only the abnormal returns for the Italian lira are statistically different from zero in the 1990s. Even optimizing on the testing set produces lower returns in the 1990s than were available in previous years. Such results indicate that at least half of trading rule profit available in the 1970s and 1980s has disappeared due to changing market conditions. That is, markets have adjusted and eliminated temporary market inefficiencies. Although it is difficult to distinguish the impact of optimization from changing markets, results indicate as an upper limit that no more than one-half of in-sample trading rule profits can be attributable to within sample optimization. The actual impact of optimization may be smaller, meaning that some of the profitability attributable to optimization may have been eliminated due to increased efficiency in the currency markets. Regardless of the source of trading rule profits, abnormal returns from simple moving average technical trading rules are diminishing over time. Currency traders should perhaps look for different or more complicated technical trading rules to earn temporary abnormal returns in today's currency markets. The search for such rules might be an interesting topic for future research.

NOTE

This chapter was presented at the First International Conference on Banking and Finance: Issues and Strategies, Kuala Lumpur, August 18, 2000.

REFERENCES

Brooks, C. (1997). "Linear and Nonlinear (Non-) Forecastability of High-frequency Exchange Rates," *Journal of Forecasting*, 16, pp. 125–145.

Cheung, Y. W., and C. Y. P. Wong. (1997). "The Performance of Trading Rules on Four Asian Currency Exchange Rates," *Multinational Finance Journal*, 1, pp. 1–22.

Dacco, R., and S. Satchell. (1999). "Why Do Regime-Switching Models Forecast So Badly?" *Journal of Forecasting*, 18, pp. 1–16.

Dooley, M. P., and J. Shafer. (1983). "Analysis of Short-run Exchange Rate Behavior: March 1973-November 1981." In D. Bigman and T. Taya (Eds.), *Exchange Rate and Trade Instability*. Cambridge, MA: Ballinger.

Kho, B. C. (1996). "Time-varying Risk Premia, Volatility, and Technical Trading Rule Profits: Evidence from Foreign Currency Futures Markets," *Journal of Financial Economics*, 41, pp. 249–290.

LeBaron, B. (1999). "Technical Trading Rule Profitability and Foreign Exchange Intervention," *Journal of International Economics*, 49, pp. 125–143.

Lee, C. I., and I. Mathur. (1996). "Trading Rule Profits in European Spot Cross Rates," *Journal of Banking and Finance*, 20, pp. 949–962.

Levich, R. M., and L. R. Thomas. (1993). "The Significance of Technical Trading-rule Profits in the Foreign Exchange Market: A Bootstrap Approach," *Journal of International Money and Finance*, 12, pp. 451–474.

Lui, Y. H., and D. Mole. (1998). "The Use of Fundamental and Technical Analyses by Foreign Exchange Dealers: Hong Kong Evidence," *Journal of International Money and Finance*, 17, pp. 535–545.

Meese, R. A., and K. Rogoff. (1983). "Empirical Exchange Rate Models of the Seventies: Do They Fit Out of Sample?" *Journal of International Economics*, 14, pp. 3–24.

Meese, R. A., and A. K. Rose. (1990). "Nonlinear, Nonparametric, Nonessential Exchange Rate Estimation," *American Economic Review*, 80, pp. 192–196.

Neely, C. J. (1997). *Technical Analysis in the Foreign Exchange Market: A Layman's Guide*. Review—Federal Reserve Bank of St. Louis, pp. 1–15. St. Louis, MO: Federal Reserve Bank of St. Louis.

Neely, C. J., and P. Weller. (1998). "Technical Trading Rules in the European Monetary System." Working paper, Federal Reserve Bank of St. Louis. St. Louis, MO: Federal Reserve Bank of St. Louis.

Neely, C. J., P. Weller, and R. Dittmar. (1997). "Is Technical Analysis in the Foreign Exchange Market Profitable? A Genetic Programming Approach," *Journal of Financial and Quantitative Analysis*, 32, pp. 405–426.

Siddiqui, S. (1998). "A Qualitative Threshold Model of Daily Exchange Rate Movements," *Economics Letters*, 59, pp. 243–248.

Sweeney, R. (1986). "Beating the Foreign Exchange Market," *Journal of Finance*, 41, pp. 163–182.

Szakmary, A. C., and I. Mathur. (1997). "Central Bank Intervention and Trading Rule Profits in Foreign Exchange Markets," *Journal of International Money and Finance*, 16, pp. 513–535.

CHAPTER 7

Analyzing the Asian Crisis: Was It Really a Surprise?

Michel-Henry Bouchet, Ephraim Clark, and Bertrand Groslambert

INTRODUCTION

On July 2, 1997, the Thai baht was ignominiously devalued by 20 percent despite weeks of desperate moves to prop up the currency, including central bank intervention of 8.7 billion on the spot market, and $23 billion in forward contracts, interest rate increases from 12 percent to 18 percent and restrictions on foreign speculators. By the end of the year the baht crisis had spread around the world. The median devaluation of the five East Asian tigers hardest hit by the crisis—Indonesia, Korea, Malaysia, the Philippines, and Thailand—was 80 percent. The International Finance Corporation's (IFC) emerging stock market index dropped by 20 percent between June and December and its Asian index fell by 53 percent. By the end of the year the baht had depreciated by 93 percent, the Hong Kong dollar, the Korean won, and the Taiwan dollar were under attack and their stock markets were nosediving, currencies and equity prices in Eastern Europe and Latin America were falling, and in November, Korea, the world's eleventh largest economy, became the recipient of the world's largest ever rescue package.

What happened? Conventional wisdom has it that in spite of a benign international background with high rates of growth in world trade and declining spreads on international borrowing, international investors suddenly awoke to the reality of structural weaknesses in the private financial sector including resource misallocation and maturity and currency mismatches as well as public sector economic mismanagement regarding the exchange rate, financial regulation, and implicit or explicit government guarantees. The rude awakening caused a crisis of confidence that the three countries, vulnerable because of the buildup of private sector, short-term, unhedged debt, were unable to overcome. Nevertheless, it is generally agreed that when the reckoning did come, the countries' underlying economic and financial situation did not warrant the humiliating treatment inflicted on it by the international financial markets. It is noted that public borrowing was subdued, most of the countries were running a fiscal surplus, inflation was low relative to most other developing countries, and savings rates were high. With this in mind, conventional wisdom has it that the Asian crisis was a mindless overreaction by international investors.

There are several shortcomings to this attractive conventional view, which seems to fit the facts in general. First of all, it fails to explain how otherwise sophisticated international investors could have remained oblivious so long to events that were known and had been developing over an extended period. It also fails to explain what caused them to overreact when they finally did get wise. Finally, it fails to explain what caused a crisis that was uniquely Asian in nature to spread to the other emerging markets in general, including those as far afield and economically different as Latin America and Eastern Europe.

In this chapter we address these questions. We give evidence for the conventional conclusion that the region's underlying economic and financial situation did not warrant the humiliating treatment inflicted on it by the international financial markets. Although the region's economic and financial situation definitely did warrant a substantial readjustment of its importance in international investors' portfolios, it did not warrant the spectacular readjustment that actually occurred. The spectacular scale of the readjustment, however, was not a mindless overreaction to suddenly perceived changes in the countries' political fragility. On the contrary, we show that the countries' evolving economic, financial, and political fragility was recognized and compensated for as far back as 1994.

The chapter is organized as follows. In the section entitled "Financial Crises, Herd Instinct, and Spillover Effect," we give a brief overview of the institutional response to the spillover effect in the aftermath of the Asian financial crisis. In the section entitled "The Economic and Financial Situation: A Brief Overview," we look at the three countries' economic, financial, and political situation, with particular emphasis on international short-term borrowing. This analysis generally confirms the conventional consensus of overall well-being with significant but manageable problems. In the section entitled "The Empirical Study, " below, we use option pricing theory to analyze how the situation was perceived by the market. More specifically, we ask what was the perceived level of risk and was the level rising or falling. Contrary to the conventional view, we find that international investors perceived Indonesia and Malaysia as very risky and that the perceived risk was growing. The perceived risk for the Philippines was high but falling. In the conclusion, we present our concluding remarks.

FINANCIAL CRISES, HERD INSTINCT, AND SPILLOVER EFFECT

Today, buoyant world economic growth has already put the 1997 Asian financial crisis in economic history books. The dust has settled on the international rescue packages. In mid-August 2000, the Philippines came back to the Samourai market with a Y35 billion five-year deal, the first benchmark yen bond issue since December 1996, and Malaysia asked lenders to shave 70bp off a past loan's margin. Amnesia is a key feature of international capital markets, probably more so than the well-known "herd instinct." The two concepts are closely related, however. It seems indeed that, after focusing on the same group of borrowers, capital markets quickly forget that creditors' behavior is at the root of past financial turmoil. Investor overreaction is well illustrated by George Soros's diagnosis in January of 1998 that "the international financial system was suffering a systemic breakdown" with an immediate risk of "worldwide deflation."[1] Investors are prompt to lose their tempers once they lose financial assets.

The crisis in Asia seemed like a containable regional problem in July of 1997, when Thailand abruptly devalued its currency by 20 percent. It then led to the biggest confidence crisis since the Mexican peso shock at the end of 1994. Sharp liquidity downturns around the world made investors wary of countries that rely heavily on foreign capital inflows. Spillover from Asia's crisis clouded a number of welcome developments in Latin America when investor anxiety hit this region as well as other emerging market groups. Rating agencies severely downgraded sovereign and corporate debt, and investors feared the real prospect of defaults and moratoriums in countries such as Korea and Indonesia. All in all, Asian stock market US$ indices dropped by 58 percent during 1997, with cuts of 78 percent in Thailand, 75 percent in Indonesia, 74 percent in Malaysia, and 62 percent in Indonesia.[2] Consequently, yield spreads on many Asian bonds hit record levels at end-1997, with issues from countries such as Korea widening out to more than 1,000 basis points over treasuries.

The crisis in Asia has raised several important issues regarding the so-called international financial architecture, as well as the role of the International Monetary Fund (IMF) and the need for "early warning signals." The IMF was at the center of a storm of criticism. It did not see the crisis coming and acted too late to stem it. It is known that the IMF's 1997 Annual Report praised "Korea's continued impressive macroeconomic performance and the authorities enviable fiscal record." Moreover, when the IMF acted, its traditional belt-tightening policy measures, including a sharp increase in interest rates, led to a deflationary spillover effect in the region and elsewhere. The IMF tightened domestic credit in economies already at risk from slumping demand, currencies in free fall, and reserves close to exhaustion. Finally, the main focus of criticism was moral hazard, that is, that by its interventions the IMF allows borrowers and lenders to escape the full consequences of their recklessness, thereby encouraging other agents to follow the same course in the future. The IMF under fire argues that available data was unreliable: thus, the South Korean government actively misled capital markets about the liquidity of its reserves and the leverage of the banking system. In addition, 30 years of dynamic growth had given Asian policymakers a sense of invulnerability, illustrated for instance by the unrealistic peg of the Thai currency to the U.S. dollar.[3] The IMF could point out that, just before the crisis erupted, Institutional Investor's Country Risk rating still showed positive assessments of the Asian countries with South Korea and Malaysia standing ahead of Chile and Hong Kong, Thailand ahead of China, Greece, and Israel, and Indonesia ahead of Poland, Hungary, and Tunisia.[4] And Standard & Poor's (S&P) as well as Moody's maintained their credit rating for most Asian countries until mid-1997.

The purpose of the chapter is not to revisit the question of what went wrong in Asia. Research literature from the international financial institutions (IFIs), commercial banks, and the academic community provides ample room for analysis of the macro and micro roots of the crisis, notably large current account deficits and deep-seated structural weaknesses in domestic financial markets.[5] One key policy mistake, indeed, was to allow banks and corporations to borrow extensively abroad without prudential controls on foreign exchange exposure. The chapter's aim is to assess capital markets behavior and to observe whether investors were caught by surprise by the abrupt financial crisis. There is a broad consensus that international investors did not anticipate any of the three crises that erupted in the 1980s, in Latin America, the Mexican crisis of 1994–1995, nor the Asia crisis of 1997–1998.[6] According to many authors, surprise is one of the key factors behind ramification and spillover effects. They argue that despite rising investor sophistication, there is a tendency to treat emerging markets as a single asset class in times of uncertainty.

Our analysis differs from mainstream research conclusions. We looked at two key variables of capital markets, namely, risk premium and implied volatility to assess whether private investors discriminate among sovereign borrowers. The chapter leads to clear-cut conclusions in the three countries under consideration, Indonesia, Philippines and Malaysia. First, a sharp rise in the risk premium and implied volatility can be observed for those countries that (1) exemplified strong macroeconomic imbalances throughout the 1990s (thus, well before the inception of the 1997 crisis), and (2) exemplified protracted inertia to adjust macroeconomic policies to get rid of structural weaknesses and restore private sector confidence. This is particularly the case of Indonesia. Second, the risk premium and implied volatility remain stable for those countries that either embark on robust IMF-supported adjustment programs (e.g., the Philippines) or adopt ad hoc and heterodox but successful adjustment measures (e.g., Malaysia).

THE ECONOMIC AND FINANCIAL SITUATION: A BRIEF OVERVIEW

Each of the eight main Asian countries (China, Hong Kong, Singapore, Indonesia, Malaysia, Philippines, Korea, and Thailand) exemplified very different macroeconomic situations when the crisis erupted in the second half of 1997. China, for instance, witnessed dynamic growth rates close to 10 percent a year throughout the period 1993–1999 and the yuan's exchange rate resisted speculative attacks thanks to some US$149 billion in official reserves, equivalent to nine months of import coverage.

The contrast is striking regarding the three countries under consideration in this chapter. The case of Indonesia stands out as an intricate and often opaque combination of financial fragility, structural and institutional weaknesses on the one hand, and deeply rooted macroeconomic distortions on the other. One can distinguish four main problems.

- First, Indonesia's current account deficit averaged 3 percent of gross domestic product (GDP) in the years 1990–1997, with a peak of 3.8 percent, equivalent to more than US$8.6 billion, in the year 1996 before the crisis eruption. This large and rising deficit is entirely attributable to mounting interest payments on foreign debt, given that the country enjoyed trade surpluses despite one of the lowest trade openness ratios in the region.[7]

- Second, the change in GDP deflator averaged 10 percent during the same period, a very high rate for the region. Inflation stemmed from large increases in domestic demand.

- Third, Indonesia's financial system suffered from weak supervision, a highly indebted corporate sector, and market distortions that translated into large portfolios of non-performing assets as well as undercapitalization. The government had been reluctant to take stern measures against recalcitrant debtors and to speed up privatization. Indonesia's large conglomerates provide case studies for inefficient investment and crony capitalism. Bold restructuring measures were announced only in mid-2000 under strong pressures from the IFIs, paving the way for the release of a US$400 million IMF loan.

- Last but not least, Indonesia suffered from a typical external debt overhang, coupled with a deep maturity mismatch. The country's debt to exports ratio was the highest in the region, averaging 230 percent in the period, culminating at 256 percent in 1997. Moreover, Indonesia relied heavily on short-term borrowing from international banks. One can observe a drastic rise in "original" short-term bank liabilities from less than US$12 billion at end-1990 to nearly US$32 billion at end-1997, to drop sharply to US$20 billion in the following year of credit crunch.[8] Moreover, Indonesia's ratio of short-term debt to total bank debt remained consistently above 50 percent throughout this period (Figure 7.1).

Regarding the Philippines, a large current account deficit was rooted in a substantial trade deficit that reached US$11 billion in 1997. With a healthy fiscal surplus, the annual current account deficit stemmed from buoyant domestic demand. The Philippines's imbalances were quickly tackled by the government, contrary to Indonesia.

- First, the Philippines's SDRs1 billion IMF stand-by arrangement was approved by the IMF's Board as early as March 1998, following the expiration of the previous extended facility by the end-1997. In addition, the World Bank provided a large financial sector adjustment loan. One can also observe that the Organization for Economic Co-operation Development's (OECD) export credit agencies provided massive support for the Philippines's exports by increasing officially guaranteed or insured trade-related bank claims by 88 percent between end-1996 and end-1998. Thanks to international support, the Philippines managed to turn current account deficits that averaged close to 5 percent of GDP each year in the 1994–1997 period to a 2 percent surplus in 1998. With export growth boosted by gains in competitiveness, domestic economic expansion slackened only little and indeed became the strongest in the region.

- Second, the Philippines's financial sector had been under the World Bank's scrutiny since late 1988. The financial fragility of the central bank had grown over the years to the point that it became bankrupt in 1993 and it had to be recapitalized

Figure 7.1
"Original" short-term bank liabilities

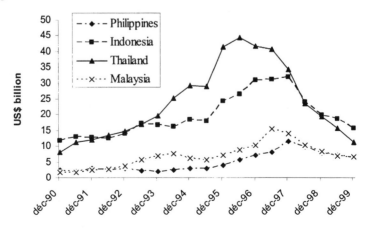

and fully restructured. The crisis, however, did not spread to the entire financial system as in Thailand, Indonesia, or even Korea.

- Third, the Philippines had benefited from a US$4.5 billion Brady-type London Club debt restructuring in 1989, with substantial debt relief. Hence, the country's debt/exports ratio dropped from close to 200 percent in 1993 to "only" 106 percent in 1997. Moreover, our analysis shows that adjusted short-term debt remained steady throughout the 1990–1996 period at less than US$5 billion even though the ratio of short-term to total debt rose due to a drop in the denominator (i.e., total debt).

As for Malaysia, in the face of sizeable capital outflows, of equity capital in particular, the authorities opted for currency depreciation as the main line of defense, accompanied by administrative measures to control capital flows and cushion equity prices. Monetary tightening was moderate. More importantly, preemptive banking reform measures meant that the country was able to forestall a real crisis without radical surgery of its financial system. Its unique approach reflected a desire to avoid the systemic dislocation and social upheaval that have beset other Asian countries. Moreover, Malaysia's reluctance to rely on short-term debt meant its banks never experienced the same degree of turmoil as those elsewhere in the region.[9] Malaysia's ratio of short-term debt decreased during the mid-1994/end-1996 period at levels well below those of neighboring countries.

All in all, Malaysia's macroeconomic management was relatively sound in the aftermath of the regional crisis, despite the IMF's criticism of the country's unorthodox policy measures and resistance to the IMF's shock therapy. Malaysia's policymakers intend to be rewarded for having tackled the country's problems boldly. In mid-August 2000, the country asked international lenders to cut the margin on a US$1.35 billion dual currency loan due to mature in 2003 by shaving almost 70bp off the initial loan margin, currently 120bp over US$ London Inter Bank Offered Rate (LIBOR) (Figure 7.2).

THE EMPIRICAL STUDY

The Data

Since our methodology is based on a market value approach, it is necessary to dispose of mark to market data in order to conduct an empirical study. Unfortunately, as noted by Kamin and Von Klein (1999), no readily available alternative to Brady bond-based measures of average emerging market country spreads exists. Consequently, because the only Asian country with Brady bonds is the Philippines, we had to build a specific index to evaluate the market assessment of their external debt.

Figure 7.2
Ratio of short-term bank debt to total bank debt

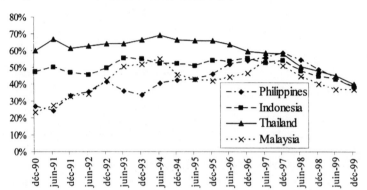

For that, we used the International Securities Market Association (ISMA) database. ISMA provides weekly market prices for all world-wide issued eurobonds. For each country, we compute the issued amount weighted average of the yield to maturity of every US$ bond listed in the ISMA Weekly Eurobond Guide, at the end of each year. We then take this rate as a proxy for the average yield to maturity of a whole country's external debt. The period runs from 1993, corresponding to one year before the Mexican crisis, until the end of 1997, six months after the beginning of the Asian crisis.[10]

We wish to study the five main countries directly concerned by the Asian crisis, namely, Indonesia, Korea, Malaysia, the Philippines, and Thailand. But in a first step, due to lack of reliable data, we can only focus on Indonesia, Malaysia, and the Philippines. Macroeconomic data is missing for Korea in 1995 and 1996, when this country was excluded from World Bank database, being considered as a developed country because its GDP per inhabitant in US$ reached the threshold of $10,000. For Thailand, ISMA market data is missing from 1993 through 1995.

Observed Market Risk Premium on Asian External Debt from 1993 to 1997

We compute the observed risk premium at the end of each year, by subtracting the US T-bond yield with the nearest maturity to the country's debt duration from the average yield to maturity computed from ISMA data. Tables 7.1, 7.2, and 7.3 and Figures 7.3 and 7.4 summarize the information.

Based on the observed risk premium, it seems that, by the end of 1996, the markets had begun to anticipate some problems for Indonesia and

Figure 7.3
Average yield to maturity on external debt—ISMA data

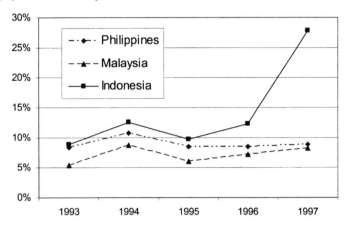

Table 7.1
Average Yield to Maturity on External Debt

	1993	1994	1995	1996	1997
Indonesia	8,90%	12,52%	9,72%	12,32%	27,88%
Malaysia	5,44%	8,70%	6,08%	7,19%	8,18%
Philippines	8,35%	10,80%	8,52%	8,43%	8,79%

Source: ISMA Weekly Eurobond Guide 1993–1997.

Table 7.2
Relevant U.S. T-Bond Yields According to Each Country's Duration

	1993	1994	1995	1996	1997
Indonesia	4,88%	7,61%	5,36%	5,99%	5,65%
Malaysia	4,88%	7,72%	5,39%	6,10%	5,69%
Philippines	5,20%	7,72%	5,36%	6,10%	5,69%

Source: Bloomberg.

In order to get the risk premium, we compute the duration of each country's debt for each year, and we take the U.S. Treasury bond(T-bond) yield with the nearest maturity to each country's external debt duration. We then subtract the average yield to maturity from the relevant U.S. T-bond yield.

Table 7.3
Observed Market Risk Premium

	1993	1994	1995	1996	1997
Indonesia	4,02%	4,91%	4,36%	6,33%	22,23%
Malaysia	0,56%	0,98%	0,69%	1,09%	2,49%
Philippines	3,15%	3,08%	3,16%	2,33%	3,10%

Figure 7.4
Observed risk premiums

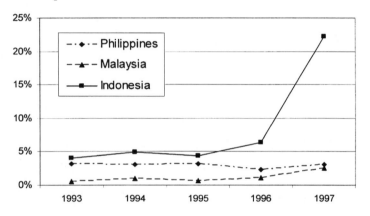

Malaysia. Indonesia experienced an increase of its risk premium from 436 to 633 basis points between 1995 and 1996 and Malaysia's risk premium rose by 58 percent over the same period to a higher level than in 1994 in the wake of the Mexican peso crisis. The Philippines's risk premium, however, was falling. At the end of 1997, the risk premium was obviously strongly impacted by the events of mid-1997, although the Philippines seems to have been less exposed than its neighbors and better able to manage the crisis. In any case, all three countries suffered a dramatic rise in their premium. In this sense, we could conclude as did the World Bank (1998) that: "Rating agencies and international institutions failed to adequately assess the region's economic vulnerabilities. . . . Markets and market observers failed to anticipate the scope and severity of the crisis." In the following section we use the concept of implied volatility to test whether or not this statement was, in fact, true.

Implied Volatility on Asian External Debt from 1993 to 1997

Clark (1991) derived a method for measuring the market value of a national economy and showed how it can be applied for estimating and managing many types of international risk. We use the Clark (1991) macroeconomic estimation method and the Black-Scholes (1973) option pricing formula[11] to compute the implied volatility of the three economies in question, in order to get an instantaneous measure of risk at different times.[12] This instantaneous measure of risk represents the market's perception of the riskiness of each economy at each point in time.

The procedure goes as follows.

1. We apply the Clark estimation method using data from International Financial Statistics to calculate the market value of the three economies for each year over the period 1993–1997. This variable represents the underlying asset in the Black-Scholes formula.

2. We use data from the World Bank Debt Tables to calculate the Macaulay (1938) duration of each economy's outstanding foreign debt at the end of each year. The strike price for each year is estimated as the present value of projected external debt service and the risk-free rate is the U.S. Treasury bond (T-bond) with the maturity the nearest to the duration of the external debt.

3. We use the observed yield to maturity (ISMA rate) to estimate the market value of the debt in the formula: Market value of the debt $\approx$ Face value of debt $\times$ $e^{-\text{duration x YTM}}$.

4. We use the market value of the debt to calculate the value of the call in the formula: Market Value of the Call $=$ Market Value of the Economy $-$ Market Value of the Debt.

5. We calculate the economy's implied volatility by running the option pricing formula backwards with the call price as given and volatility as the unknown.[13]

The results given below in Table 7.4 and Figure 7.5 represent the market's perception of the riskiness of each economy at the end of each year.

From these results, we can observe that the market considered these countries as extremely risky as far back as 1993 with implied volatility ranging from 41 percent to 68 percent between 1993 and 1996. Furthermore, by 1996 implied volatility for Indonesia and Malaysia was at the levels reached at the height of the Mexican peso crisis in 1994. This suggests

Table 7.4
Implied Volatility

Year	1993	1994	1995	1996	1997
Indonesia	55,0%	63,3%	56,2%	67,8%	85,4%
Malaysia	43,6%	54,1%	47,0%	53,2%	54,0%
Philippines	41,4%	49,8%	46,9%	46,2%	40,3%

Figure 7.5
Implied volatility

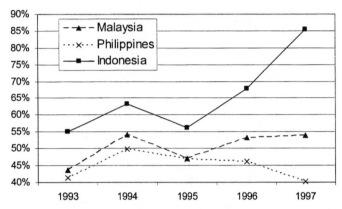

that the market anticipated as early as 1996 the potential difficulties that would eventually materialize in 1997. Only the Philippines has a decreasing implied volatility over the period and it is the Philippines that was least affected when the crisis did hit.

These outcomes are consistent with the economic performance of the three countries during the crisis. It could seem surprising to rate the Philippines as the lowest risk before 1997 but in light of the actual 1997 events, this was, on the contrary, a very shrewd assessment. Indeed, as evidenced by *a posteriori* results, even though the Philippines had not been able to achieve its neighbors' economic performance over the last decade, it did not suffer their specific weaknesses to the same extent. One of the main causes of the Asian problems arose from its financial sector's vulnerability. In fact, if we look at the financial ratios in Table 7.5, the Philippines resembles the Latin American countries more than the Asian countries. This could explain why its implied volatility actually decreased in 1997 as the Asian crisis unfolded (Table 7.5).

Therefore, contrary to most previous statements on this topic, we conclude that the market was sensitive to the five countries' growing economic and political problems. Furthermore, it was able to discriminate between each country's specific features as well. Thus, we conclude that while the rating agencies and international institutions failed to adequately assess the region's economic vulnerabilities, the markets themselves were able to accurately assess the situation for the region in general and for individual countries in particular.

CONCLUSIONS

In this chapter we use standard options pricing techniques and the Clark (1991) macroeconomic estimation methods to analyze investors'

Table 7.5
Ratios of Short-term Debt to Total Debt and to Reserves in East Asia and Latin America, Mid-1997 (%)

Country	Short-term debt / total debt	Short-term debt / reserves
Indonesia	24	160
Korea, Rep. of	67	300
Malaysia	39	55
Philippines	19	66
Thailand	46	107
Argentina	23	108
Brazil	23	69
Chile	25	44
Colombia	19	57
Mexico	16	126

Source: Bank for International Settlements data; IMF International Financial Statistics; and World Bank data, from Global Development Finance 1999.

anticipations concerning three countries—Indonesia, Malaysia, and the Philippines—before, during, and after the Asian crisis of 1997. We find that implied volatilities were generally high for all three countries over the whole period. By 1996, just before the crisis, implied volatilities were at levels comparable to those at the height of the Mexican peso crisis at the end of 1994. However, the market did seem to discriminate shrewdly among the three countries. Indonesia had the highest implied volatility and was the hardest hit by the crisis. Malaysia was hit second hardest and had the second highest implied volatility. The Philippines, which was only marginally affected by the crisis, had the lowest implied volatility and it was falling before, during, and after the crisis. We conclude that the market was sensitive to the three countries' growing economic, financial, and political problems and was able to judiciously discriminate among them. In this context, the "crisis" looks more like a rational portfolio rebalancing due to the evolving economic situation in each of the three countries rather than a mindless, indiscriminate panic.

NOTES

1. Soros, G. (1998). "Avoiding a Breakdown," *Financial Times* (January 1) 23–24.
2. IFC Emerging Markets Index. (1997). *Financial Times* (December 8) 11–14.

3. "Defending the Fund." (1998). Interview of Michel Camdessus. *Financial Times* (February 9).

4. (1997). *Institutional Investor* (September), p. 118.

5. See among many others: P. Krugman, Sachs. J. Mathieson, L. Richards, and B. Shara. (1998). "Crises Financières des Marchés Emergents," *Finance & Development* (December), pp. 28–31; Aghevli, B. (1999). "La Crise Asiatique: Causes et Remèdes," *Finance & Development* (June 1999), pp. 28–31.

6. See, for instance, Mathieson, Richards, and Sharma, *op. cit.*

7. Indonesia's openness to trade ratio reached 20 percent in 1996 compared with 29 percent for Korea, 79 percent for Malaysia, 31 percent in the Philippines, and 35 percent in Thailand, according to the Bank for International Settlements, Basle, Switzerland, 68th Annual Report, June 1998.

8. Short-term bank claims are adjusted to obtain original short-term debt by eliminating residual short-term debt that incorporates current debt service payments to banks. Data come from BIS sources. U.S. banks alone cut their overall lending to Philippines by one third during the December 1996–March 1999 period, according to FFIEC data.

9. Only for two banks, Sime and Bank Bumiputra, was the situation critical. The first was absorbed into RHB Bank and the second merged with Bank of Commerce. Overall, a rising stock market helped to boost the collateral value of bank loans.

10. We intend to extend the period of study up to 1998 as soon as macroeconomic data becomes available.

11. The formulas are

$$C_0 = V_0 N(d_1) - Ee^{-rt}N(d_2)$$

$$d_1 = \frac{1n(V_0 / E) + (r + \sigma^2 / 2)t}{\sigma\sqrt{t}}$$

$$d_2 = \frac{1n(V_0 / E) + (r + \sigma^2 / 2)t}{\sigma\sqrt{t}}$$

where C_0 is the market value of the bond, V_0 is the present value of the underlying security, E is the exercise price, and $N(d)$ is the value of the standardized normal cumulative distribution evaluated at d, r is the continuously compounded riskless rate of interest, σ is the standard deviation of the underlying security's continuously compounded annual rate of return, and t is the time to maturity or the duration of the call.

12. In the Appendix we outline the Clark (1991) macroeconomic estimation method.

13. For more details on implied volatility, see Cox and Rubenstein (1985, pp. 278–279).

REFERENCES

Bank for International Settlements. *International Banking Statistics, Quarterly Reports,* all issues 1996–2000.

Black, F., and M. Scholes. (1973). "The Pricing of Options and Corporate Liabilities," *Journal of Political Economy,* 81, no. 3, pp. 637–659.

Clark, E. A. (1991). *Cross Border Investment Risk: Applications of Modern Portfolio Theory.* London: Euromoney Publications.

————. (2000). "Agency Conflict and the Signalling Snafu in the Mexican Peso Conflict of 1994," *International Journal of Public Administration,* 23, nos. 5–8, pp. 837–876.

Clark, E. A., and B. Marois. (1996). *Managing Risk in International Business.* London: International Thomson Business Press.

Cline, W., and K. Barnes. (1997). "Spreads and Risk in Emerging Markets Lending," *Institute of International Finance Research Paper,* 97, no. 1 (November).

Cox, J. C., and M. Rubenstein. (1985). *Options Markets.* Englewood Cliffs, NJ: Prentice Hall.

Dadush, U., D. Dasgupta, and D. Ratha. (2000). "The Role of Short-term Debt in Recent Crises," *Finance and Development,* 37, no. 4.

"Defending the Fund." (1998). Interview of M. Camdessus. *Financial Times* (February 9).

Edwards, S. (1986). "The Pricing of Bonds and Bank Loans in International Markets: An Analysis of Developing Countries' Foreign Borrowing," *European Economic Review,* 30, no. 3, pp. 565–589.

Euromoney/Deutsche Bank. (2000). *Guide to Asian Debt Markets.* New York/Zurich, Switzerland.

Fitch IBCA. (1998). (January 13). Washington, D.C.

Frankel, J. A. (1998). "The Asian Model, the Miracle, the Crisis and the Fund." Delivered at the U.S. International Trade Commission, April 16, Washington, D.C.

International Monetary Fund. (1995–2001) *International Financial Statistics,* several issues.

ISMA. (1992–1999). *Weekly Eurobond Guide,* several issues.

Kamin, S. B., and K. Von Klein. (1999). "The Evolution and Determinants of Credit Markets Spread," International Finance discussion paper, no. 653. Board of Governors of the Federal Reserve System (November). Washington, D.C.: Federal Reserve System.

Krugman, P. (1994). "The Myth of Asia's Miracle," *Foreign Affairs,* 73, no. 6 (November/December), pp. 62–78.

————. (1998). "What Happened to Asia?" Retrieved August 18 from http://web.mit.edu/krugman/www/DISINTER.html.

Macaulay, F. R. (1938). *Some Theoretical Problems Suggested by Movements of Interest Rates, Bond Yields and Stock Prices in the U.S. since 1856.* New York: National Bureau of Economic Research.

Milesi-Ferretti, G. M., and A. Razin. (1996). "Current Account Sustainability: Selected East Asian and Latin American Experiences." Working paper WP/96/11. Washington, D.C.: International Monetary Fund.

World Bank. (1998). Global Development Finance CD-ROM (formerly World Debt Tables).

APPENDIX

ESTIMATING MACROECONOMIC MARKET VALUE

The methodology for measuring a national economy's market value was first developed in Clark (1991). It involves presenting economic activity as a series of expected cash flows in a convertible currency such as dollars. Start with the following definitions:

b_t = the dollar value of income from the sale of the economy's output of final goods and services for period t.

a_t = the dollar value of the economy's expenditure on final goods and services for period t.

X_t = the dollar value of exports including all goods and services, other income, and unrequited transfers for period t.

M_t = the dollar value of imports including all goods and services except dividends and interest paid abroad, other income, and unrequited transfers for period t.

D_t = the dollar value of dividends and interest paid abroad in period t.

F_t = the net inflow (outflow) of foreign capital including operations by the monetary authority.

V_t = the dollar value of the economy at the beginning of period t.

r = the economy's internal rate of return.

$R = 1 + r$.

E is the expectations operator.

Macroeconomic accounting discipline is imposed through the transactions involving the external sector by the balance of payments identity:

$$X_t - M_t + D_t + F_t = 0 \tag{7.1}$$

Define b_t and a_t as:

$$b_t = X_t + (C_t - M_{ct}) \tag{7.2}$$

and

$$a_t = M_t + (C_t - M_{ct}) \tag{7.3}$$

where C is the dollar value of domestic consumption and M_c represents the dollar value of imports of consumption goods. From (7.2) and (7.3) it is clear that $(b_t - a_t)$ will always be equal to $(X_t - M_t)$, which, as can be seen from (7.1), is an expression of balance of payments accounting discipline.

Suppose that all transactions take place on the first day of each period and that the capital markets are in equilibrium so that the economy's cost of capital is equal to its internal rate of return, r. The value of the economy measured in dollars at the beginning of time T is:

$$V_t = E[(b_r - a_r) + (b_{T+1} - a_{T+1})R^{-1} + \ldots + (b_n - a_n)R^{-(n-T)}] \quad (7.4)$$

Equation (7.4) is the expression for the economy's net present value measured in units of foreign exchange. It is market oriented in so far as it is cast in terms of expected values of future cash flows. It also reflects international criteria for resource allocation. The reason is straightforward. Remember that $(b_t - a_t)$ will always be equal to $(X_t - M_t)$, the difference between exports and imports. The prices of exports and imports are generally derived in the international marketplace. Thus, V_T, the discounted value of the $X_t - M_t$, reflects these prices.

It is important to see the relationship between (7.4) and the traditional national accounting equation. Taking the formula for V_{t+1} gives:

$$V_{t+1} = E[(b_{T+1} - a_{T+1}) + (b_{T+2} - a_{T+2})R^{-1} + \ldots + (b_n - a_n)R^{-(n-\,')}] \quad (7.5)$$

Substituting (7.5) into (7.4) gives:

$$V_T = (b_T - a_T) + V_{T+1}R^{-1} \quad (7.6)$$

Since b_T and a_T are known because they take place on the first day of the period, the expectation operator before $(b_T - a_T)$ disappears.

Multiplying (7.6) by $1 + r$ to obtain the value of the economy at the end of period T and rearranging, yields the national accounting equation for period T:

$$r(V_T + a_T - b_T) + a_T = b_T + (V_{T+1} - V_T) \quad (7.7)$$

where $r(V_T + a_T - b_T)$ represents profits before interest and dividends paid abroad, a_T represents cost, b_T represents income and $(V_{T+1} - V_T)$ represents net investment. Equation (7.7) says that profits plus cost [on the left-hand side (LHS) of the equation] are equal to income plus investment [on the right-hand side (RHS) of the equation]. It can be more easily recognized if we substitute (7.2) and (7.3) into (7.7) and rearrange:

$$r(V_T + M_T - X_T) + C_T = X_T - M_T + C_T + (V_{T+1} - V_T) \quad (7.8)$$

The RHS of (7.8) is immediately recognized as a derivative presentation of net national product: exports minus imports plus consumption plus net investment. The difference between this presentation and the traditional format is that interest and dividends paid abroad are not included and net investment is an expected value since it depends on V_{T+1}. The LHS of the equation shows the economy's earnings before interest and dividends paid abroad plus consumption. Consumption, then, appears directly as a cost. However, it does not represent the total cost. Total cost would include expenditure on imports of investment goods.

The individual V_t's in the foregoing accounting format cannot be observed directly for two reasons. First, we are dealing with expected future flows and, second, a country's national accounts are presented in domestic currency rather than foreign currency. The market information does, however, exist so that they can be estimated. The estimation procedure involves using the exchange rate to link the V_t's to the domestic currency statistics presented in the national accounts.

The domestic currency equivalent of (7.4) is:

$$V'_T = E[(b'_T - a'_T) + (b'_{T+1} - a'_{T+1})R'^{-1} + \ldots + (b'_n - a'_n)R'^{-(n-T)}] \quad (7.9)$$

where the primes denote domestic currency values and $R' = 1 + r'$. r' is the economy's internal rate of return in domestic currency. Since $b - a$ equals the $X - M$, equation (7.9) can be rewritten using the exchange rate. Let

$$X'_t = S_t X_t$$

and

$$M'_t = S_t M_t$$

where S_t is the spot exchange rate at time t expressed as the number of units of domestic currency for one unit of foreign currency. Then

$$V'_T = E[S_T(X_T - M_T) + S_{T+1}(X_{T+1} - M_{T+1}) \\ R'^{-1} + \ldots + S_n(X_n - M_n)R'^{-(n-T)}] \quad (7.10)$$

Using interest rate and forward rate parity and assuming linear independence, it is easy to show that:

$$V_T = \frac{V'_T}{S_T} \quad (7.11)$$

and at the end of the period

$$V_{T+1} = \frac{V'_{T+1}}{S_{T+1}} \quad (7.12)$$

Equations (7.11) and (7.12) mean that the economy's NPV measured in units of foreign currency is equal to the NPV in domestic currency divided by the exchange rate. It is important to note that the effects of expectations on future cash flows are captured in the exchange rate through the mechanisms of interest rate and forward rate parity.

Now write V'_T and V'_{T+1} using historical values showing what has been invested in the economy from time 0 to time $T-1$

$$V'_T = -(b'_0 - a'_0)R^T - (b'_1 - a'_1)R^{T-1} - \ldots - (b'_{T-1} - a'_{T-1})R \quad (7.13)$$

$$V'_{T+1} = -(b'_0 - a'_0)R^{T+1} - (b'_1 - a'_1)R^T - \ldots - (b'_T - a'_T)R \quad (7.14)$$

Historical and expected measures of V'_T and V'_{T+1} will be equivalent if all discounting and compounding is done at the economy's internal rate of return. Making this assumption means that V'_T can be estimated directly from readily available statistical data. It is simply the sum, from period 0 to the end of period $T - 1$, of the domestic currency value of net investment at market prices, which itself is a component of the traditional presentation of the national accounts (or it can be estimated from gross fixed capital formation). This can be written:

$$V'_T = \sum_{t=0}^{T-1} (V'_{t+1} - V'_t) \tag{7.15}$$

and at the end of the period T it is:

$$V'_{T+1} = \sum_{t=0}^{T} (V'_{t+1} - V'_t) \tag{7.16}$$

Applying (7.11), (7.12), (7.15), and (7.16) gives the macroeconomic market value.

CHAPTER 8

Banking and Regulatory Reform in Postcrisis Asia

Mohamed Ariff and Michael T. Skully

INTRODUCTION

Since 1997, the Asian financial crisis has wiped billions of dollars from the region's share markets and transformed what were strongly growing economies into ones with slow or even negative growth rates. While share prices and economies are recovering, the opportunity cost of the crisis remains. Billions of dollars of lost production are simply gone. The personal suffering experienced by both business and population similarly cannot be erased. Many financial institutions have ceased to exist and unemployment in the banking sector is likely to worsen. As with most crises, the Asia crisis also has a good side. While bankers may be suffering, it has proved of an immediate benefit to financial consultants, accountants, and lawyers. Events have similarly provided excellent opportunities for academic research and will continue to do so for some decades. One other possible long-term benefit, for which one can but hope, is that of an improved banking and bank regulatory system. By examining policies both before and during the crisis, countries should become better placed to deal with similar problems in the future. This chapter considers some of these. After a brief overview of the banking problem with nonperforming loans, the various responses to crisis are examined, first in respect to banking reforms and second in respect to regulatory reforms. The chapter ends with some concluding statements.

THE NONPERFORMING LOAN PROBLEM

Commercial banks in Asia have experienced significant problems with nonperforming loans. There are considerable difficulties in making cross-country comparisons on nonperforming loans due to differences in definitions, regulations and accounting practices. Morris Goldstein (1998) provided an excellent indication of these problems when he compared a range of estimates for various Asian countries. As shown in Table 8.1, there were major differences between how these market experts perceive the situation.

Nonperforming loans (NPLs) are those in which the clients have not fulfilled the conditions of the advance. Typically, this means that they have been late with their payments. When only one payment is missed, there

Table 8.1
Estimates of Nonperforming Bank Loans in Asia

Study	Thailand	Korea, South	Indonesia	Malaysia	Philippines	Singapore	Hong Kong
Jardine Flemming (1997) PNPL/TL	19.3	Na	16.8	15.6	13.4	3.8	Na
Ramos (1998), Goldman Sachs ANPL/TL PNPL/TL	18.0 >25.0	14.0 >25.0	9.0 >25.0	6.0 12.0–25.0	3.0 10.0–15.0	2.0 >8.0	2.0 >8.0
Jen (1998), Morgan Stanley ANPL/TL	18.0	14.0	12.5	6.0	NA	NA	NA
Peregrine (1997) ANPL/TL	36.0[a]	30.0	15.0	15.0	7.0	4.0	1.0
Enschweiler (1998), JP Morgan ANPL/TL	17.5	17.5	11.0	7.5	5.5	3.0	1.8
BIS (1997), official estimate for 1996 ANPL/TL	7.7[b]	0.8	8.8	3.9	na	na	2.7

na = not available
PNPL = Peak nonperforming loans (1998–1999)
ANPL = Actual nonperforming loans (1997 or 1998)
TL = Total loans
a. Includes finance companies
b. Estimate for 1995

Source: Morris Goldstein, 1998, p. 10.

is perhaps no need for concern. It is when several payments have not been made that a loan is categorized as nonperforming. These loans have a number of effects on banks.

Initially, the bank may expect the client to resume their payments and so will continue to charge interest on the account and credit these earnings to its operational income. After a few months of nonpayment, this no longer makes sense and the loan is moved from accrual (of interest) to nonaccrual. Interest is still charged to the client, but the amount is not credited to the bank's earnings. At the same time, the bank will make provisions against these loans in the likelihood that it will not be repaid.

A specific provision is a simple accounting technique that withdraws a certain amount of funds from the bank's retained earnings or current profit and places it in a special reserve against this account, producing a loss. The longer the loan has been nonperforming, the larger this provision will become until the entire loan (or the exposure less realizable collateral for a secured loan) will be covered.

Where a bank has relatively few NPLs, these provisions do not present a problem. However, where a major part of its loan portfolio is having problems, the impact of provisioning can be quite significant.

As mentioned earlier, the standard minimum capital a bank is expected to have must equal at least 8 percent of its risk-weighted assets. With provisions (after a specific amount), each dollar of provision reduces the bank's capital similarly by a dollar. This may not seem much, but the impact is significant. For example, if a bank provides fully against a $100 loan, it will experience a $100 reduction in bank capital. This now means, due to the 8 percent capital adequacy ratio that it can now support $1,250 less in its loan portfolio than before.

Where banks experience major problems with their existing loans, it is usually at least partly a function of economic conditions. As further provisions are required, the bank's ability to lend is reduced further. Not surprisingly, few banks are keen to lose additional capital and so they will tighten their credit standards accordingly. As the funds become less available and interest rates rise, other clients who were borderline defaults become unable to service their debt and the bank soon needs to increase its provisions. This further reduces its ability to lend and makes it even more cautious with its advances. This process can spiral downward quickly when the banks are forced to sell off the loan collateral and in the process force the property prices down below their initial collateral valuations. So the more the banks foreclose, the more they lose and the more difficult bank lending becomes. This cycle produces what is called a credit crunch.

The overall effect of nonperforming loans is illustrated in Table 8.2 through changes in average credit ratings for Asian banks over the credit crisis. A financial strength rating is a form of credit rating designed to show the relative risk of placing a deposit or otherwise becoming a creditor of a specific bank. It considers the institution's position without the support of any government guarantees or deposit insurance schemes. The highest rating is "A" while the lowest is an "E." While depositors should feel quite safe with a B ranking, a D rank should be cause for concern. Indonesian depositors, therefore, would seem to have considerable cause for concern as their banks have achieved the lowest possible ranking. This explains why the Indonesian government felt it necessary to guarantee its financial institution deposits and other liabilities.

Besides the impact of credit ratings and lending abilities, bad debts also hamper a bank's ability to compete against other, more financially sound institutions. There is an inverse relationship between a bank's financial strength and its cost of funds. So in respect to price competition, these institutions will be poorly placed to match their competitors (particularly the larger, international banks). As their competitors will logically seek only the bank's better clients, these institutions will lose their more profitable customers and so become even weaker than before. Poor profitability may similarly hamper a bank's ability to invest in new technology as well as marketing and training. So the downward spiral discussed earlier may have a longer-term effect as well.

APPROACHES TO BANKING REFORM

The governments' initial response to the crisis was to remove the potential danger of systemic collapse. Most did so by providing a blanket

Table 8.2
Financial Strength Ratings

	Mid-1996	End-1996	Mid-1997	End-1997	Mid-1998
China	D	D	D	D	D
Indonesia	D	D	D	D	E
Korea	D	D	D	D	E+
Malaysia	C+	C/C+	C/C+	D+	D
Philippines	D+	D+	D+	D+	D+
Singapore	B	B	B	C+/B	B
Thailand	C+	C+	C+	D	E+

Source: Moody's Investor Services, 1998.

guarantee of the deposit and other liabilities of local banks and other significant deposit institutions. In addition, the regulator seized problem banks and some were subsequently liquidated. This section examines how the governments tried to revive those institutions that remained. A multifaceted approach was attempted addressed at resolving the nonperforming loans and shortage of liquidity on the asset side of the balance sheet and insufficient regulatory capital on the liability side.

Dealing with the Asset Side

Good lending policies help banks ensure a healthy assets side of their balance sheet. Many banks in Asia, however, are experiencing the costs of bad lending. The goal then is to resolve the bad loans and find ways to earn revenue from other assets.

Nonperforming Loans

In the normal course of banking, loan officers will make mistakes. Some clients who should not have gotten loans receive them anyway. Other clients who were good lending candidates when they applied have since had their business deteriorate. Still others fail through no direct fault of their own such as with the Asian financial crisis and its resulting waves of corporate collapses. Where the number of these bad debts is relatively modest, it is something that bank management is expected to address. Where major portions of the loan portfolio is nonperforming, however, then the task becomes somewhat overwhelming. The management becomes all involved in the debt collection business and ceases to be a true lender. In crisis times, such as recently experienced, governments prefer more, rather than less, lending as this is needed to restart the economy. Thus in order to remove these distractions, the standard rescue formula follows a "good bank, bad bank" approach. This entails creating asset management companies (AMCs) which then purchase the NPLs from the more troubled banks. The AMCs then concentrate on resolving the NPLs while the banks, now free of these duties, can concentrate on their surviving clients.

While asset management companies were established in a number of crisis impacted countries, the approaches differed. In the case of Indonesia and Malaysia, for example, a central government body was established for this purpose (Indonesian Bank Restructuring Agency, IBRA, and Danaharta, respectively). In contrast, Thailand adopted a split approach with a government body to address finance company NPLs and individual bank by bank AMCs for the commercial banks. Korea initially followed the national route but in April 2000 KAMCO opted for a number of individual joint ventures with foreign entities. China took only the bank by bank approach with each troubled bank having its own personal AMC (see Table 8.3).

Intuitively, the central approach might seem the most effective. One could establish the infrastructure needed to foreclose or otherwise obtain the necessary back payments. Where the re-scheduling requires writing off some debt (a haircut), a single entity would be likely to represent all of the major credits. Furthermore, and this certainly proved the case in Indonesia, the national "bad bank" could be given special legal powers not normally afforded to commercial banks. These AMCs' operations vary from country to country, but of these, Malaysia's Danaharta presents the most interesting example.

Pengurusan Danaharta Nasional (the asset management company) was established in May 1998 to remove the larger NPLs from local financial institutions with high bad debt problems (individual NPLs of over MYR 5 million from banks with over 10% NPLs). It was given special legal powers to foreclose, impose conditions, and appoint administrators not normally available to banks. While it bought NPLs at market rather than face value, Danaharta then shared 20/80 any recoveries over the purchase price with the selling bank. At the end of June 1999 Danaharta had acquired some 36 percent of then total NPLs at an average discount of 57 percent.

Other country AMC programs have generally been less effective with the liquidation of the AMC portfolios slowed by legal and other difficulties.

Securitization for Performing Assets

While the removal of bad loans from a bank loan portfolio may seem logical, the idea of removing some of the good loans, too, may not. Nevertheless securitization is an interesting way of dealing with problems on both the asset and liability side of the balance sheet. Healthy banks are expected to hold an amount of regulatory capital equal to at least 8 percent of their risky asset holdings. If a bank's capital has largely been written

Table 8.3
Asian Approaches to the Asset Management Companies

China	Individual Bank AMCs
Indonesia	Indonesian Bank Restructuring Agency
Korea	Korean Asset Management Company
Malaysia	Danaharta
Thailand	Finance Companies — Financial Restructuring Agency
	Commercial banks — Individual AMCs

off, there is insufficient capital available to support any additional new lending. Where not enough new capital funds are forthcoming, one alternative to fulfill client loan demand is through securitization.

Securitization involves the creating and sale of new financial assets backed by the security of existing loans. The bank effectively packages up a certain portion of its loan portfolio for resale to a separate special purpose vehicle, which funds this purchase through the sale of capital market securities. The end product is that while the bank originates these loans, the assets are sold rather than retained on the balance sheet. This would allow a troubled bank then to continue some lending even against a fairly depleted capital basis. As the originating bank would receive a fee for arranging the loan and, in most cases, be contracted for annual fees to manage the loans, these revenues could then be applied against other expenses.

A whole range of assets can be securitized. The key is that these assets had a common loan documentation standard, have fully amortizing payment streams, hold historically proven portfolio characteristics, are homogeneous in nature, and follow a well-defined asset originating process. All these factors then make the securitized assets suitable for credit rating.

Unfortunately, the Asian crisis came at a bad time for the region's securitization industry. In most countries, the legal and institutional structure was only being (or just) established in 1997. So with the crisis, the industry's further development has been placed on hold. As Asia Money 1998/1998 reported, Indonesia and Thailand, had held their first two programs each, one in 1996 and one in 1997 (Automobile Securitized Finance No. 1 and Indonesia Motor Vehicle Funding 19971; and SitcarsFunding Ltd and Thai Cars). Korea, too, had only just started with one issue (KE International) in 1996, as did China with the securitization of the cash flow payments expected under its Zhu hai highway project. As these raisings were all denominated in U.S. dollars, the collapse of their respective currencies made few issuers willing or able to accept any additional exposures. Similarly, recent losses in emerging market debt have meant potential investors would demand too high a premium to justify the raising.

The two markets where securitization has had and continues to show progress is Japan and, to a much lesser extent, Hong Kong. The Japanese market is slightly older with, following a change in regulations, a number of yen denominated issues in 1996. These issuers have continued to tap the local market and have been helped by improved regulatory conditions. Hong Kong, too, has had some government assistance, most notably the Hong Kong Mortgage Corporation, but its success is more a reflection of a range of international bank affiliated issuers and securitized assets (home mortgages, commercial mortgages, credit cards, and car loans) and, given the HK dollar link with the U.S. dollar, the ability to use U.S. dollar denominated paper.

Few securitization programs related to Asian financial assets to date have actually been sold in their local financial market. Instead most have been dominated in U.S. dollars and sold overseas. So while securitization offers some promise, it has not yet had a major impact in the current bank reform measures.

Dealing with the Liabilities Side

From a regulatory viewpoint, regulatory capital is the critical component of the liability side of a bank balance sheet. It serves a traditional role as a cushion whereby shareholders lose money before depositors. The problem was that the Asia crisis NPL writeoffs and provisions effectively removed much, if not all, of many banks' regulatory capital and created a deficit position instead.

Nationalization

Where a commercial bank has a severe NPL problem, it might prove too difficult to attract new additional private capital. If so, the government might need to assume total ownership. This may seem particularly attractive where the bank's actual closure will result in substantial losses to the taxpayer. The argument is that as the government will need to provide so much of the funding, it might as well take over the entire institution. Under the government's wing, the otherwise dead bank may well be restored to life and then, after a suitable period of government ownership, be sold off to the private sector.

Given the scope of the recent crisis, defacto nationalisation was an option selected in many countries including Indonesia, Japan, Korea, Malaysia, and Thailand. In each case, the intention is that these institutions will eventually be sold to private interests. In Korea, for example, the government has worked to recapitalize the two nationalized banks and it plans to sell them in the near future. Others may need to wait somewhat longer.

Nationalization certainly shows that a government is willing to act, but the problem is that it will need to act in respect to the bank's management and to act in reselling the institution quickly. The danger is that governments are often less willing to make such hard decisions once the public confidence crisis has been solved. Finally, when selling these institutions, the government must be careful not to make too many performance and risk related guarantees to the new purchasers.

Temporary Government Equity Investment

Where the NPL writeoffs are not so severe, the existing shareholders might survive with just a little additional outside assistance. Again, some short-term capital investment may prove (in the long run at least) potentially less expensive for the taxpayers. By boosting a troubled bank's regulatory capital to the appropriate level, the recapitalized bank can then provide at least some lending support for its better clients and perhaps help other marginal NPLs to restructure.

While Indonesia and Thailand have both made selective new equity investments, Malaysia's experiences are the most interesting. Its government equity investments were conducted via a special purpose vehicle, Danamodal Nasional. It injected new capital through a variety of instruments (ordinary shares, preference shares, and exchangeable subordinate capital loans) into 10 troubled financial institutions and in the process their average risk-weighted capital adequacy ratio moved from 9.8 percent at the end of August 1998 to 13.9 percent at the end of June 1999.

Danamodal intended to earn an internal return on its investments of 12 percent per annum and recover its funds within five years. These funds could simply be repaid or the securities sold back to the institutions' initial owners, new shareholders (foreign banks restricted to a maximum of 30 percent), or the general public. As of the end of June 1999, Danamodal had provided some MYR 6.2 billion in new capital (3.5 to banks, 2.4 to finance companies, and 0.3 to merchant banks). Some have since repaid part of these funds and further returns may result from the planned mergers.

Other Private Sector Equity Investment

In each of the crisis countries, regulators have called on the banks' existing shareholders to provide additional funds or potentially lose their total investment. Where the bank has negative equity, investing new money is not so attractive. Nevertheless some shareholders have sought to retain their bank ownership. Alternatively, the needed private capital can be found from new shareholders. Here Thailand has been the most aggressive with its major banks, like Bangkok Bank and Siam Commercial, having both local and international share and other capital issues. Similarly, Thailand has been more progressive in allowing foreign banks to take a major shareholding, or expand their interests, in Thai banks. Some of these investments include the Development Bank of Singapore in the Thai Danu Bank, HSBC in Bangkok Metropolitan Bank, and Standard Chartered in Nakornthon Bank.

Mergers with Other Banks or Financial Institutions

An alternative source of private capital is through mergers. Where some banks have survived the crisis well, they might be persuaded (or directed) to merge with their less successful competitors. The resulting combined institution would result in not only improved capital ratios (from the troubled bank viewpoint) but also access to potential better management skills. There may even be some direct economic benefits such as reducing over capacity or reducing costs via branch consolidations, enhanced technology or other potential synergies. However, even in the absence of direct benefits, the regulator could claim that the weaker institution at least appeared to have been rescued.

These "savior" type mergers are not confined to just rescuing banks. Malaysia has used a similar approach to resolving its post crisis finance company problems; designating a bank as a de facto sponsor of a troubled finance company or companies. More recently, Korea has allowed the Korea Exchange Bank to merge with its merchant bank affiliate, the Korea International Merchant Bank. Similarly in Thailand, many of the remaining finance companies will eventually be merged with an existing local bank or acquired by foreign financial institutions.

Not all of these are mergers in the traditional sense. Malaysia's famous plan to merge 55 institutions into just 10 (initially only 6) banks is certainly merger by fiat. It remains to be seen, despite lots of press releases, whether all of these Malaysian mergers eventuate. Korea's Financial Supervisory Commission avoided these potential squabbles among merging institutions by simply revoking the licenses of five troubled banks (Donghwa, Dongnam, Daedong, Chungchong, and Kyungki). It then transferred their assets to five more sound ones (Shinhan, Housing & Commercial, Kookmin, Hana, and Koram, respectively).

Even prior to the crisis, many countries had tried to encourage mergers among their banks and other institutions. Prior to deregulation, for example, Indonesia had long offered incentives for private banks to merger. In order to open additional branches, for example, Indonesian banks had first to merger with a set number of other banks. The same was true to gain a foreign exchange license. These policies were in part based on the rational objective of increasing the capital base of these otherwise generally small institutions.

Other countries have taken similar, but less direct, action by gradually increasing the paid-up capital that their banks must have to continue operations. The banks might of course raise these funds themselves, but a merger might also help reach the threshold. Singapore, for example, introduced an SGD 1.5 billion paid-up capital requirement to force mergers within the four major banking groups (the Tat Lee and Keppel Bank merger also resulted). Malaysia took a slightly different approach in 1994 for more paid-up capital through a new two-tier licensing system where only the larger institutions qualified for tier one status. Tier one banks enjoy certain privileges not available to the tier two deposit-taking institutions.

Deposit Insurance

As mentioned earlier, an immediate measure to counter systemic collapse, as well as the deteriorating credit standing of troubled local banks, was a general government guarantee of the banking sector's liabilities. As Malaysia's Deputy Minister of Finance, Wong See Wah (August 1999) explained, the blanket guarantee of all deposits in the banking system " . . . was critical to maintain confidence and avoid widespread bank runs." While this stopped the problem from worsening, it presents an interesting challenge for the country concerned. Eventually, they will need to convert what is now billions of dollars in effectively risk-free assets into ones (depending on the asset, issuer, and country) with potentially considerable risk. A gradual transition would seem the logical approach—no guarantees on deposits or other liabilities created after a certain date. The worry is what will happen at that time. A politically attractive alternative is to reduce but not remove the coverage. It is here that deposit insurance becomes attractive. Rather than all liabilities, only deposits would retain specific protection. Furthermore, this depositor protection would be available only up to a certain limit. More importantly, this protection would be restructured so that ideally the financial institutions and their clients rather than the taxpayer would pay it.

As shown in Table 8.4, deposit insurance is not unknown in Asia. Japan, Taiwan, and the Philippines have long had some form of deposit insurance. The Philippines scheme currently covers up to 100,000 pesos or around US$2,500 per account (some 93 percent of all bank accounts in the Philippines) compared to Taiwan's net total deposits (NTD) 1,000,000 or approximately, US$30,0000. Indonesia introduced government protection in early 1998 with plans to formalize this scheme over 1999–2000. Vietnam has similarly introduced a scheme in August 2000. Malaysia and Thailand were still considering the matter. Only in Hong Kong (it was seriously considered in 1992) and in Australia (the Wallis Report rejected it) is there currently no form of explicit deposit insurance.

The danger is that many government officials may view deposit insurance as way to solve their banking crisis. By itself, however, it will do

Table 8.4
Explicit Deposit Insurance in Asia Pacific

Australia	None
China	May consider deposit insurance
Hong Kong	Considered, but no formal plans
Indonesia	Government guarantees
Korea	Korea Deposit Insurance Corporation
Japan	Deposit Insurance Corporation
Malaysia	Selected guarantees
Philippine	Philippines Deposit Insurance Corporation
Singapore	POS Bank guarantee (non-post DBS merger)
Thailand	Government guarantees
Taiwan	Central Deposit Insurance Corporation
Vietnam	Vietnam Deposit Insurance Agency

little but potentially postponing and compounding the actual problem. As potential depositors look to the insurance coverage, they are not so concerned about the bank's risk, which arises from the management quality of the bank.

Another difficulty to resolve is that, as Kane (1986) pointed out, in most countries deposit insurance is not insurance at all but rather a full guarantee to depositors for all or up to a stated amount of deposits. Instead, it must be structured so that some market risks must remain. As the president of the Philippines Deposit Insurance Corporation, Ernest Leung (Dumlao, 1998) commented, "full insurance cover takes away the incentives for depositors to ascertain for themselves the condition of the bank and the risk of closure." Banks may then select more risky undertakings knowing that their funding costs, at least in respect to insured deposits, will not be affected. If successful, the managers and shareholders benefit. If they are not, both groups lose but it is the depositor insurer (usually the taxpayer) that covers any deficit. This moral hazard danger is well proven across a range of developed markets. So to revitalize market discipline, any insurance coverage must come with a requirement that these institutions raise at least a specified portion of their funding through uninsured, subordinate debt issues.

While the U.S. system has not yet required this, the costs to the taxpayers of the savings and loan association crisis would have been dramatically lessened if they had. Only where larger depositors, other credits, shareholders, and managers are forced to face the real risks can moral hazard dangers be minimized.

An alternative, adopted by Hong Kong in 1995, it to require that any bank liquidations give preference to small depositors up to a certain amount (to HKD 100,000 in Hong Kong) or all depositors in the case of Australia. This places further pressure on nondepositors but depends on the existence of a range of credit groups to be successful. If the latter becomes required, then it may offer substantial advantages over the traditional U.S. model.

It would be pleasant to suggest that recent moves for governments to limit their overall exposures reflect an understanding of market discipline. Sadly, it is a more accurate reflection to say that governments are finally starting to understand their potential risk exposures and are moving quickly to limit them. In Japan, for example, where its Deposit Insurance Corporation has provided full protection to depositors regardless of amount, a 10 million yen upper limit per depositor will commence in April 2001. Similarly, Korean deposit insurance protection was reduced to W 20 million (including accrued interest) on new deposits with any institution that fails prior to 2001. The scheme would be continued in 2001 as announced.

The danger is that deposit insurance may come to be viewed as a solution rather than just a band-aid. Deposit insurance will only work if the financial sector works, too. It is likely to increase the need for regulation, not reduce it. As Jeffrey Tan of RAM (Adbullah, October 13, 1999), explained, "there would need to be better enforcement of banking laws preventing banks from making related-party loans and better corporate governance." Otherwise as Goodhart (1988) warned, such schemes will simply force the larger and better-managed institutions into "subsidising the small and risky units."

APPROACHES TO REGULATORY REFORM

The problem of course is not entirely a function of bad bankers. Bad regulators are similarly at fault. However rather than allocate blame, a new system should be implemented. One centered on the four principles of transparency, ability, regulatory dominance, and independence or the TARDI principles.

Transparency

Transparency, or rather the lack of transparency, has been one of the key lessons from the crisis. If banks and their regulators were forced to disclose the true position of their finances, the current problems would have been caught much earlier. Transparency forces both bankers and regulators alike to do their jobs. Financial institutions must release detailed market-related accounts on a quarterly basis. As financial institutions are preparing weekly or fortnightly balance sheets for regulatory purposes, this rich information source should not be hidden from the market. The threat that the depositors will shift their funds based on these disclosures will force bankers to work for both depositors and shareholders. Poor reporting only postpones corrective actions. This empowers the regulators and the regulated to increase moral hazard actions and increases the likelihood that taxpayers rather than just shareholders suffering. If publicly listed companies are required to reveal the company's financial status to the shareholders, why should there not be a report to the depositors who have a majority claim on the assets of the banks? In some respects, the Reserve Bank of New Zealand has set the example by disclosing in due course all information that it receives from its regulated banks. In contrast, Bank Indonesia has discovered that its own bank secrecy legislation unintentionally curtails any disclosure it might seek about any of its banks.

Ability

The ability of bankers and regulators is equally important. The rapid pre-crisis expansion of the local banking industries in Asia meant that the demand for good staff greatly exceeded supply. This caused some staff to be promoted beyond their abilities. Still others attracted by higher and higher salaries "bank hopped" building their resumes but not their depth of experience. The enforcement of certain minimum education and experience standards for senior bank staff would force the industry to invest more in training and in graduates. It would likewise help to limit future overexpansions. In contrast with the private sector, most state bank employees and regulatory officials have traditionally been poorly paid. Similarly, in these days, where performance related compensation is popular, these employees fall further behind. Regulators must be sufficiently rewarded to attract and retain good quality staff but this remains a problem both for regulators and government banks. The costs have been very apparent with the nonperforming loan problems experienced in China, Indonesia, and Korea. This can be redressed by funding tertiary training, expanding macro-economy based bank training and has been partly addressed by a range of Asian Development Bank and World Bank institutional strengthening programs. In the meantime expertise could come from multinational banks already in these countries. A more urgent task is to create incentives to capture a core of dedicated men and women with abilities to remain and serve at the middle and top levels of the central banks and security commissions. Singapore authorities have a rule that prevents the very handsomely remunerated central bank managers from seeking employment in any private sector banks for eight years. Retaining and rewarding the central banker with ability is a remedy for the mediocrity found in some central banks whose staff leave the central banks to seek greener pastures.

Regulatory Dominance

This means that it is the regulators that control the industry, rather than the reverse. It requires that one prudential regulator is responsible for all financial institutions and that this regulator has been given the necessary power to perform its responsibilities. It will cover all aspects rather than just the banks or other specified institutional types. As the Wallis Inquiry in Australia concluded, the system needs to be sufficiently flexible so that it captures all of the institutions offering similar financial products/activities. So insurance, provident funds, and other nonbank financial institutions should be placed under the same regulatory umbrella as the banking system. Both the UK and Australia have moved in this direction that has freed the central bank to concentrate on the macroeconomic management.

Independence

This means that the regulator not only has the legal independence but the real power to implement decisions. Over 1997–1998, there were a number of resignations and sackings of senior regulators in Indonesia, Malaysia, and Thailand. Had these officials had real independence, corrective action might have been taken sooner. Germany, the UK, the United States, and New Zealand provide some excellent examples as to how this might be accomplished and the Japanese and the Philippines have certainly taken an important step in this direction. The past history of intervention by politicians and well-connected business people must not be repeated.

CONCLUSION

The banking sector in Asia has undergone dramatic change. Over the last three decades it has been transformed from a system subjected to substantial direct controls and other restraints on competition to one where competition is a fact of day-to-day business. The regulatory system has changed with the banking industry, but unfortunately not exactly at the same speed. It has been a follower rather than a leader. This is unfortunate as a number of inappropriate practices were allowed to develop and other poor policies not corrected. These have resulted, and will result, in substantial losses to local taxpayers, but the true costs, the costs of reduced or negative economic growth, are much higher. It would be nice to conclude that these problems have now been identified and so these regulatory systems have been corrected, but sadly the evidence remains mixed. With recovery, the previous pressure for significant change has waned and it is all too likely that a major portion of the needed reforms will be simply forgotten until Asia Crisis II comes by to remind us.

REFERENCES

Abdullah, D. O. (1999). "KL Central Bank Studying Set-up of Deposit Insurance Scheme," *Business Times,* 23 October.

Ariff, M., and Khalid, A. (2000). *Liberalisation, Growth and Asian Financial Crisis.* Cheltenham, MA: Elgar Publishing.

Delhaise, P. F. (1998). *Asia in Crisis: The Implosion of the Banking and Finance Systems.* Singapore: John Wiley and Sons.

Dumlao, D. (1998). "38 Troubled Banks Lose PDIC Insurance." *Philippines Daily Inquirer,* 22 October.

Goldstein, M. (1998). "Halifax II Reforms." In *The Asian Financial Crisis: Causes, Cures, and Systemic Implications* (pp. 45–64). Washington, DC: Institute for International Economics.

Goodhart, C. (1988). *The Evolution of Central Bank.* Cambridge, MA: MIT Press.

Kane, E. (1986). "Appearance and Reality in Deposit Insurance: The Case for Reform," *Journal of Banking and Finance,* 23 (June), pp. 175–189.

———. (2000). "Designing Financial Safety Nets to Fit Country Circumstances," Keynote speech delivered at the Asia Pacific Finance Association Meetings, Tokyo, July 13, 2000.

Moody's Capital Markets. (2000). *Annual Report.*

Wong See Wah. (1999). "How Malaysia Tackled the Financial Crisis." Speech given at the University of Xiamen, Fujian, China, August 6.

CHAPTER 9

Bank Operating Strategies and Impact of Crisis: The Malaysian Case

Mohd Nordin Asudalli and Obiyathulla Ismath Bacha

INTRODUCTION

Malaysia's banking sector appears to have suffered its second major crisis within the last two decades. The first major crisis was in 1985. In both instances, the banking crises had been preceded by a period of rapid economic growth and asset inflation, particularly in the broad property sector. In both instances too, the banking crises had been the result of externally induced economic shocks. Whereas the first crisis was due largely to a drop in prices of export commodities, the recent crisis was the result of a sudden depreciation in the ringgit and the policy response to that speculative currency attack.

That the banking sector, despite very vibrant precrisis growth remains fragile, points at underlying vulnerability. The seven-year period (1990–1996) preceding the recent crisis had seen rapid growth in bank assets and total loans and advances. While assets had grown a cumulative 272 percent over the period, total loans and advances had cumulative growth of 259 percent.[1] In addition to rapid growth in loans and assets, what appears to have contributed to banking system vulnerability was the direction of lending.

Loan portfolios were skewed toward the broad property sector (Construction, Properties, and Real Estate); slightly more than half of all bank lending had been directed to this sector. Additionally, share financing for the purchase of shares, though small in proportion had grown rapidly. It has been these two sectors that had seen the quickest deterioration in asset quality and contributed the most to the Nonperforming Loan (NPL) problem.

This is not surprising given the fact that both the above sectors are highly sensitive to interest rate movements. Defense of the currency necessitated sharp and severe rate hikes, coupled with the general loss of confidence and uncertain economic environment, both stocks and the grossly overbuilt property sectors went through a near meltdown. What was surprising was the extent to which the banking sector had exposed itself to these vulnerable sectors.

Objective and Motivation

Despite the systemic nature of the crisis, it is clear that some banks suffered more than others. Though the macroeconomic shocks were beyond the control of individual banks, their vulnerabilities were dependent on their assets profile, their precrisis growth strategies, and their chosen funding strategies.

The objective of this study is to determine whether the differential impact of the crisis on individual banks was due to differences in asset profile, growth strategy, and funding strategy. We address the following research questions:

Was there significant difference in the loan profile of the worst affected versus least affected banks, in particular, exposure to the vulnerable sectors?

Were there any differences in the earnings of banks that grew rapidly precrisis with those that were more conservative?

Did the fast growing banks suffer larger earnings contraction during the crisis?

Did banks that chose a higher leverage strategy earn more precrisis and did they suffer more during the crisis?

What were the differentiating features between the worst hit versus least affected banks?

The Malaysian Banking System—An Overview

Malaysia's financial system can be divided into two broad categories, the banking system and the nonbank financial intermediaries. Like most developing economies, the financial system is lopsided, with the banking sector being far larger than the others. The banking sector accounted for 70 percent of the total assets of the financial system as at end 1998.[2] Within the banking system[3] the commercial banks are the main players accounting for 76 percent of total loans and 71 percent of all deposits. As at end June 1999, there were a total of 34 commercial banks (excluding Bank Islam Malaysia) with 1,735 branches nationwide. This includes 13 locally incorporated foreign banks. Following Bank Negara Malaysia (BNM) requirement in 1994, foreign banks were locally incorporated. In essence, the foreign banks simply became wholly owned subsidiaries of their foreign parent as opposed to having been mere branches. The 1994 exercise saw 14 foreign banks incorporating locally and 2 foreign banks being bought out by Malaysian entities. These were Security Pacific Asian Bank, which became Arab-Malaysian Bank Berhad, and United Overseas Bank, which became Phileo Allied Bank Bhd. A listing of commercial banks, their asset size, and year of establishment is shown in Appendix 9.1.

This chapter is divided into six sections. The section entitled "Review of Literature," below, provides a review of relevant literature. "Data and Methodology" outlines our data and methodology. The section "Factors Differentiating the Performance of Commercial Banks" presents the results and discusses the implications. The next section, entitled "Comparison between the Five Worst Affected and the Five Least Affected Domestic Banks," compares the five worst and least affected banks and provides an overall comparison of domestic and foreign banks. The final section, entitled "Conclusion," concludes the chapter.

REVIEW OF LITERATURE

Many factors have been identified as contributors to banking crises. Goldstein and Turner (1996) list eight factors that cause banking crises in emerging economies. They are (1) macroeconomic volatility, external and internal; (2) lending booms, asset price collapses, and surges in capital inflows; (3) increased bank liabilities with large maturity or currency mismatches; (4) inadequate preparation for financial liberalization; (5) heavy government involvement and loose control of connected lending; (6) weaknesses in accounting, disclosure and legal frameworks; (7) distorted incentives; and (8) exchange rate regimes. We outline below some of the key relationships between the above factors and banking crises.

Macroeconomic Volatility, External and Internal

Banks operate with high leverage and hold relatively small amounts of cash. Deposits are redeemable at par, and depositors are assured that they can get immediate access to liquidity. These characteristics make the banking business vulnerable to large relative price changes and to losses of confidence. According to the authors, one of the external sources of large fluctuations is the change in the terms of trade. When banks' customers suddenly find that the terms of trade have turned sharply against them, their ability to service existing loans is likely to be impaired. Caprio and Klingebiel (1996) report that 75 percent of the developing countries in their sample, which experienced a banking crisis, suffered a terms-of-trade decline of at least 10 percent prior to the crisis. Other things being equal, countries with relatively low export diversification are more susceptible to a banking crisis.

Volatility in international interest rates, and induced effects on private capital flows also contribute to a banking crisis. Not only do fluctuations in international interest rates affect the cost of borrowing for the emerging market but they also alter the relative attractiveness of investing in the market. For Asian developing countries that are members of the Asia Pacific Economic Council (APEC), net inflows in capital account roughly doubled [as a share of host-country gross domestic product (GDP)] from the 1984–1988 period to the 1989–1993 period. Incompletely sterilized capital inflows boost banks' deposits and tempt banks to increase lending even at the expense of lower credit quality. This plants the seeds of trouble when the boom collapses. And when capital flows out unexpectedly as a result of a loss of confidence, there is the possibility that banks will face serious liquidity problems to meet the sudden withdrawal of bank deposits.

The third type of external volatility comes from changes in real exchange rates. Real exchange rate volatility can cause difficulties for banks either directly when there is currency or maturity mismatch between bank liabilities and assets or indirectly when exchange rate volatility creates large losses for bank borrowers. Kaminsky and Reinhart (1996) observe that sharp real exchange rate appreciation typically precedes a banking crisis.

Domestically, both growth and inflation rates are often highly volatile. One of the strongest conclusions of the empirical literature on early-warning signals of financial crisis is that sharp contractions in economic activity increase the probability of banking crises. Caprio and Klingebiel (1996) report that volatility of growth and inflation rates exhibited a rising trend over the 1960–1994 period for countries experiencing systemic banking crises over the period, no such trend was evident for countries experiencing less severe or no banking difficulties.

Lending Booms, Assets Price Collapses, and Surges in Capital Inflows

Excessive credit creation and unsound financing during the expansion phase of a business cycle can trigger a banking crisis when the bubble bursts. Three features of recent experience provide support for this argument. First, both bank lending booms and declines in equity prices have often preceded banking crises. Second, those emerging economies that received the largest net private capital inflows are also those that experienced the most rapid expansion in their commercial banking sectors. And finally, part of the capital inflows in the 1990s might be regarded as a bubble built on overoptimism about the effects of policy reform in host countries. Kaminsky and Reinhart (1996) find the sharp declines in equity prices to be among the best leading indicators of banking crises.

Exchange Rate Regime

The exchange rate regime can affect vulnerability to speculative attack, the way in which the real value of impaired bank assets is adjusted downward. It is noted that a sharp appreciation of the real exchange rate has been shown to be a useful leading indicator of banking crises.

This author has previously argued elsewhere that the Malaysian banking crisis was catalyzed by the Asian currency crisis but was aggravated by the policy response to the currency crisis. In response to the speculative attack on the ringgit and in attempting an orderly depreciation, the central bank, BNM, had to sharply raise interest rates. This action transmitted the currency problem into a banking one. The extent of potential damage to domestic banking as a result of this will depend on how vulnerable the banking sector is. If the domestic banking sector is not too leveraged, has well-diversified portfolios, is not exposed to highly leveraged borrowers, and does not have acute asset-liability mismatches, then it would likely withstand the interest rate shock better. Otherwise, a systemic banking crisis could result.

According to the author, there were several factors that caused the vulnerability of the Malaysian banking sector. Among these were, excessive credit growth, overleveraging and asset inflation commercial banks assets grew at an average of 20.7 percent per annum from 1990 to 1997, or cumulative growth of 272 percent. During the same period the total loans and advances grew 20.1 percent on average per year for a cumulative growth of 259 percent. This close resemblance implies that almost all the asset side expansion of commercial banks came from growth in loans and advances.

The excessive credit growth had induced asset inflation. While the overall inflation level as measured by consumer price index (CPI) remained relatively low, that is, averaging around 4 percent per annum, isolated pockets of inflation were visible particularly in the real estate/property sector and the stock market. The broad property sector is highly cyclical whereas stocks are prone to volatility. In addition, both sectors are highly interest rate sensitive. Any increase in interest rates therefore would cause serious problems to a banking system exposed to these sectors.

Some researchers explain the key determinant of strong and uninterrupted loan growth in relation to the profit-maximizing behavior of the Malaysian banking system between 1988 and 1997. Between 1993 and 1997, banking sector loans grew at an annual compounded rate of 25 percent while the Malaysian economy grew at an average of 8 percent per annum. Credit growth picked up consistently from less than 10.0 percent in early 1993 to a high of 28 percent in late 1995, hovering at that level for the next two years with the broad property sector accounting for almost 40 percent of new loans. In absolute amounts, bank credit soared from RM0.77 billion in 1988 to RM41.9 billion in 1997, averaging RM40.3 billion a year. Using regression analysis, they show that some 96 percent of variation in bank Profit Before Tax (PBT) is explained by loan growth.

The 10-year period, 1988–1997 is shown to have been highly conducive to such a buildup in loan growth due to strong loan demand, strong liquidity growth, and a noninterventionist and supportive regulatory stance (fiscal as well as monetary).

The authors suggest the loan/deposit ratio (LDR) as a tool to check excessive rate of loan growth. A lower LDR reduces the excesses of leverage risk, of over-investment and of over-heating pressure. A regulatory LDR limit can be seen as a prompt corrective indicator, requiring banks to recognize early the risks associated with rising profitability, future NPLs, and a weaker balance sheet and income statement.

Lee (1998) explains the impact of the October 1997 revision of the BNM/GP3 guidelines on NPLs of financial institutions. BNM/GP3 are guidelines on the treatment of interest and nonperforming accounts issued by BNM to the financial institutions. Following the revision, assets are to be classified NPL if they had been unserviced for three months as opposed to six months previously. Using BNM reports, the author shows the impact of these changes on the NPL status of banks. If the three-month criterion is applied to the banking system as a whole, the percentage of NPLs would be at 6.8 percent at the end of 1997 from 3.6 percent in mid-97 under the six-month criteria. Essentially this amounts to a near doubling of NPLs over a six-month period.

However, these guidelines restored the six-month classification after imposition of capital controls in September 1998 but effective from January 1, 1998.[4] Therefore, the NPLs and provision for doubtful and bad debts figures for 1998 and 1999 are comparable to the figures prior to the crisis. As such any increase would be attributable to a deterioration in the quality of loans and not to changes in the classification of NPLs.

Financial Liberalization and Risk Management

Thillainathan (1998) argues that the banking industry in Asia, including Malaysia, is more traditional and inward-looking compared to that of the West. In the West, the emergence of fund managers and non-bank-based financial institutions has displaced the banking sector as the biggest mobilizer of savings on the one hand, and as the biggest investor and lender on the other.

The restrictions and the underdevelopment of capital markets and non-bank financial institutions makes Asia overly dependent on its banking sector. Given the influence of the banks on money supply and the high-risk nature of the banking business, this overdependence has increased the macroeconomic vulnerabilities and risk profile. Further, as the banks engaged in payment functions the overreliance has also increased the exposure of Asian economies to systemic risk.

The high-risk nature of banking can arise from the high gearing and asset liability mismatch that characterize this industry. The high gearing may in fact create incentives for risky or imprudent lending. The massive asset-liability mismatches can convert a liquidity crisis into a solvency crisis. A run on banks can cause a multiple contraction in credit and hence lead to macroeconomic instability.

This is unlike the situation in the fund management industry where the risks are borne by the investors. Any difference in the liquidity needs and the maturity profile of the investment portfolio can be met by the liquidation of the underlying assets. Such liquidations will lead to price volatility, where the risk has to be borne by investors. However, as any fund outflow has to be exactly matched by the inflow, liquidity and systemic risks are minimized.

A well-developed financial sector is likely to minimize the mismatches between provider and end-users of funds and transfer the remaining risk to those who are willing to bear them, which is not necessarily the bank. The underdevelopment of the capital markets causes over-concentration of risks in the banks and lack of risk management products prevents the banks transferring the risks to those who are better able to bear them.

High gearing, which is the characteristic of the banking industry, may have been made possible only because of the implicit government guarantee on deposits. In the absence of this guarantee, the market's tolerance level for gearing would have been lower. Although this implicit guarantee is needed to stimulate a high rate of deposits for the country, it has resulted in the problem of "moral hazard" to the banking sector, namely, of bankers having an incentive to engage in more risky lending.

It has been argued that banking crises in Asia were due to the particular structural characteristics of Asian financial systems, often referred to as the "Asian model" of capitalism. First, Asian countries generally favor a centralized and behind-the-scenes relationship between financial institutions, business, and government for the intermediation and allocation of capital. In general, a large share of lending and investment decisions were not made by a decentralized open capital market via arms-length transactions, but rather by personal and business relationships or government influence.

Second, financial institutions and other agents were lacking the incentive to manage risk effectively. Banks' capital was usually small, which makes the owners' risk relatively little for lending into excessively risky projects. Depositors were offered implicit or explicit deposit insurance and therefore did not monitor the lending decisions of the banks. The banks themselves were typically given implicit guarantees of a government bailout in the event of adverse financial conditions. The presence of such financial insurance posed a clear moral hazard problem that distorted the incentives to carry out a proper risk assessment of investment projects.

DATA AND METHODOLOGY

All data for this study is obtained from the annual reports of the respective banks, several issues of BNM Monthly Statistical Bulletin, and BNM annual reports. The study covers the nine-year period from 1990 to 1998.[5] It covers all domestic commercial banks in Malaysia but excludes Bank Islam Malaysia Berhad (BIMB) because of the different nature of its business; and Sime Bank Berhad (SIME) because of the nonavailability of data for 1998, the year in which the bank was bought over by RHB Bank Berhad. The most recent annual report available for SIME was that of March 1997, which was before the currency crisis. Although, BIMB, and SIME are excluded, their data is retained in the study for the purpose of comparison. The study also includes five foreign banks incorporated in Malaysia. Our sample therefore consists of 21 domestic and 5 foreign banks. The list of banks and their financial year-end date is shown in Appendix 9.1.

In mid-1997, BNM required the commercial banks to include data on loans and advances analyzed by economic sectors in their annual reports. This requirement was only effective from the financial year-end (FYE) of December 1997. The banks, whose annual account date falls before December, did not include the data in their 1997 annual reports. For these banks, the earliest data available for loan portfolios by economic sectors is from the year 1997, that is, from their 1998 reports, as the banks are required to provide previous year figures for comparison. For the other banks, the data available is from the year 1996.

The data from annual reports is on a yearly basis. Since the currency crisis started in mid-1997, which was also the middle of the accounting year for the majority of commercial banks, the data does not show the immediate impact of the currency crisis. In addition, the balance sheet items are at a single point of time, that is, the balance sheet date, which may not represent the true situation on the other dates. Differences of accounting year make the data on income statements not directly comparable, especially absolute numbers. We therefore use percentages in all comparisons and evaluations.

The period under study, 1990 to 1999, is divided into two subperiods, namely, the period prior to the crisis and the period of the crisis. Since data collected is from banks' annual reports, which come once a year, and the currency crisis started in mid-year, that is, July 1997, this study has adjusted the duration of the subperiods in accordance with the advent of the crisis. For banks whose FYE fall before July 1, data for the period prior to crisis is taken from annual reports of 1991–1997, while data for the period during the crisis is from 1998 to 1999. For banks whose FYE fall after July 1, the period prior to crisis is from 1990 to 1996 while the period during crisis is from 1997 to 1998.

The annualized growth of PBT is used as the measure to assess how vulnerable banks were to the currency crisis. The banks are ranked according to the annualized growth of PBT during the period of crisis with the largest contraction in growth indicating the most affected banks (see Appendix 9.2). Besides PBT, this study uses growth in total assets, provision for doubtful and bad debts, interest income and expenses, Return on Equity (ROE), Total Debt Ratio (TDR), and loans/deposits ratio (LDR) as measures where appropriate.

We use a parametric and a nonparametric statistical test procedure to measure the significance of a difference of means between two distributions. The distributions tested are between the worst affected banks and least affected banks. All statistical tests use one-tailed tests.

Given the small population size, the Student's t-test is used as the parametric test while for nonparametric test procedure, we use the Mann-Whitney U-test methodology. The nonparametric statistical procedure is useful in making inferences in situations where serious doubt exists about the assumption that both populations are normally distributed. The test procedure involves ranking the n_1 and n_2 observations independently from the two populations from the smallest (rank = 1) to the highest (rank = $n_1 + n_2$). Ranking for tied observations are averaged and the rank is assigned to each of the tied observations. Then the sum T_A of the ranks for sample A and the sum T_B of the ranks for sample B are calculated. The rank sums are used in constructing the test statistic.

The logic is that if distribution A is shifted to the right of distribution B, then the rank sum T_A should exceed T_B. The Mann-Whitney U-test statistic will use one of the two quantities UA or UB shown by the formulas below:

$$U_A = n_1 n_2 + \frac{n_1(n_1 + 1)}{2} - T_A$$

$$U_B = n_1 n_2 + \frac{n_2(n_2 + 1)}{2} - T_B$$

where:

$$n_1 = \text{Number of observations in sample A}$$

$$n_2 = \text{Number of observations in sample B}$$

$$U_A + U_B = n_1 n_2$$

T_A and T_B = Rank sums for samples A and B, respectively

All Mann-Whitney U-tests in this study except the fifth test are to detect a shift in the A distribution to the right of the B distribution and will reject the null hypothesis of "no difference in the population distributions" if U_A is less than U_0. For the fifth test, the test is to detect a shift in the B distribution to the right of the A distribution and will reject the null hypothesis of "no difference in the population distributions" if U_B is less than U_0. (From the distribution function of U for the Mann-Whitney Tests; U_0 is the Argument, $P(U \leq U_0)$.)

Proportion of Loan Portfolio in Vulnerable Sectors and Impact on Performance.

In addressing the first research question, the percentage of Gross Non-performance Loans (GNPL) for each economic sector is used as a measure to determine vulnerability of the sectors. The GNPL is nonperformance loans before deducting interest-in-suspense and provision for doubtful and bad debts. We find that GNPL had increased for all economic sectors during the crisis period. Overall, GNPL increased from 3.56 percent in June 1997 to 12.10 percent in December 1999 with the highest increase recorded in September 1998 at 14.11 percent. The severity of the impact was not equal for all economic sectors. The most vulnerable sectors were the Purchase of Securities, Real Estate, and Construction while the least vulnerable were the Electricity, Gas and Water, Residential Property, and the Agriculture, Hunting, Forestry, and Fishing sectors (see Appendix 9.3).

GNPL for the Purchase of Securities sector increased from 1.02 percent before the currency crisis in June 1997 to 13.22 percent in December 1999 with the highest rate recorded in September 1998 at 32.94 percent. The amount of loans approved for this sector was relatively small at about 8 percent of the total loans approved by commercial banks. Nevertheless, it contributed the highest in terms of amount and percentage to the GNPL particularly during the third quarter of 1998. The GNPL for the Construction sector increased from 4.37 percent in June 1997 to 19.31 percent in December 1999 while the GNPL for the Real Estate sector increased from 8.27 percent to 18.21 during the same period. (See Appendix 9.3.)

The consolidated percentages of loan portfolios to the Construction, Real Estate, and Purchase of Securities sectors by bank are shown in Appendix 9.4. The percentages of loan portfolios to these sectors during the crisis years are averaged and used as a measure to determine which banks had the higher exposure to these vulnerable sectors (see Appendix 9.5). The five domestic banks that had the highest rate of exposure (denoted by**) are grouped together and compared against the five domestic banks that had the lowest exposure (denoted by*). Then, the means of annualized growth of PBT of both groups are tested using the Student's t-test and Mann-Whitney U-test methodologies at 95 percent confidence level.

Effect of Loan Portfolios in Vulnerable Sectors on the Annualized Growth of PBT

$$H_o: L_{LP} - L_{SP} = 0$$
$$H_a: L_{LP} - L_{SP} > 0$$

where

L_{LP} is the annualized rate of PBT contraction by the group of banks that had large portfolios in vulnerable sectors.

L_{SP} is the annualized rate of PBT contraction by group of banks that had small portfolios in vulnerable sectors.

The null hypothesis is that the group that had a large proportion of their loan portfolio in vulnerable sectors, had no difference in the annualized rate of PBT contraction than the group that had the lower proportion. The null hypothesis can be rejected if statistical results show that the mean is bigger, implying that the banks with a large loan portfolio in vulnerable sectors performed worse than others that had a lower proportion.

Effect of Loan Growth on Bank Performance

We next use the LDR[6] to examine whether loan growth had any effect on the performance of banks before and during the currency crisis. Deposits from customers is the major source of funds for the banking sector, while at the same time constituting the biggest item of their liabilities. Besides deposits, banks use money market funds and subordinated loans to finance their loan portfolios. The amount of shareholder funds is relatively small compared to the loan portfolios of banks because of the leveraged nature of the banking business. The LDR indicates how aggressive a bank is in managing its loan growth. A high ratio would indicate aggressiveness.

Banks that could not raise enough deposits but wished to have greater loan growth borrow money from the Interbank market, issue subordinated loans, or raise new capital. Some banks may prefer to use Interbank market funds rather than raising subordinated loans or new capital as it is easier to get funds from that source. Additionally, borrowed funds give higher returns to shareholders given the financial leverage.

The LDR of each domestic bank for the nine-year period was averaged to indicate which banks had the higher ratio during the period (see

Appendix 9.6). Next, the five banks with the highest LDR (denoted by **) are grouped into one group, while the five banks with the lowest ratio are grouped into another group. Two statistical tests for each parametric and non-parametric method are conducted using these grouped samples. The first test is to assess the effect of the LDR on the annualized growth of PBT in the period **before the crisis;** and the second test to assess the annualized rate of PBT contraction **during the crisis** period.

Effect of Loan Growth (LDR) on the Annualized Growth of PBT in Period before the Crisis

$$H_o: P_{HL} - P_{LL} = 0$$
$$H_a: P_{HL} - P_{LL} > 0$$

where

P_{HL} is the annualized growth of PBT in the period before the crisis for the group of banks that had high LDR.

P_{LL} is the annualized growth of PBT in the period before the crisis for the group of banks that had low LDR.

The null hypothesis is that the group with the higher LDR had no difference in the annualized growth of PBT in the period before the crisis than the group that had the lower LDR.

Effect of Loan Growth (LDR) on the Annualized Rate of PBT Contraction during the Crisis

$$H_o: P_{HL} - P_{LL} = 0$$
$$H_a: P_{HL} - P_{LL} > 0$$

where

L_{HL} is the annualized rate PBT contraction during the crisis for the group of banks that had high LDR.

L_{LL} is the annualized rate of PBT contraction during the crisis for the group of banks that had low LDR.

The null hypothesis is that the group with the higher LDR has no difference in the annualized rate of PBT contraction during the crisis than the group that had lower LDR.

Effect of Leverage on the Performance of Banks

In examining a bank's overall leverage on performance, we examine the effect of the TDR[7] on the ROE[8] before and during the crisis. TDR indicates the percentage of debt used by banks to finance their total assets. Here, all nonequity items including deposits are considered part of a bank's leverage. Theoretically, the banks with higher leverage should have had higher returns in the precrisis period, but suffered more during the crisis. To see if this is true, we rank the banks by the extent of their leverage prior to the crisis (see Appendix 9.7). The five banks with the highest TDR (denoted by **) are grouped into one group while the five banks with the lowest ratio (denoted by *) are grouped into another group. Two statistical tests for each parametric and nonparametric method are done to ascertain the effect of TDR on the ROE of banks before and during the crisis. We then test for statistical difference in ROE between the two groups; first in the precrisis period, and second during the crisis.

Effect of Leverage on ROE in the Period before the Crisis

$$H_o: R_{HL} - R_{LL} = 0$$
$$H_a: R_{HL} - R_{LL} > 0$$

where

R_{HL} is the ROE before the crisis for the group of banks that had high TDR.
R_{LL} is the ROE before the crisis for the group of banks that had low TDR.

The null hypothesis is that the group with the higher TDR had no difference in ROE in the period before the crisis than the group that had a lower TDR.

Effect of Leverage on the ROE during the Crisis

$$H_o: R_{HL} - R_{LL} = 0$$
$$H_a: R_{HL} - R_{LL} < 0$$

where

R_{HL} is the ROE during the period of the crisis for the group of banks that had high TDR.
R_{LL} is the ROE during the period of the crisis for the group of banks that had low TDR.

The null hypothesis is that the group with a higher TDR had no difference of ROE during period of the crisis than the group that had a lower TDR.

FACTORS DIFFERENTIATING THE PERFORMANCE OF COMMERCIAL BANKS

In this section we describe the results of our statistical tests and expound on some of the implications. Relevant data on individual banks within the groups is provided in tabular format. Given space constraints, a summary of the parametric test results for all five of the above tests are provided in Appendix 9.8. Appendix 9.9 is a similar summary of the non-parametric Mann-Whitney U test.

Result: Effect of Loan Portfolios in Vulnerable Sectors on the Annualized Growth of PBT (Test 1)

Appendices 9.8 and 9.9 show the summary results of our parametric *t*-test and the nonparametric Mann-Whitney U-test. Both tests reject the null hypothesis at the 95 percent level. It appears that banks with a large loan portfolio in the Construction, Real Estate, and Purchase of Securities sectors going into the crisis experienced a larger rate of PBT contraction, or performed worse than banks that had a lower proportion exposed to these sectors.

The Construction, Real Estate, and Purchase of Securities were the most susceptible sectors during the currency crisis. These sectors were especially sensitive to increases in interest rates, inflation, and depreciating exchange rates. For example, the construction of commercial buildings declined 54.8 percent[9] in 1998. This resulted from the sharp decline in demand for such properties and the consequent collapse of asset prices. When the price of real estate and stocks collapsed, the value of loan collateral collapsed forcing many borrowers to default on payments. The sharp value declines meant that they were financially better off losing the collateral than paying the loans.

Table 9.1, which shows data on provision for doubtful and bad debts,

Table 9.1
Average Growth of Doubtful and Bad Debt Provision

High proportion of Portfolio in Vulnerable Sectors		Low Proportion of Portfolio in Vulnerable Sectors	
Bank	*Avg. Ann. Growth of Doubtful and Bad Debts Provision (%)*	*Bank*	*Avg. Ann. Growth of Doubtful and Bad Debts Provision (%)*
Arab Bank	246.96	HL Bank	110.43
Perwira	455.24	Public	181.12
Eon Bank	351.47	Pacific	116.76
Utama	457.90	Sabah Bank	12.12
Bumiputra	863.07	Maybank	141.94
Average	*474.93*	*Average*	*112.47*

supports this argument. Banks that had a higher proportion of loan portfolio to these high-risk sectors also had a higher growth in doubtful and
bad debts provision. Average annual growth of the provision for the
group was 474.93 percent compared to 112.47 percent for the group that
had a lower exposure to these vulnerable sectors.

RESULT: EFFECT OF LOAN GROWTH (LDR) ON
PBT GROWTH BEFORE CRISIS (TEST 2)

Results of our test on the effect of loan growth on precrisis PBT growth
are shown in Appendices 9.8 and 9.9. Both the Student's t-test and the
Mann-Whitney test fail to reject the null hypothesis. Thus, there is no
evidence that banks with a higher LDR performed any better in the period
before the crisis.

Annualized growth of PBT in the period before the crisis is 74.16 percent
for the group of banks with higher LDR and 30.77 percent for the group
of banks with lower LDR. That we find no difference in PBT growth
despite such a large variance in LDR between the two groups is quite
possibly due to the stable, regulated interest rate regime. In such an environment, even banks that had to rely on interbank funds could make
profits on the interest spreads despite a smaller source of funds from customer deposits.

Nevertheless, this strategy did not necessarily make them perform better than those banks that had a lower LDR. By borrowing money from
the Interbank market, the higher LDR banks had incurred higher cost of
funds compared to the banks that have the ability to attract more deposits
from customers. Substantial portions of customer deposits provide banks
with free funds due to the floats created.

Result: Effect of LDR on the Rate of PBT Contraction
during Crisis (Test 3)

As expected, however, banks with higher LDRs suffered significantly
more in the period of the crisis. As Appendices 9.8 and 9.9 show, the null
hypothesis is rejected in both tests. It appears that banks in the group with
higher LDRs experienced a significantly larger contraction in PBT than
banks in the low LDR group.

This is not surprising given that banks with a high LDR are more reliant
on interbank funds and therefore much more exposed to interest rate risk.
Interest rate risk is closely related to the way banks manage their assets
and liabilities. Perhaps the best way to understand the role of asset/lia-
bility management is to view it within the context of the overall sources
and uses of funds. Banks get their funds from deposits from customers
(demand deposits, saving deposits, fixed and investment deposits, and

negotiable instrument of deposits), short-term borrowing (including the placement of other banks), long-term borrowing such as through selling of subordinated loans, and equity capital (including retained earning).

From this pool of funds, banks must make a choice between acquiring assets that serve the needs of the bank for meeting legal requirements, earning, and income providing liquidity. The Statutory Reserve Requirement (SSR) imposed by BNM must be met prior to purchasing of earning assets and fixed assets for operations. Banks earn income from the interest differential between the interest paid to the suppliers of funds (depositors and lenders) and interest received from users of funds (borrowers). The difference is called "net interest income," which contributes the majority of most banks' income.

It is the nature of the banking business that the durations of deposits and loans are not equal. Deposits are usually of relatively shorter duration than loans. Therefore, banks are at an inherent disadvantage during a period of rising interest rates because they have to raise deposit rates earlier than they can raise loan interest rates. Failing to raise deposit rates could cause discontinuation of existing deposits and an inability to attract new ones. As regards loans, banks could not increase the rates quickly, as the loans have a longer maturity. They can escape this interest rate risk if their loans are on floating rates, but could face credit risk as many borrowers could not afford to pay higher loan installments.

When the recent currency crisis started in July 1997, Bank Negara increased interest rates in an effort to defend the ringgit. The increase affected the banks' net interest incomes due to a mismatch of durations of loans and deposits. While the effect of this mismatch was felt by all banks, the banks that had used interbank funds to finance their loan portfolios would certainly suffer more. This, due to the higher costs of funds in the money market. Furthermore, purchased funds have different characteristics than core deposits. For core deposits, the volume of funds is relatively less sensitive to changes in interest rates. Whereas the banks determined the prices of core deposits or were price-setters, they were price-takers for the interbank funds.

To substantiate this argument, Table 9.2 compares the average annual growth of interest incomes against the average annual growth of interest expenses during the period of the crisis. The table shows the difference in interest income and expense growth rates. There are two interesting features to note. First, the fact that the differences are all negative implies that all banks experienced a higher growth in interest expenses than income. That is, costs increased faster than revenue, even for banks with low LDRs. The second obvious feature is the fact that higher LDR banks suffered significantly more. Going by the average numbers, approximately twice more.

Table 9.2
Percentage Change in Interest Spreads

High LDR Banks		Low LDR Banks	
Bank	Avg. Ann. Growth of Interest Income less Avg. Ann. Growth of Interest Expenses(%)	Bank	Avg. Ann.Growth of Interest Income less Avg. Ann. Growth of Interest Expenses(%)
BSN Comm.	-28.70	Public	-9.18
Arab Bank	-16.87	Hock Hua	-16.87
Sabah Bank	-19.29	Ban Hin Lee	-9.04
Oriental	-22.64	Intl. Bank	-14.04
Eon Bank	-14.48	HL Bank	-4.52
Average	*-20.40*	*Average*	*-10.73*

Results: Effect of TDR on ROE in the Period before the Crisis (Test 4)

The results of our test of the effect of leverage on precrisis ROE is shown in Appendices 9.8 and 9.9. Both tests reject the null hypothesis that there is no difference in ROE. It appears that banks that had a larger TDR had a bigger ROE or gave better returns to shareholders than banks that had a lower TDR during the period prior to the currency crisis. Higher TDR means that the bank used a higher percentage of debts to finance their assets or, alternatively, that a lower percentage of equity was used.

Results: Effect of TDR on the ROE during Crisis (Test 5)

Despite the fact that banks with higher total debt ratios performed better in terms of ROE in the precrisis period, it appears that they did no worse than the less leveraged banks during the crisis. Both our tests (Appendices 9.8 and 9.9) fail to reject the null hypothesis.

Annualized rate of PBT contractions experienced by banks during the period of crisis was mainly due to an increase in the provision for doubtful and bad debts, and a squeeze in the interest rate margin. The banks that had high exposure to credit and interest rate risks incurred the greater contraction regardless of their TDR level. Part of the reason for nonsignificance may be due to the fact that the doubtful and bad debt portions were more dependent on the sectors to which the banks had lent rather than on how the bank had financed its loan portfolio.

COMPARISON BETWEEN THE FIVE WORST AFFECTED AND THE FIVE LEAST AFFECTED DOMESTIC BANKS

In this section, we carry out on overall evaluation of all the banks in our study sample. Essentially, we compare the five worst crisis affected banks with the five least crisis affected banks. The performance measure used is PBT. We examine two differentiating features, (1) loan profile/ credit risk and (2) exposure to interest rate risk.

The first group of worst affected banks consists of Bank Bumiputra, Arab Malaysian Bank, Utama Bank, BSN Commercial, and Oriental Bank. The second group consists of Southern Bank, Public Bank, International Bank, Hock Hua Bank, and Malayan Banking (see Table 9.2).

Loan Profile and Credit Risk

In analyzing the loan profile and the potential credit risk, we examine the proportion of loan portfolio in the earlier mentioned vulnerable sectors. Additionally, we also compare the rate of growth in doubtful and bad debt provision during the crisis. Table 9.3 shows the comparative percentage of loans in vulnerable sectors for each group. The average percentage of loan portfolios to Construction, Real Estate, and Purchase of Securities sectors for the worst and least affected groups is 28.42 percent and 21.90 percent, respectively.

Though the proportion of loans to the vulnerable sectors does not seem all that different between the two groups, we see a big difference between the groups in the case of bad debt growth. As Table 9.4 shows, the mean rate of growth in bad debt during the crisis period is 402.47 percent and

Table 9.3
Percentage of Loan Portfolio in the Construction, Real Estate, and Purchase of Securities Sectors

The Worst Affected Domestic Banks		The Least Affected Domestic Banks	
Bank	*Avg. Loan Portfolio to Vulnerable Sectors (%)*	*Bank*	*Avg. Loan Portfolio to Vulnerable Sectors (%)*
Bumiputra	26.82	Southern	23.17
Arab Bank	36.40	Public	18.02
Utama	29.88	Intl. Bank	23.47
BSN Comm.	26.41	Hock Hua	23.98
Oriental	22.57	May bank	20.87
Average	*28.42*	*Average*	*21.90*

127.78 percent, respectively. The worst affected banks had growth in bad debts more than three times that of the least affected banks. That this happened despite exposures to the vulnerable sectors that were not too different between the two groups, implies the following. It appears that the worst affected banks not only had somewhat higher exposure to vulnerable sectors but more importantly had poorer quality loan portfolio.

Exposure to Interest Rate Risk

In examining exposure to interest rate risk, we compare the LDRs of the two groups of banks. As argued earlier, LDR is an indicator of how much a bank relies on interbank funds. Since such funds are highly responsive to rate movements, banks reliant on such funds would be subject to higher interest rate risk. Table 9.5 shows the LDR and averages for the two groups. Going by the average numbers the worst affected banks clearly had a significantly larger LDR.

Given the numbers in Table 9.5, one would expect banks that relied on interbank funds to suffer a bigger squeeze in their interest spreads. Indeed this is borne out in Table 9.6. The worst affected group of banks suffered close to an 18 percent squeeze in interest spreads as opposed to 13.6 percent for the other group.

Comparison between Domestic and Selected Foreign Banks

In this section, we will compare the average performance of all domestic banks against five selected foreign banks. Overall, the domestic banks were more severely affected than the foreign banks. All domestic banks

Table 9.4
Average Growth of Doubtful and Bad Debts Provision during Crisis

The Worst Affected Domestic Banks		The Least Affected Domestic Banks	
Bank	*Avg. Growth of Doubtful and Bad Debts Provision During Crisis (%)*	*Bank*	*Avg. Growth of Doubtful and Bad Debts Provision During Crisis (%)*
Bumiputra	863.07	Southern	63.31
Arab Bank	246.96	Public	181.12
Utama	457.90	Intl. Bank	129.66
BSN Comm.	219.98	Hock Hua	122.86
Oriental	224.46	Maybank	141.94
Average	*402.47*	*Average*	*127.78*

Table 9.5
Average Loan/Deposit Ratio

The Worst Affected Domestic Banks		The Least Affected Domestic Banks	
Bank	*Avg. Loan/Deposit Ratio (%)*	*Bank*	*Avg. Loan/Deposit Ratio (%)*
Bumiputra	98.08	Southern	91.68
Arab Bank	162.22	Public	49.28
Utama	91.22	Intl. Bank	88.10
BSN Comm.	170.87	Hock Hua	57.61
Oriental	112.05	Maybank	101.29
Average	*126.89*	*Average*	*77.59*

Table 9.6
Difference in Growth between Interest Income and Interest Expense during Crisis

The Worst Affected Domestic Banks		The Least Affected Domestic Banks	
Bank	*Avg. Ann. Growth of Interest Income less Avg. Ann. Growth of Interest Expenses (%)*	*Bank*	*Avg. Ann. Growth of Interest Income less Avg. Ann. Growth of Interest Expenses(%)*
Bumiputra	-12.48	Southern	-6.38
Arab Bank	-16.87	Public	-9.18
Utama	-8.93	Intl. Bank	-14.04
BSN Comm.	-28.70	Hock Hua	-16.87
Oriental	-22.64	Maybank	-21.54
Average	*-17.92*	*Average*	*-13.60*

recorded profit growth contraction while two out of the five foreign banks recorded profit growth during the currency crisis. The foreign banks that recorded profit growth were Chase Manhattan Bank Berhad and Citibank Berhad. By group, the annualized growth of PBT for domestic banks contracted by 67.51 percent compared to that of the foreign banks' group which contracted by 5.39 percent. The fact that both groups had experienced annualized profit growth contraction during the period of the crisis indicates that the crisis was systemic in nature.

Exposure to Credit Risk

Domestic banks had a larger exposure to the vulnerable sectors compared to the foreign banks group. The average percentage of loan portfolio to the Construction, Real Estate, and Purchase of Securities for both groups during the crisis was 24.46 percent and 14.79 percent, respectively (see Appendix 9.4). The difference was significant enough to cause differentiation in performance between both groups of banks.

Foreign banks had a higher percentage of loan portfolio in the Manufacturing and Residential Property sectors. The Manufacturing sector was badly affected at the beginning of the crisis. However, it recovered earlier than other sectors with the increase in exports when the ringgit became undervalued. Residential Property was among the least affected sectors during the crisis.

Exposure to Interest Rate Risk

Both groups of banks had about an equal percentage of LDR. The average LDR for domestic banks was 100.07 percent while for the foreign banks it was 101.94 percent. Therefore, we cannot say that either group of banks had a more aggressive approach in promoting loan growth by borrowing money from the Interbank market.

The foreign banks group had a higher proportion of loan portfolio in the Residential Property sector. Since loans to residential property were at floating rates, they largely escaped the interest rate risk.

CONCLUSION

Clearly, the recent banking crisis was systemic in nature, and even good banks were affected by the crisis. There were several factors affecting the banks' performance. While some of these factors were beyond the control of the banks such as the changes in exchange rates, interest, and inflation rates; others were within the control of the banks such as decisions on loan portfolios, and asset/liability management and leveraging. While the macroeconomic factors caused the systemic effect, the factors under the control of the banks caused the differentiation in performance among the banks.

We examined a number of micro-level bank determined factors. These included (1) profile of loan portfolios, (2) the effect of loan growth on bank earnings precrisis and during crisis, (3) the effect of leverage on bank shareholders earnings precrisis and during crisis; finally, (4) we compare the worst affected banks with the least affected and identify the differentiating features. In addition, (5) we compare domestic bank performance to that of a select group of foreign banks in Malaysia.

With regard to the first issue, we find a direct relationship between the profile of loan portfolios and performance as measured by PBT growth. Banks that had a higher percentage of their loan portfolio in the Construction, Real Estate, and Securities sectors experienced a significantly larger contraction in PBT growth.

Regarding the effect of loan growth on PBT growth, we find no difference between banks with higher LDRs and those with lower LDRs in the precrisis period. However, banks with high LDRs performed significantly worse during the crisis, this effect being mainly due to the higher cost of funds and the consequent squeeze on margins during the crisis.

In examining the effect of leverage on shareholder earnings, we find that banks with high TDR had significantly higher ROE precrisis. However, we find no difference in ROE between banks with high and low TDR during the crisis. All banks appear to have suffered equally. In comparing the five worst affected banks with the least affected ones, we find that the worst affected banks had (1) loan portfolios more skewed to the vulnerable sectors, (2) higher LDRs, and (3) higher overall leverage as measured by the TDR.

When comparing our sample of domestic banks to selected foreign banks we find that the domestic banks as a whole had significantly higher exposure to the risky sectors. Domestic banks as a group had disbursed 24.48 percent of their total loans to Construction, Real Estate, and Securities whereas foreign banks only 14.79 percent to these sectors. In terms of LDRs, there was little difference between foreign and domestic banks.

Our findings appear to be broadly consistent with findings cited in earlier research. As per Goldstein and Turner (1996) a lending boom and asset price collapse certainly preceded the Malaysian banking crisis. The asset price collapse was catalyzed by an external currency shock and was translated into a banking problem by the policy response. There is also consistency with Kaminsky and Reinhart (1996) that sharp declines in equity prices are among the best indicators of a potential banking crisis. Malaysia's equity market collapse did precede the banking problems.

What can we learn from all this? The main lesson is that policy initiatives must be aimed at avoiding banking sector vulnerability. Broadly speaking, these should have the following three objectives, (1) curtailing lending booms in order to avoid the consequent asset price collapses, (2) enforcing limits on direction of bank lending, and (3) reducing moral hazard by capping excessive leveraging and the provision of implicit guarantees.

NOTES

1. See Obiyathulla (1998).
2. BNM (1999), "The Central Bank and the Financial System in Malaysia."

3. The banking system is made up of commercial banks, finance companies, merchant banks, and discount houses.

4. BNM Annual Report 1998, p. 140.

5. Where data is available 1999 numbers are also used.

6. LDR = (Gross loans/Deposits from customers) × 100

7. TDR = (Total Assets – Total Equity) / Total Assets × 100

8. ROE = Net Income/Shareholders's funds × 100

9. BNM Annual Report 1998, p. 127.

REFERENCES

Bank Negara Malaysia (BNM). (1998). Annual Reports, 1997 and 1998. Kuala Lampur, Malaysia.

———. (1999). "The Central Bank and Financial System in Malaysia, a Decade of Change 1989–1999."

Caprio, G., and D. Klingebiel. (1996). "Bank Insolvencies: Cross-Country Experience." Policy research working paper 1620. Washington, DC: World Bank.

Goldstein, M., and P. Turner. (1996). "Banking Crises in Emerging Economies: Origins and Policy Options," *BIS Economic Chapters*, no. 46 (October). Basle, Switzerland: Bank for International Settlements.

Kaminsky, G., and C. Reinhart. (1996). "The Twin Crises: The Causes of Banking and Balance-of-Problems." International finance discussion paper 544. Board of Governors of the Federal Reserve System.

Lee, Khee Joo. (1998). "Non-performing Loans—The Latest Revision of BNM/GP3," *Accountant National*, Vol. 14, No. 2, pp. 123–132. (June).

Obiyallah, Ismath Bacha. (1998). "Malaysia: From Currency to Banking Crisis," *Malaysian Journal of Economic Studies*," 25, nos. 1 and 2 (June/December).

Thillainathan, R. (1998). "Reforming the Financial Sector and Promoting Capital Market Development," *Banker's Journal Malaysia*, no. 108 (December), Institute Bank–Bank Malaysia.

APPENDIX 9.1

List of Commercial Banks in Sample

Bank Name	Year of Commencement in Malaysia	Total Assets as end of Financial Year 1998/99 - (RM million)	Code Used in this Chapter	Financial Year-end
MALAYSIAN BANKS				
1 ARAB-MALAYSIAN BANK BERHAD[1]	1957	12,614.6	ARABBANK	31 Mac
2 BAN HIN LEE BANK BERHAD	1935	6,820.8	BANHINLEE	31 Dec
3 BANK BUMIPUTRA MALAYSIA BERHAD[2]	1966	38,164.7	BUMIPUTRA	31 Mac
4 BANK OF COMMERCE (M) BERHAD[3]	1973	20,382.7	COMMERCE	31 Dec
5 BANK UTAMA (M) BERHAD	1976	7,140.9	UTAMA	31 Dec
6 BSN COMMERCIAL BANK (M) BERHAD[4]	1975	6,565.7	BSNCOMM	31 Dec
7 EON BANK BERHAD[5]	1964	9,149.0	EONBANK	31 Dec
8 HOCK HUA BANK BERHAD	1951	4,934.6	HOCKHUA	31 Dec
9 HONG LEONG BANK BERHAD[6]	1923	15,094.5	HLBANK	30 Jun
10 INTERNATIONAL BANK MALAYSIA BERHAD[7]	1961	969.0	INTLBANK	31 Dec
11 MALAYAN BANKING BERHAD	1960	77,896.0	MAYBANK	30 Jun
12 MULTI-PURPOSE BANK BERHAD[8]	1957	7,658.5	MULTIBANK	31 Dec
13 ORIENTAL BANK BERHAD[9]	1937	8,866.7	ORIENTAL	31 Mac
14 PERWIRA AFFIN BANK BERHAD	1976	15,343.1	PERWIRA	31 Dec
15 PHILLEOALLIED BANK (M) BERHAD[10]	1966	10,605.8	PHILLEOALLIED	31 Jan
16 PUBLIC BANK BERHAD	1966	31,581.9	PUBLIC	31 Dec
17 RHB BANK BERHAD[11]	1965	51,285.2	RHBBANK	31 Dec
18 SABAH BANK BERHAD	1979	2,670.1	SABAHBANK	31 Dec
19 SOUTHERN BANK BERHAD	1965	8,193.1	SOUTHERN	31 Dec
20 THE PACIFIC BANK BERHAD	1922	10,955.7	PACIFIC	31 Dec
21 WAH TAT BANK BERHAD	1955	724.7	WAHTAT	31 Dec
FOREIGN BANKS				
1 CITIBANK BERHAD	1959	13,719.5	CITIBANK	31 Dec
2 HSBC BANK MALAYSIA BERHAD	1884	25,187.3	HSBC	31 Dec
3 STANDARD CHARTERED BANK (M) BHD	1875	17,009.1	CHARTERED	31 Dec
4 OCBC BANK (MALAYSIA) BERHAD	1932	15,882.4	OCBC	31 Dec
5 THE CHASE MANHATTAN BANK (M) BHD	1964	1,126.1	CHASE	31 Dec

APPENDIX 9.2

The Impact of Currency Crisis on the Banks' Annualized Growth of Profit Before Tax (PBT)

	Annualized Growth of PBT		Ranking by Most Affected	Ranking by Least Affected
	Before Crisis*	After Crisis+		
Domestic Banks				
BUMIPUTRA	30.83	-221.95	1	20
ARABBANK	166.44	-197.75	2	19
UTAMA	182.89	-158.76	3	18
BSNCOMM	55.87	-156.03	4	17
ORIENTAL	50.11	-108.47	5	16
PHILLEOALLIED	28.13	-83.13	6	15
PACIFIC	42.66	-58.59	7	14
EONBANK	82.63	-51.90	8	13
COMMERCE	29.76	-46.46	9	12
PERWIRA	49.90	-42.76	10	11
SABAHBANK	15.74	-41.13	11	10
MULTIBANK	47.36	-37.84	12	9
BANHINLEE	40.05	-31.48	13	8
WAHTAT	25.00	-27.60	14	7
HLBANK	36.48	-26.37	15	6
MAYBANK	25.98	-21.59	16	5
HOCKHUA	30.20	-12.92	17	4
INTLBANK	17.75	-11.83	18	3
PUBLIC	29.34	-9.29	19	2
SOUTHERN	22.54	-4.35	20	1
Foreign Banks				
OCBC	41.11	-34.95	1	5
HSBC	52.25	-22.68	2	4
CHARTERED	26.03	-9.93	3	3
CITIBANK	18.30	6.22	4	2
CHASE	30.11	34.38	5	1

Global Financial Markets

APPENDIX 9.3

Percentage of NPL by Sector

	1997			1998				1999			
	June	Sept	Dec	Mac	June	Sept	Dec	Mac	June	Sept	Dec
Agriculture, hunting, forestry, and fishing	4.31	4.16	4.17	4.29	6.19	7.96	9.19	9.44	9.75	9.57	7.64
Mining and quarrying	3.37	10.64	10.32	3.63	8.76	9.83	13.86	18.21	25.40	17.91	14.91
Manufacturing	4.61	4.16	4.98	6.62	9.45	13.17	12.77	14.04	14.02	13.11	12.99
Electricity, gas, and water	0.14	0.20	0.60	3.13	10.21	5.57	0.77	0.64	1.09	0.79	0.53
Construction	4.37	3.35	4.63	10.04	13.45	17.82	17.08	19.12	22.13	20.31	19.31
Real estate	8.27	6.98	7.55	12.09	18.21	21.14	22.10	19.27	21.51	19.79	18.21
Purchase of landed property											
(of which : 1) Residential property	3.48	3.17	4.31	6.16	6.63	7.23	6.92	7.23	7.52	7.57	7.43
2) Non-residential	3.15	2.83	4.16	5.92	7.94	11.21	10.40	10.41	10.38	11.73	11.42
General commerce	3.32	3.64	4.54	6.62	8.22	10.72	10.37	11.69	11.79	13.55	12.68
Transport, storage, and communications	1.88	2.07	2.81	6.47	7.50	14.61	13.14	11.93	11.16	11.78	12.67
Finance, insurance, and business services	1.29	1.49	3.12	4.00	7.73	9.75	10.21	11.73	11.35	13.11	11.35
Purchase of securities	1.02	1.78	5.84	12.56	24.31	32.94	21.26	16.81	17.35	17.84	13.22
Purchase of transport vehicles	0.87	6.18	5.12	2.61	1.91	9.61	13.76	17.11	20.07	24.75	26.82
Consumption credit	6.36	4.54	6.43	10.71	12.97	15.38	14.97	14.78	14.02	13.20	13.24
Others	2.37	3.43	8.57	11.57	14.41	17.70	12.59	10.24	11.88	10.82	9.60
	3.56	3.35	4.89	7.63	10.93	14.11	12.45	12.63	13.10	13.06	12.10

APPENDIX 9.4

Loan Portfolios for the Construction, Real Estate, and Purchase of Securities Sectors

		Outstanding Loan (RM ,000)			Annual Growth (%)		Share of Total (%)			Average of
		1996	1997	1998	1997	1998	1996	1997	1998	97& 98
	Domestic Bank									
1	ARABBANK	1,759,839	3,157,011	2,849,208	241.68	-31.99	27.92	37.41	35.40	36.40
2	BANHINLEE	862,565	944,773	996,606	9.53	5.49	23.51	20.68	20.69	20.69
3	BUMIPUTRA	5,712,154	7,583,417	n.a	89.83	n.a	24.50	26.82	n.a	26.82
4	COMMERCE	2,138,664	3,406,449	3,319,720	174.30	20.13	21.09	27.86	24.11	25.98
5	UTAMA	881,571	1,328,945	1,268,051	228.90	-8.48	29.60	31.27	28.49	29.88
6	BSNCOMM	636,649	1,326,015	1,223,931	399.46	156.08	18.90	27.62	25.19	26.41
7	EONBANK	687,545	1,836,292	1,908,001	688.20	15.41	25.52	35.02	33.18	34.10
8	HOCKHUA	781,430	748,076	778,200	-24.91	25.62	27.71	24.23	23.73	23.98
9	HLBANK	1,251,742	1,411,198	1,324,935	68.20	163.06	15.56	14.53	13.47	14.00
10	INTLBANK	137,957	151,383	166,839	66.60	-18.87	25.64	22.57	24.36	23.47
11	MAYBANK	9,562,075	11,119,712	8,970,206	40.69	-63.23	24.66	23.77	17.96	20.87
12	MULTIBANK	1,106,302	1,417,809	1,481,167	28.16	4.47	25.05	22.70	24.84	23.77
13	ORIENTAL	1,102,425	1,431,311	1,278,692	149.35	-22.54	20.31	22.58	22.57	22.57
14	PERWIRA	1,924,185	1,911,360	2,522,475	3.62	156.29	22.21	18.06	24.29	21.18
15	PHILLEOALLIED	1,712,556	1,461,537	1,635,454	-58.43	22.92	33.12	22.77	24.18	23.47
16	PUBLIC	3,069,584	2,042,576	2,558,802	100.78	89.78	26.74	16.58	19.46	18.02
18	SABAHBANK	454,148	404,069	418,699	104.41	-13.22	28.67	19.95	19.84	19.89
19	SOUTHERN	788,682	1,121,204	1,194,723	140.51	17.01	21.08	24.33	22.01	23.17
20	PACIFIC	1,174,071	1,449,556	1,116,158	69.42	-61.90	19.81	20.68	16.43	18.56
21	WAHTAT	164,116	117,621	113,696	-74.48	-17.89	37.39	23.39	22.18	22.78
	Average	**1,795,413**	**2,218,516**	**1,756,278**	**122.29**	**21.91**	**24.95**	**24.14**	**22.12**	**23.80**
	Foreign Bank									
1	CITIBANK	530,103	459,628	389,412	-13.29	-15.28	11.23	7.51	5.15	6.33
2	HSBC	2,052,650	2,734,092	3,312,340	33.20	21.15	17.35	19.04	19.82	19.43
3	CHARTERED	546,292	810,825	876,077	48.42	8.05	6.84	7.78	7.39	7.59
4	OCBC	3,202,671	3,099,282	3,384,530	-3.23	9.20	35.00	26.20	28.66	27.43
5	CHASE	31,989	36,574	43,741	14.33	19.60	10.51	10.71	15.68	13.19
	Average	**1,272,741**	**1,428,080**	**1,601,220**	**12.21**	**12.12**	**16.19**	**14.25**	**15.34**	**14.79**

APPENDIX 9.5

Average Percentage of Loan Portfolios for the Construction, Real Estate, and Purchase of Securities Sectors (1990–1999)

		% of Loans	Annualized Growth of PBT during Crisis	
	Domestic Bank			
1	HLBANK	14.00	-26.37	*
2	PUBLIC	18.02	-9.29	*
3	PACIFIC	18.56	-58.59	*
4	SABAHBANK	19.89	-41.13	*
5	MAYBANK	20.87	-21.59	*
6	BANHINLEE	20.99	-31.48	
7	PERWIRA	21.18	-42.76	
8	ORIENTAL	22.57	-108.47	
9	WAHTAT	22.78	-27.60	
10	SOUTHERN	23.17	-4.35	
11	INTLBANK	23.47	-11.83	
12	PHILLEOALLIED	23.47	-83.13	
13	MULTIBANK	23.77	-37.84	
14	HOCKHUA	23.98	-12.92	
15	COMMERCE	25.98	-46.46	
16	BSNCOMM	26.41	-156.03	**
17	BUMIPUTRA	26.82	-221.95	**
18	UTAMA	29.88	-158.76	**
19	EONBANK	34.10	-51.90	**
20	ARABBANK	36.40	-197.75	**
	Average	*23.82*	*-67.51*	
	Foreign Bank			
1	CITIBANK	6.33	6.22	
2	CHARTERED	7.59	-9.93	
3	CHASE	13.19	34.38	
4	HSBC	19.43	-22.68	
5	OCBC	27.43	-34.95	
	Average	*14.79*	*-5.39*	

** Denotes the five banks with the highest percent of loan portfolios in the vulnerable sectors.

* Denotes the five banks with the lowest percent of loan portfolios in the vulnerable sectors.

Note: These two groups were compared for difference in PBT growth. (For results, see Tables 9.8 and 9.9.)

APPENDIX 9.6

Average of Loan/Deposits Ratio and Annualized Growth of PBT

		Average LDR	Annualized Growth of PBT Before Crisis	Annualized Growth of PBT During Crisis	
	Domestic Bank				
1	PUBLIC	49.28	29.34	-9.29	*
2	HOCKHUA	57.61	30.20	-12.92	*
3	BANHINLEE	80.83	40.05	-31.48	*
4	INTLBANK	88.10	17.75	-11.83	*
5	HLBANK	88.60	36.48	-26.37	*
6	MULTIBANK	89.75	47.36	-37.84	
7	UTAMA	91.22	182.89	-158.76	
8	PACIFIC	91.22	42.66	-58.59	
9	SOUTHERN	91.68	22.54	-4.35	
10	WAHTAT	97.86	25.00	-27.60	
11	BUMIPUTRA	98.08	30.83	-221.95	
12	PHILLEOALLIED	99.81	28.13	-83.13	
13	COMMERCE	101.18	29.76	-46.46	
14	MAYBANK	101.29	25.98	-21.59	
15	PERWIRA	103.05	49.90	-42.76	
16	EONBANK	110.94	82.63	-51.90	**
17	ORIENTAL	112.05	50.11	-108.47	**
18	SABAHBANK	115.81	15.74	-41.13	**
19	ARABBANK	162.22	166.44	-197.75	**
20	BSNCOMM	170.87	55.87	-156.03	**
	Average	*100.07*	*50.48*	*-67.51*	
	Foreign Bank				
1	CHARTERED	91.27	26.03	-9.93	
2	CITIBANK	92.25	18.30	6.22	
3	HSBC	93.42	52.25	-22.68	
4	OCBC	100.07	41.11	-34.95	
5	CHASE	132.67	n,a	34.38	
	Average	*101.94*	*27.54*	*-5.39*	

** Denotes the five banks with the highest LDR.

* Denotes the five banks with the lowest LDR.

Note: These two groups were tested for significant difference in PBT growth. (For results, see Tables 9.8 and 9.9.)

APPENDIX 9.7

Average Total Debt Ratio and Average Return on Equity

		Average TDR Before Crisis	Average ROE Before Crisis	Average TDR During Crisis	Average ROE During Crisis	
	Domestic Bank					
1	RHBBANK	0.81	30.34	0.92	44.14	
2	ORIENTAL	0.82	35.38	0.97	-578.20	*
3	PHILLEOALLIED	0.88	13.99	0.94	12.73	*
4	INTLBANK	0.89	37.09	0.93	42.33	*
5	EONBANK	0.90	35.98	0.86	7.06	*
6	SOUTHERN	0.90	31.37	0.86	24.10	*
7	SABAHBANK	0.91	28.93	0.91	19.03	
8	WAHTAT	0.91	32.93	0.91	42.64	
9	BSNCOMM	0.92	37.78	0.96	-151.43	
10	PUBLIC	0.92	35.63	0.92	43.20	
11	HLBANK	0.92	55.02	0.89	21.01	
12	MAYBANK	0.92	39.03	0.91	48.64	
13	PACIFIC	0.92	21.93	0.92	24.32	
14	BANHINLEE	0.92	44.77	0.92	32.93	
15	HOCKHUA	0.93	51.53	0.88	32.15	
16	BUMIPUTRA	0.94	37.85	0.96	-29.05	
17	UTAMA	0.94	47.18	0.89	-18.02	**
18	MULTIBANK	0.94	57.34	0.93	32.44	**
19	ARABBANK	0.94	25.41	0.98	-2668.01	**
20	COMMERCE	0.94	46.27	0.93	24.41	**
21	PERWIRA	0.96	46.79	0.91	26.38	**
	Average	*0.91*	*37.74*	*0.92*	*-141.29*	
	Foreign Bank					
1	CHASE	0.80	22.53	0.80	41.30	
2	CITIBANK	0.91	49.61	0.91	57.83	
3	HSBC	0.92	56.31	0.94	31.11	
4	OCBC	0.92	33.34	0.92	26.72	
5	CHARTERED	0.93	63.18	0.93	56.71	
	Average	*0.90*	*44.99*	*0.90*	*42.73*	

** Denotes the five banks with the highest TDR before crisis.

* Denotes the five banks with the lowest TDR before crisis.

Note: These two groups were tested for difference in ROE precrisis and during crisis. (For results, see Tables 9.8 and 9.9.)

APPENDIX 9.8

Summary of Parametric Test Results (Student's *t*-Test)

Test No.	Null Hypothesis Tested	*t*-critical (95%)	*t*-Stat	Finding
Test 1	Proportion of loan Portfolio to vulnerable sectors had no impact on Bank PBT contraction.	2.015	4.1534	Null hypothesis; rejected Banks with higher loan growth had larger PBT contraction during crisis.
Test 2	Loan Growth rate had no impact on PBT growth *before* the crisis.	2.1318	1.689	Cannot reject null hypothesis
Test 3	Loan Growth rate had no impact on PBT growth *during* the crisis	2.1318	3.0617	Null hypothesis; rejected. Banks with higher loan growth had larger PBT contraction during crisis.
Test 4	Leverage (higher TDR) had no impact on ROE *before* the crisis.	1.8595	2.2688	Null hypothesis; rejected. Banks with higher TDR gave better ROE pre-crisis.
Test 5	Leverage (Higher TDR) had no impact on ROE *during* the crisis.	2.1318	-1.09	Cannot reject null hypothesis

APPENDIX 9.9

Summary of Nonparametric Mann-Whitney U-Test Results

Test No.	Null Hypothesis Tested	U_A- U_0 Value (Rejection Area)	Computed U_A Value	Finding
Test 1	Proportion of loan portfolio to vulnerable sectors had no impact on bank PBT contraction.	1 and 4	1	Null hypothesis; rejected Banks with higher loan growth had larger PBT contraction during crisis.
Test 2	Loan growth rate had no impact on PBT growth *before* the crisis.	5 and 4	5	Cannot reject null hypothesis
Test 3	Loan growth rate had no impact on PBT growth *during* the crisis	0 and 4	0	Null hypothesis; rejected. Banks with higher loan growth had larger PBT contraction during crisis.
Test 4	Leverage (higher TDR) had no impact on ROE *before* the crisis.	4	4	Null hypothesis; rejected. Banks with higher TDR gave better ROE pre crisis.
Test 5	Leverage (Higher TDR) had no impact on ROE *during* the crisis.	12 and 4	12	Cannot reject null hypothesis

CHAPTER 10

Persistent Dependence in Foreign Exchange Rates? A Reexamination

John T. Barkoulas, Christopher F. Baum, Mustafa Caglayan, and Atreya Chakraborty

INTRODUCTION

Since the breakdown of the Bretton Woods system, the volatility of exchange rates has been cited as a drawback of the floating exchange rate system. At both theoretical and empirical levels, the international trade and finance literature has stressed the effects of exchange rate uncertainty on international trade flows, pricing of exports and domestic goods, market structure (entry-exit decisions), and international asset portfolios. It is also well documented that although firms can protect themselves against short-term foreign exchange risk through hedging, they are exposed to medium- and long-term exchange rate volatility.[1] Such an exposure to foreign exchange risk could affect firms' investment decisions and therefore distort the optimal allocation of resources. Knowledge of the short- and long-term time series properties of foreign currency rates can have important implications for these issues. Additionally, such an understanding can address issues of appropriateness of models of exchange rate determination and foreign currency market efficiency and predictability.

The standard tool in analyzing the stochastic behavior of exchange rates has been the autoregressive integrated moving average (ARIMA) model. Along these lines, a large body of past research [see, for example, Baillie and Bollerslev (1989)] documents that foreign currency rates are best characterized as pure unit-root (random-walk or martingale) processes, thus making predictability of exchange rate movements impossible. The failure of linear univariate and structural exchange rate models to improve upon the predictive accuracy of random-walk forecasts motivated many researchers to turn to nonlinear models.[2] Engel and Hamilton (1990) use a Markov switching model for exchange rate changes while Diebold and Nason (1990) and Meese and Rose (1990) use variants of local regression, a nearest-neighbor nonparametric technique. Kuan and Liu (1995) use feedforward and recurrent artificial neural networks to produce conditional mean forecasts of foreign exchange rates. Meese and Rose (1991) estimate structural models of exchange rate determination using a variety of nonparametric techniques. The success of these studies to explain exchange rate movements has been very limited, thus leaving the martingale model as the leading characterization of the data generating process of exchange rates.

More recently, some researchers have argued against the martingale hypothesis by pointing to the possibility of long-memory (fractional) dynamic behavior in the foreign currency market.[3] The long-memory, or long-term dependence, property describes the high-order correlation structure of a series. If a series exhibits long memory, persistent temporal dependence exists even between distant observations. Such series are characterized by distinct but nonperiodic cyclical patterns. As long memory creates nonlinear dependence in the first moment of the distribution and therefore generates a potentially predictable component in the series dynamics, its presence in foreign currency rates would cast doubt on the weak form of foreign exchange market efficiency. The price of an asset determined in a weak-form efficient market should follow a martingale process in which each price change is unaffected by its predecessor and has no memory. As long memory implies significant autocorrelations between distant observations, its presence entails that past returns can help predict future returns, and the possibility of consistent speculative profits arises.[4]

Applying rescaled-range (R/S) analysis to daily exchange rates for the British pound, French franc, and Deutsche mark, Booth, Kaen, and Koveos (1982) find positive long-term persistence during the flexible exchange rate period (1973–1979) but negative dependence (antipersistence) during the fixed exchange rate period (1965–1971).[5] More recently, Cheung's (1993) findings strengthen the evidence that persistent dependence characterizes the behavior of foreign exchange markets during the managed floating regime. Using spectral regression and maximum likelihood methods, Cheung finds support for long-memory behavior in weekly returns series for the British pound, Deutsche mark, Swiss franc, French franc, and Japanese yen over the period 1974–1987. However, he also finds that impulse responses are generally insignificant and that short- and longer-horizon long-memory forecasts fail to improve upon the naive random-walk forecasts.

This study extends previous research on foreign exchange long-memory dynamics in three respects. First, the sample employed spans a longer time period and therefore incorporates more information regarding the low-frequency (long-term) behavior of foreign exchange rates. Second, the sample is not restricted to the major currencies, but is much more comprehensive, including currency rates for eighteen industrial countries. And third, a sensitivity analysis is performed to analyze the robustness properties and temporal stability of the long-memory (fractional differencing) parameter for the foreign currency rates. We use the Gaussian semiparametric method to estimate the long-memory parameter. Contrary to previous findings of strong persistence, our evidence strongly favors the martingale model against long-memory alternatives in the foreign currency markets, thus supporting the market efficiency hypothesis in its weak form. The sensitivity analysis suggests that any evidence of long memory is temporally unstable, especially for major currency rates. However, persistent dependence appears to characterize the temporal behavior of three secondary (nonmajor) currency rates.

The rest of the paper is constructed as follows. The section entitled "Fractional Differencing Modeling and Estimation" presents the fractional model and the Gaussian semiparametric method for estimating the fractional parameter. Data, empirical estimates of the fractional parameter, and the results of the sensitivity analysis are reported and discussed in the section "Data and Long-Memory Results." We summarize and conclude in "Conclusions."

FRACTIONAL DIFFERENCING MODELING AND ESTIMATION

The model of an autoregressive fractionally integrated moving average process of order (p, d, q), denoted by autoregressive integrated moving average (ARIMA) (p, d, q), with mean μ, may be written using operator notation as

$$\Phi(L)(1-L)^d (y_t - \mu) = \Theta(L)u_t, \qquad (10.1)$$
$$u_t \sim \text{i.i.d.}(0, \sigma^2_u)$$

where L is the backward-shift operator, $\Phi(L) = 1 - \phi_1 L - \ldots - \phi_p L^p$, $\Theta(L) = 1 + \vartheta_1 L + \ldots + \vartheta_q L^q$, and $(1 - L)^d$ is the fractional differencing operator defined by

$$(1-L)^d = \sum_{k=0}^{\infty} \frac{\Gamma(k-d)L^k}{\Gamma(-d)\Gamma(k + 1)} \qquad (10.2)$$

with $\Gamma(\bar{o})$ denoting the gamma function. The parameter d is allowed to assume any real value. The arbitrary restriction of d to integer values gives rise to the standard ARIMA model. The stochastic process y_t is both stationary and invertible if all roots of $\Phi(L)$ and $\Theta(L)$ lie outside the unit circle and $|d| < 0.5$. Assuming that $d \in (0,0.5)$ and $d \neq 0$, Hosking (1981) shows that the correlation function, $p(\bar{o})$, of an ARFIMA process is proportional to k^{2d-1} as $k \to \infty$. Consequently, the autocorrelations of the ARFIMA process decay hyperbolically to zero as $k \to \infty$ which is contrary to the faster, geometric decay of a stationary autoregressive moving average (ARMA) process. For d ($\in 0,0.5$),

$$\sum_{j=-n}^{n} |p(j)|$$

diverges as $n \to \infty$, and the ARFIMA process is said to exhibit long memory, or long-range positive dependence. The process is said to exhibit intermediate memory (antipersistence), or long-range negative dependence, for ($d \in 0,0.5$). The process exhibits short memory for $d = 0$, corresponding to stationary and invertible ARMA modeling. For $d \in (0,0.5)$, the process is nonstationary (having an infinite variance) but it is mean reverting, as there is no long-run impact of an innovation on future values of the process.

We estimate the long-memory parameter using Robinson's Gaussian semiparametric (GS) method. Robinson (1995) proposes a Gaussian semiparametric estimate, GS hereafter, of the self-similarity parameter H, which is not defined in closed form. It is assumed that the spectral density of the time series, denoted by $f(\bar{o})$, behaves as

$$F(\xi) - \sim G \, \xi^{1-2H} \text{ as } \xi \to 0^+ \tag{10.3}$$

for $G \in (0,\infty)$ and $H \in (0,1)$. The self-similarity parameter H relates to the long-memory parameter d by $H = d + 1/2$. The estimate for H, denoted by $\hat{H}$, is obtained through minimization of the function

$$R(H) = \ln \hat{G}(H) - (2H - 1) \, 1 \Big/ v \sum_{\lambda=1}^{v} \ln \xi_\lambda \tag{10.4}$$

with respect to H, where

$$\hat{G}(H) = 1 \Big/ v \sum_{\lambda=1}^{v} \xi_\lambda^{2H-1} I(\xi_\lambda), \ I(\xi_\lambda)$$

is the periodogram of y_t at frequency ξ_λ, and v is the number of Fourier frequencies included in estimation (bandwidth parameter). The discrete averaging is carried out over the neighborhood of zero frequency and, in asymptotic theory, v is assumed to tend to infinity much slower than T. The GS estimator is $v^{1/2}$-consistent and the variance of the limiting distribution is free of nuisance parameters and equals $1/4_v$. The GS estimator appears to be the most efficient semiparametric estimator developed so far. It is also consistent and has the same limiting distribution under conditional heteroscedasticity (Robinson and Henry, 1999).

DATA AND LONG-MEMORY RESULTS

Data

The data set consists of U.S. dollar nominal rates of weekly frequency for the Canadian dollar, Deutsche mark, British pound, French franc, Italian lira, Japanese yen, Swiss franc, Netherlands guilder, Swedish krona, and Belgian franc and of monthly frequency for the Austrian schilling, Danish krone, Luxembourg franc, Norwegian krone, Finnish markka, Greek drachma, Portuguese escudo, and Spanish peseta. The sample period covers the post-Bretton Woods period of the floating exchange rate system. See the Appendix for details of data and sources. All subsequent analysis is performed on the first logarithmic differences (returns) of the exchange rate series.

Long-Memory Estimates

Before proceeding with the empirical evidence, we briefly make the distinction between short- and long-term dependence. Short-term dependence, or short memory, describes the low-order correlation structure of a series and is typified by quickly declining autocovariances in the time domain and significant power at high frequencies in the frequency domain. For a short-memory process, events from the distant past have negligible effect on the present. On the other hand, the long-memory, or long-term dependence, property characterizes the behavior of the series' long-lagged autocovariances. If a series exhibits long memory, there are significant correlations even between observations widely separated in time (the correlations of the series are not summable); such behavior is indicated by hyperbolically declining autocovariances in the time domain. A shock to the series persists for a long time (has a long-lasting impact), even though it eventually dissipates. For all practical purposes, a long-memory process may be considered to have an infinite span of statistical interdependence. In the frequency domain, long memory is indicated by the fact that the spectral density becomes unbounded as the frequency approaches zero. Standard ARIMA processes cannot exhibit long-term dependence as they can only describe the short-run behavior of a time series.

GS estimates of the fractional exponent for the exchange rate series are reported in Table 10.1.[6] In order to check the sensitivity of our results to the choice of bandwidth, or number of harmonic frequencies used in estimation, we report d estimates for $v = T^{0.50}$ and $v = T^{0.55}$.[7] Concentrating on the major currencies, there is no evidence of long memory in any of the returns series with the exception of the French franc. For the Italian lira, rejection of the unit-root null hypothesis is obtained but it is restricted

Table 10.1
Gaussian Semiparametric Estimates of the Fractional Differencing Parameter
d for Exchange Rate Returns Series

Currency	Gaussian Semiparametric Estimates	
	$d(0.50)$	$d(0.55)$
	(A) Weekly Returns	
Canadian dollar	0.015	0.111
	(0.172)	(1.538)
Deutsche mark	0.071	0.074
	(0.815)	(1.025)
British pound	-0.007	0.031
	(-0.080)	(0.429)
French franc	0.177	0.181
	(2.033)*	(2.508)*
Italian lira	0.110	0.149
	(1.263)	(2.064)*
Japanese yen	0.025	0.095
	(0.287)	(1.316)
Swiss franc	0.041	0.068
	(0.471)	(0.942)
Belgian franc	0.119	0.146
	(1.367)	(2.023)*
Netherlands guilder	0.074	0.093
	(0.850)	(1.288)
Swedish krona	0.079	0.148
	(0.907)	(2.050)*

to a particular estimation window size, thus lacking robustness. This evidence for the major currency rates does not confirm the long-memory evidence reported in Booth et al. (1982) and Cheung (1993). For the remaining currencies, consistent evidence of long memory is apparent for the Danish krone, Luxembourg franc, Portugese escudo, and Spanish peseta. For the Belgian franc, Swedish krona, Finnish markka, and Greek drachma, weak evidence of fractional dynamic behavior is found, but only for a specific estimation window size. For all other exchange rate series, the martingale hypothesis is robust to long-memory alternatives.

The overall evidence can be summarized as follows. The returns series for major currencies appear to be short-memory processes, which exhibit a rapid exponential decay in their impulse response weights. There is no convincing evidence that these series are strongly autocorrelated, which

Table 10.1 (*Continued*)
Gaussian Semiparametric Estimates of the Fractional Differencing Parameter
d **for Exchange Rate Returns Series**

Currency	Gaussian Semiparametric Estimates	
	$d(0.50)$	$d(0.55)$
	(B) Monthly Returns	
Austrian schilling	0.185	0.202
	(1.480)	(1.850)
Danish krone	0.253	0.228
	(2.024)*	(2.089)*
Luxembourg franc	0.302	0.284
	(2.416)*	(2.603)*
Norwegian krone	-0.009	0.090
	(-0.072)	(0.824)
Finnish markka	0.185	0.257
	(1.480)	(2.355)*
Greek drachma	0.321	0.218
	(2.486)*	(1.949)
Portugese escudo	0.386	0.299
	(3.088)*	(2.740)*
Spanish peseta	0.266	0.344
	(2.128)*	(3.153)*

Notes: The sample period is January 11, 1974 to December 29, 1995 for a total of 1,147 returns observations for the weekly currency rates. The sample period is September 1973 to December 1995 for a total of 268 returns observations for the monthly currency rates, except for the Greek drachma, which spans the period April 1975 to December 1995 for a total of 248 returns observations. $d(0.50)$ and $d(0.55)$ give the *d* estimates corresponding to estimation window size $v = T^{0.50}$ and $v = T^{0.55}$, respectively. The t – statistics are given in parentheses. The superscript * indicates statistical significance for the null hypothesis $d = 0$ at the 5 percent level or less.

could give rise to improved predictability.[8] However some evidence of long-term dependence appears to characterize the temporal patterns of some nonmajor currencies.

Sensitivity Analysis

To ascertain the robustness and temporal stability properties of the long-memory coefficient, a sensitivity analysis is performed on each exchange rate series. The analysis of subsamples should provide us with insights as to whether long memory is a genuine feature of the data generating process underlying the foreign exchange rate series. It will also enable us to compare our findings with those reported in earlier studies. We apply the GS method to an initial sample of exchange-rate changes spanning the period 1974–1983 and then on samples generated by adding 26 weekly observations, so that the fractional exponent is reestimated every six months until the full sample period is exhausted.[9]

If the analysis is restricted to the 1974–1987 sample period investigated by Cheung, the GS results obtained here do confirm his long-memory evidence on the five major currency returns series. With increasing sample size, however, there does not appear to be any consistent evidence favoring long memory, across both window size and time, for almost all major currency rates. Only the French franc rejections of the no long-memory null hypothesis are invariably obtained over time. Therefore, the long-memory evidence for the major currency rates generally vanishes when the sample period is expanded, thus suggesting temporal parameter instability.

Based on the results of the sensitivity analysis, the exchange rate series analyzed by Cheung appear to be short-memory processes over the extended sample periods. His evidence of long memory appears to be a function of the particular sample period used in his analysis and does not generalize to a temporally expanded data set. Over time, the presence of long memory ranges from very weak and sporadic to nonexistent. This temporal instability of the long-memory evidence helps explain Cheung's negative findings based on impulse response function analysis and out-of-sample forecasting. If long memory is not a robust feature of the stochastic behavior of major foreign currency rates, then fitting an ARFIMA model to the series is unlikely to produce superior out-of-sample forecasts as compared to benchmark random-walk forecasts. In summary, the evidence supports the martingale model—and the market efficiency hypothesis in its weak form—for major foreign currency rates over the floating exchange rate period (with the French franc being the only exception).

For the rest of the currencies, generally consistent, stable evidence of long-term persistence is obtained for the Luxembourg franc, Portuguese escudo, and Spanish peseta and weaker evidence for the Greek drachma. The sensitivity analysis produces negative evidence for long memory for all other foreign currency rates with any long-memory evidence being sporadic and fragile.[10]

The observed deterioration in the overall evidence of persistent dependence over time could well reflect the increasing breadth and sophistication of foreign currency markets in the past decade. It could also reflect the reduced role of central bank interventions in the foreign exchange market in the 1990s. Additionally, the development of active spot, futures, and options markets in secondary currencies and the development of financial markets in a number of emerging economies has led to greater efficiencies in global currency markets. These trends are consistent with martingale behavior.

CONCLUSIONS

Using Robinson's Gaussian semiparametric estimator, we test for stochastic long memory in the returns series for currencies of eighteen industrial countries. For major currency rates previously studied in the literature, there is no convincing evidence in support of long-memory dynamics. A sensitivity analysis suggests that, when evidence of long memory is obtained, it is sporadic and generally temporally unstable. The evidence of long memory in major currency rates reported in Booth et al. (1982) and Cheung (1993) would appear to be an artifact of the sample period and currencies considered in those studies. For all but three of the broader set of currencies analyzed here, we find that the unit-root hypothesis is robust to long-memory alternatives, providing strong support for martingale behavior of currency rates and, therefore, for foreign exchange market efficiency.

NOTES

1. There are limitations and costs associated with firms' hedging strategies. For example, size and limited maturity of forward contracts may make it difficult for firms to hedge their foreign exchange risk.

2. Absence of risk-neutral behavior, the nature of the policy regime, time deformation, and misspecification of the functional form of the structural exchange rate model are some of the plausible sources of nonlinearity in foreign exchange rates.

3. Long-memory methods have been applied extensively to financial asset price series: for stock prices (Lo, 1991), futures prices (Barkoulas, Labys, and Onochie, 1999), commodity prices (Barkoulas, Labys, and Onochie, 1997), Eurocurrency deposit rates (Barkoulas and Baum, 1999), for example. See Baillie 1996 for a survey of fractional integration methods and applications in economics and finance.

4. The presence of fractional structure in asset returns raises a number of theoretical and empirical issues. As long memory represents a special form of nonlinear dynamics, it calls into question linear modeling and invites the development of nonlinear pricing models at the theoretical level to account for long-memory behavior. Mandelbrot (1971) observes that in the presence of long memory, the arrival of new market information cannot be fully arbitraged away and martingale models of asset prices cannot be obtained from arbitrage. In addition, pricing derivative securities with martingale methods may not be appropriate if the underlying continuous stochastic processes exhibit long memory. Statistical inferences concerning asset pricing models based on standard testing procedures may not be appropriate in the presence of long-memory series.

5. The classical rescaled-range (R/S) method has a number of drawbacks (see Lo, 1991).

6. Another frequently used periodogram-based method to estimate the fractional differencing parameter d is the spectral regression method suggested by Geweke and Porter-Hudak (1983). The Geweke and Porter-Hudak fractional ex-

ponent estimates are broadly consistent with the GS estimates for our sample exchange rate series and our inferences therefore remain unaltered. The GPH results are not reported here but they are available upon request from the authors.

7. Monte Carlo simulations have shown that such bandwidth choices provide a good balance in the tradeoff between bias (which tends to increase with bandwidth) and sampling variability (which tends to decrease with bandwidth). Henry and Robinson (1999) provide heuristic approximations of the minimum mean squared error optimal bandwidth. Inferences drawn below remain unaltered for other plausible bandwidth choices.

8. Alternative estimation methods of long-memory models include Sowell's (1992) exact maximum likelihood method, Fox and Taqqu's (1986) frequency domain approximate maximum likelihood method, and the conditional sum of squares (CSS) method (Chung and Baillie, 1993). The maximum likelihood methods are computationally burdensome, especially in light of the repeated estimation in the sensitivity analysis, and rely on the correct specification of the high-frequency (ARMA) structure to obtain consistent parameter estimates. Given the near whiteness of the exchange-rate returns series, the periodogram-based method employed here is not likely to suffer from biases due to the presence of strong short-term dependencies in the series dynamics (Agiakloglou, Newbold, and Wohar, 1993). Since the main finding in this study is the absence of long memory in exchange rate series, its validity should not be questioned on the basis of the particular estimation method employed here as the presence of any high-frequency dependencies would only bias the inference toward finding long memory.

9. The same procedure was performed on the monthly data, with qualitatively similar results.

10. The corresponding figures for these currencies are not presented here but are available on request from the authors.

REFERENCES

Agiakloglou, C., P. Newbold, and M. Wohar. (1993). "Bias in an Estimator of the Fractional Difference Parameter," *Journal of Time Series Analysis*, 14, pp. 235–246.

Baillie, R. (1996). "Long Memory Processes and Fractional Integration in Econometrics," *Journal of Econometrics*, 73, pp. 5–59.

Baillie, R., and T. Bollerslev. (1989). "Common Stochastic Trends in a System of Exchange Rates," *Journal of Finance*, 44, pp. 167–181.

Barkoulas, J., and C. F. Baum. (1997). "Fractional Differencing Modeling and Forecasting of Eurocurrency Deposit Rates," *Journal of Financial Research*, 20, no. 3, pp. 355–372.

Barkoulas, J., C. F. Baum, W. Labys, and J. Onochie. (1997). "Fractional Dynamics in International Commodity Prices," *Journal of Futures Markets*, 17, no. 2, pp. 735–755.

———. (1999). "Long Memory in Futures Prices," *Financial Review*, 34, pp. 91–100.

Booth, G. G., F. R. Kaen, and P. E. Koveos. (1982). "R/S Analysis of Foreign Exchange Markets under Two International Monetary Regimes," *Journal of Monetary Economics*, 10, pp. 407–415.

Cheung, Y. W. (1993). "Long Memory in Foreign-Exchange Rates," *Journal of Business and Economic Statistics*, 11, pp. 93–101.

Chung, C.-F., and R. T. Baillie. (1993). "Small Sample Bias in Conditional Sum of Squares Estimators of Fractionally Integrated ARMA Models," *Empirical Economics*, 18, pp. 791–806.

Diebold, F., and J. Nason. (1990). "Nonparametric Exchange Rate Prediction?" *Journal of International Economics*, 28, pp. 315–332.

Engel, C., and J. D. Hamilton. (1990). "Long Swings in the Dollar: Are They in the Data and Do Markets Know It?" *American Economic Review*, 80, pp. 689–713.

Fox, R., and M. S. Taqqu. (1986). "Large-sample Properties of Parameter Estimates for Strongly Dependent Stationary Gaussian Time Series," *Annals of Statistics*, 14, pp. 517–532.

Geweke, J., and S. Porter-Hudak. (1983). "The Estimation and Application of Long Memory Time Series Models," *Journal of Time Series Analysis*, 4, pp. 221–238.

Henry, M., and P. M. Robinson. (1999). "Bandwidth Choice in Gaussian Semiparametric Estimation of Long Range Dependence." Working paper, Department of Economics, London School of Economics, London, England.

Hosking, J. R. M. (1981). "Fractional Differencing," *Biometrika*, 68, pp. 165–176.

Kuan, C-M., and T. Liu. (1995). "Forecasting Exchange Rates Using Feedforward and Recurrent Neural Networks," *Journal of Applied Econometrics*, 10, pp. 347–364.

Lo, A. W. (1991). "Long-term Memory in Stock Market Prices," *Econometrica*, 59, pp. 1279–1313.

Mandelbrot, B. (1971). "When Can a Price Be Arbitraged Efficiently? A Limit to the Validity of the Random Walk and Martingale Models," *Review of Economics and Statistics*, 53, pp. 225–236.

Meese, R. A., and A. K. Rose. (1990). "Nonlinear, Nonparametric, Nonessential Exchange Rate Estimation," *American Economic Review Papers and Proceedings*, 80, pp. 192–196.

———. (1991). "An Empirical Assessment of Nonlinearities in Models of Exchange Rate Determination," *Review of Economic Studies*, 80, pp. 192–196.

Robinson, P. (1995). "Gaussian Semiparametric Estimation of Long Range Dependence," *Annals of Statistics*, 13, pp. 1630–1661.

Robinson, P., and M. Henry. (1999). "Long Memory Conditionally Heteroscedastic Errors in Semiparametric Estimation of Long Memory." Working paper, Department of Economics, London School of Economics, London, England.

Sowell, F. (1992). "Maximum Likelihood Estimation of Stationary Univariate Fractionally-integrated Time-series Models," *Journal of Econometrics*, 53, pp. 165–188.

APPENDIX

For the U.S. dollar nominal rates for the Canadian dollar, Deutsche mark, British pound, French franc, Italian lira, Japanese yen, Swiss franc, Netherlands guilder, Swedish krona, and Belgian franc, the frequency of observation is weekly and the sample spans the period January 4, 1974 to December 29, 1995 for a total of 1,147 returns observations. These weekly rates represent Friday noontime bid prices from the New York foreign exchange market and were obtained from the Federal Reserve Board of Governors. When Friday prices are not available Thursday prices are used. [The construction of the data set of weekly observations follows Cheung (1993)]. For the U.S. dollar nominal rates for the Austrian schilling, Danish krone, Luxembourg franc, Norwegian krone, Finnish markka, Portuguese escudo, and Spanish peseta, the frequency of observation is monthly and the sample covers the period August 1973 to December 1995 for a total of 268 returns observations. For the Greek drachma, the sample period starts at April 1975 (248 returns observations) as, prior to this date, the currency was under a fixed exchange rate regime relative to the U.S. dollar. The source of the monthly exchange rates is the International Monetary Fund's *International Financial Statistics* database. Data availability dictated the choice of the frequency of observation.

CHAPTER 11

Transfer Pricing and Investment Incentives: Asian and North American Linkages

Lawrence W. Nowicki

INTRODUCTION

The number of special investment regimes and special economic areas with targeted investment incentives, for example, in-bond assembly and economic processing zones, free-trade and investment zones, continued to increase throughout the world toward the end of the 1990s. More than 800 such zones were already in existence in more than 100 developing and developed countries at this time [United Nations Conference on Trade and Development (UNCTAD), 1998]. From the host country perspective, the primary objective behind the creation of such areas is to attract inward flows of foreign direct investment (FDI). Insofar as such an investment policy is part of a transparent, rules-based policy framework, it represents a real progress over one-on-one, closed door negotiations between a government and potential investors (Oman, 2000). Job creation, upgrading of managerial skills, technology transfers, and improved export performance are several major expected effects.

These special investment regimes and areas are often tax-free or low-tax areas. From the perspective of the multinational enterprise (MNE) as direct investor, these regimes and areas represent new vehicles for transferring value and income among the units of the firm. However, they are not mere tax havens, since there is some type of industrial activity that occurs, whether it involves production manufacturing, assembly of components into finished or semifinished products, warehousing, and logistics, or a combination of the above activities. In addition, the investment incentives that can be provided by the host country need not be fiscal. As an alternative, they can include financial incentives such as outright grants as well as miscellaneous types of investment incentives such as the provision of dedicated infrastructure and training (UNCTAD, 1996).

The working hypotheses of this research are as follows. The investment incentives of special economic processing zones and free zones represent an environmental variable capable of exercising a strong influence on the prevalence and frequency of transfer pricing manipulations away from the "arm's length price" or "arm's length standard" (ALS) recommended by the Organization for Economic Co-operation and Development (OECD) (1995) Transfer Pricing Guidelines. These manipulations involve the over- or underpricing of sales of components and finished goods between the subsidiary of an MNE located within a special zone and other units of the MNE. These other units can be located either in the same country as the subsidiary inside a zone, or in another country. However, governments can be expected to respond to such manipulation by attempting to tighten their regulations on transfer pricing as far as they are able, within the limits of their scarce financial resources. We examine the hypothesis, developed by UNCTAD (1999), that developing countries are less able to develop, implement, and enforce such regulations. The first section examines the cases of two Asian countries, China and Malaysia. The next section examines the North American cases of Mexico and Puerto Rico, while "General Conclusions" presents several conclusions.

ASIA: THE CASES OF CHINA AND MALAYSIA

The experiences of China and Malaysia are presented in this section. China is of central importance to research linking transfer pricing strategies and investment incentives for two particular reasons. First, China has been a leading destination of flows of FDI in recent years. Second, a significant number of MNEs have reported losses for their operations in China, a situation that has led the government to a consideration of the issue of transfer pricing. The government subsequently accused MNEs of using transfer pricing to shift profits out of China.

A review of the literature on the subject reveals several problems with existing research. For example, Lin, Lefebvre, and Kantor (1993) claim that transfer pricing manipulations are popular in the Asia Pacific region. However, the authors subsequently fail to present empirical data to support their affirmation.

In a second article, Chan and Chow (1997) focus on transfer pricing practices in China. They note that a host of fiscal incentives exist for inward investors in China, and especially in open cities and special economic zones (SEZs). One problem with their research, however, is that no attempt is made to distinguish between investment inside and outside the SEZs and open cities. The authors simply note that the Shenzhen SEZ has the most aggressive tax audits on transfer pricing in China despite a severe lack of enforcement resources: a staff of fewer than 12 persons is responsible for overseeing more than 1,000 MNEs. Chan and Chow merely argue that, given the low tax rates of the Chinese SEZs, and with everything else being equal, MNE income should be shifted into the zones—rather than out of the zones, as argued by many other observers—from parent countries such as Japan, the United States, Germany, and the United Kingdom in order to minimize the overall level of taxation.

Tang (1997) chooses to widen the analysis, incorporating several strategic and other nonfinancial variables into an analysis of transfer pricing practices in China and elsewhere. Contrary to Chan and Chow, this research concludes that there are many reasons to shift profits out of China, for example, in order to quickly recover investment before political and currency risks materialize. Tang also argues that MNEs can be expected to transfer income elsewhere in order to avoid sharing profits with local joint venture partners.

The reasoning of Tang has the advantage of integrating an array of elements that actually enter into consideration in corporate strategizing, decision making, and transfer pricing. For example, Tang observes that foreign MNEs rushed to beat a 1996 deadline for importing capital equipment on a duty-free basis. However, he fails to note that the Pudong New Development Zone, a popular investment location adjacent to Shanghai, was in fact exempt from this new tax. As with other authors, Tang thus fails to clearly distinguish between investment inside special investment areas and investment flows occurring elsewhere in China.

The Case of Malaysian Free Zones and Industrial Estates

In the Malaysian case, Marappan and Jomo (1994) present detailed evidence concerning the transfer pricing practices of some inward direct investors. These investor firms include several large Japanese-owned electronics and electrical MNEs with investments in Malaysia that were undertaken inside as well as outside the country's network of free zones and related industrial estates. Malaysia is an interesting case due to its heavy use of fiscal incentives and other investment incentives to promote export-led growth on the basis of these free zones and industrial estates. The catalytic role played by such economic processing zones in achieving industrialization and high rates of economic growth has been recognized and discussed elsewhere (Nowicki, 1997, 1998; Porter, 1998; Sachs, 2000).

At the federal level, these fiscal incentives for MNEs have included:

- a special pioneer tax status;
- "post-pioneer" reinvestment allowances; and
- the novel extension of duty-free status for imported parts to indirect exporters.

At the subnational level, the provision of subsidized infrastructure by Malaysia's various states for the free zones and industrial estates represents an additional category of investment incentive.

Price information was obtained for intrafirm sales of components and finished goods among the following units of the MNEs:

1. subsidiaries located within Malaysia's free zones and industrial estates with licensed manufacturing warehouses (LMWs). These LMWs lie outside the customs area of Malaysia and enjoy the same advantages and incentives as free zones (e.g., pioneer status, duty-free imports);

2. subsidiaries and associated companies located within Malaysia but outside Malaysia's free zones and LMWs;

3. a Singapore trading company, which functions as a regional headquarters and purchasing and marketing agent; and

4. the overseas parent from whom components may be ordered.

The OECD Guidelines (1997) and Section 482 of the Internal Revenue Code of the United States provide the basis for determining the arm's length principle or "standard" (ALS) for inter-firm transfer pricing. The transfer pricing regulations of most countries, regardless of their level of development, are based on the OECD Guidelines. To meet the ALS, the OECD established a hierarchy of acceptable methods. Three transactional methods take precedence: the comparable uncontrolled price (CUP), resale minus, and cost plus (C+) methods. Transactional profit methods, including the transactional profit split and the transactional net margin method (TNMM), are considered methods of last resort.

Marappan and Jomo (1994) employ a transactional method, the directly comparable uncontrolled price (CUP) method, to verify whether transfer pricing manipulations away from an OECD-acceptable arm's length price did indeed occur. Such manipulations would involve the over- or under-pricing of sales of components and finished goods between the subsidiary of an MNE located within a special zone or LMW, and other units of the MNE. These other units could be located either in Malaysia or in another country. To carry out their study, the prices for sales to, and purchases from, affiliated parties were compared with the prices on sales to, and purchases from independent parties. For the purposes of this research, four of their most interesting results are worth presenting in detail:

- *Result One:* Overpricing of Imports into Malaysia from Parent. The MNE makes refrigerators and components in Malaysia, with copper tubing being imported from the Japanese parent. There are two ways to import these parts: direct import from Japan, versus the use of a Singapore trading company. In the case of direct imports, the authors calculate that these imports were overpriced by an average of 16 percent. The probable reason that higher prices were charged concerns tax differentials: the tax rate on Malaysia-Japan remittances is greater than the tax rate on Singapore-Japan remittances.

- *Result Two:* Use of Free Zone to Transfer Income Overseas. A free zone subsidiary's sale prices to associated "sister" companies located within Malaysia but outside the free zone, are higher than the prices to independent buyers. The key reason: profit is transferred to the free zone from nonzone units. Profit is then transferred out of Malaysia by exporting to the Singapore trading arm. A key mechanism: subsidiaries in free zones and LMWs charge export sales prices that aren't scrutinized by customs, since no duties or taxes are due.

- *Result Three:* Comparable Pricing of Local Sales versus Underpricing of Exports. Due to competition, sale prices to a local sales unit are approximately equal to the arm's length price, that is, the sale prices to outside firms. However, sale prices to the parent and to Singapore are significantly undertransfer priced. The reason: profit outflow to Singapore and the parent.

- *Result Four:* Use of LMW and Third Country (Singapore) to Transfer Income to Parent. This MNE produces televisions in a zonelike LMW. As a result, Singapore transfer prices are from 8 percent to 17 percent lower than prices for local market sales. These lower prices are not offset by the value of services rendered by the Singapore subsidiary, e.g. with the provision of moulds to the Malaysian unit. The authors thus argue that the Singapore operation is merely an extension of the parent in Japan.

To conclude, it is to be noted that Marappan and Jomo's highly insightful study was made possible due to access to an extremely rare source of information: the actual, "insider" sale prices given on invoices, documents, declaration forms, and bills of transfer made available to one of the authors while employed by Malaysia's Customs and Excise Department.

NORTH AMERICA: THE CASES OF MEXICO AND PUERTO RICO

Mexico's in-bond program or "maquiladora" industry involves the assembly, by plants known as maquilas, of mostly foreign-made parts into finished and semifinished products prior to their reexport from Mexico. The primarily foreign-based MNEs participating in this program have enjoyed preferential treatment for their investments since its creation in 1965. As owners of maquila operations, MNEs have been able to take advantage of a combination of fiscal, financial, and infrastructure incentives. In terms of industry growth over time, these MNEs created more than 350,000 direct jobs with their maquila plants by 1988; approximately one million jobs had been created in about 3,000 maquilas by 1998. As of 2000, there were more than 3,500 such plants throughout Mexico, producing about 50 percent of the country's exports and earning close to 13 billion U.S. dollars in foreign exchange annually. Almost 60 percent of these maquila plants are located along the U.S-Mexico border. Large corporations such as General Motors, Ford, General Electric, and Sony have several such plants in multiple locations.

From the perspective of tax administration and transfer pricing regulations at the national level, it is interesting to note that Mexico provided no guidelines for taxpayers regarding a transfer pricing standard prior to 1992. With the amended corporate income tax code of 1992, any one of the OECD's three traditional transactional methods for establishing an arm's length price—the CUP, the resale price and C +—are now allowed, in addition to one transactional profit method, the profit split method. Some observers believe that most maquila plants have applied the C + method, adding a small profit of between 1 percent and 5 percent to total costs (Engle, 1997; Tang; 1997). However, the director of Mexico's tax policies during the Zedillo administration, Ricardo Gonzalez Orta, notes that international audit teams looking into compliance with OECD transfer pricing practices found that transactional profit methods were in fact being applied (OECD, 1997). Orta notes that transactional profit methods have been applied in the past due to practical difficulties associated with the application of traditional transaction methods. An operating margin is added by maquilas to both the costs and general and administrative expenses in order to compute their remuneration and thus the transfer price (Eden, 1998; OECD, 1997). Evidence of such alternative practices is useful in the ongoing international debates over transfer pricing methods of last resort (UNCTAD, 1999).

Despite Mexico's critical role in the U.S. economy, it is interesting to note that a U.S.-Mexico tax treaty only took effect in 1994. Of particular interest is Article 5(5), which declares that maquilas are henceforth to be considered "permanent establishments" rather than temporary cost centers for their primarily U.S.-based parents. As a result, Mexican income tax treatment was set to become the general rule for profit generated in the Mexican maquilas unless the U.S. parent could show that arm's length transactions prevail between the parent and the maquila. This critical exemption from Mexican income tax treatment of maquilas employing arm's length transfer prices was almost lost in 1999. Maquilas employing an ALS have been subject to a less onerous "safe harbor" tax equal to 5 percent of the maquila's assets. Several important events that underline the linkages that exist between transfer pricing and the special investment incentives that maquilas provide are as follows:

- 1994: The Maquila Owners' Association forms a working committee on transfer pricing, and accepts the need to employ arm's length prices for their intrafirm trade. Transfer pricing audits begin.
- 1995: Maquila exports, which will total almost 13 billion U.S. dollars by the end of the decade, must now be priced according to an ALS. Mexico's tax authority

issues its first advance transfer pricing ruling for a maquila. Such rulings are approximately equivalent to U.S.-style Advance Pricing Agreements (APAs), in which the corporate taxpayer meets with the tax administration to share its transfer pricing policy in order to minimize the probability of future audits. The transactional "cost plus" method for establishing an ALS is employed. The appearance of advance rulings coincides with Mexico's entry into the OECD.

- 1997: Documentation is now required to support arm's length pricing. For the first time, documentation on transactions between Mexican entities and entities situated in low-tax areas is also required. Observers note that documentation may play a role in rebutting the assumption that transactions between Mexican entities and related parties in low tax jurisdictions are not conducted at arm's length (Engle, 1997). Here there is a parallel and strong regulatory concern for the type of transactions previously seen to be occurring between the Malaysian and Singaporean subsidiaries of various MNEs.

- 1999: Under pressure from the U.S government and MNEs, the Mexican government backtracks on plans to convert all maquilas' tax status from temporary to permanent establishments by January 2000. The less onerous safe harbor taxes are increased. Mexico's original tax plans, if implemented, would have been very costly for U.S. firms. The uncertainty surrounding the tax plans leads to a freeze in the investments of some MNEs.

- 2000–2001: The election campaign and administration of Mexico's President Vincente Fox speak about the need to increase various business taxes, including the tax on maquila assets, in order to improve workers' housing, water supplies and other basic infrastructure along Mexico's border with the United States. Despite the uncertainty that such declarations create for MNEs, the maquila industry can be expected to continue to grow indefinitely. Growth will be less subject to criticism and controversy in locations removed from the overburdened border.

Puerto Rico and Section 936 of the United States Internal Revenue Code

The inauguration of a new governor in Puerto Rico in 2001 coincided with renewed debate over the need to reinstate the Section 936 fiscal incentives for U.S-based firms, first approved by the U.S. Congress in 1976 but dismantled by the Clinton administration and the U.S. Congress in 1996. As with China, Malaysia, Mexico, and other developing countries, these investment incentives for Puerto Rico were designed to encourage industrialization, promote economic growth and thus reduce poverty and unemployment. Section 936 represented a fifth generation of U.S. investment incentives in favor of Puerto Rico. The first four generations of incentives included: the Revenue Act of 1921, which contained a U.S. tax exemption for income from U.S. possessions such as the Philippines and Puerto Rico; the tax-free transfer of intangibles to the foreign subsidiaries of U.S. MNEs, permitted by Section 351 of the Revenue Act of 1928; the

Industrial Incentives Act of 1948, commonly known as Operation Bootstrap; and the Industrial Incentives Act of 1963, which eliminated various Puerto Rican taxes. An additional purpose behind the U.S. tax exemption of the Revenue Act of 1921 was to help U.S. MNEs compete against foreign rivals (Eden, 1998).

In terms of impact, Section 936 helped create an estimated 100,000 direct jobs and 200,000 indirect jobs between 1976 and 1990, according to Daubon and Villamil (1991), who analyze the entire Caribbean island as a single, special enterprise zone. The cost of this incentive, in terms of foregone tax revenue, was a constant source of controversy and debate. The specific incentive mechanism of Section 936 involved sheltering income earned from investments by U.S. MNEs in their Puerto Rican and other possessions corporations from U.S. tax. With Section 936, the generous foreign tax exemptions of the previous generations were converted into a foreign tax credit for investment income. By the 1990s, President Clinton and several members of Congress succeeded in passing legislation that limited what they perceived as excessive tax breaks for pharmaceutical firms and other MNEs due to Section 936.

Puerto Rico's experience with corporate transfer pricing strategies that are linked to investment incentives, and especially those of U.S.-based MNEs in the pharmaceutical industry, involve two important issues in international business and finance. These issues include the allocation of expenses and income among the units of the MNE, and the transfer, trade, and taxation of intangible goods such as technology. The Puerto Rican case holds particular lessons for MNEs and tax authorities with respect to applying the ALS to trade in intangibles, for example, the appropriate tax treatment for the transfer—rather than sale or licensing—of a drug patent by a U.S. parent firm to its low-cost, overseas manufacturing subsidiaries.

The separation of expenses and income is an issue that has involved declaring expenses in the U.S. and income in a low-tax location such as Puerto Rico. It is interesting and instructive to observe the changing ability of a U.S.-based MNE to engage in the following three practices simultaneously. First, it could write off research and development (R&D) expenses in the United States against U.S. tax. Second, it could transfer intangibles without having to recognize any taxable income, due to Section 351 of the U.S. Internal Revenue Code. Third, it could earn and declare income in low-cost manufacturing locations. These manufacturing locations will have specific advantages, e.g. tax holidays designed to spur local economic development. Section 351 has allowed MNEs to avoid recognizing U.S. taxable income if no sale or licensing occurs as an MNE transfers ownership of an intangible asset to a foreign affiliate or possessions corporation. Such transfers are considered to be contributions to capital.

With the Dole rule of 1982, that is, Section 936 (h), the U.S. federal government sought to reduce the ensuing tax losses for the U.S. Treasury per job created in Puerto Rico by allocating all of the intangibles of the Puerto Rican affiliates to the U.S. parent. However, it is interesting to note that the tax savings of many U.S. firms, as measured in dollars per job created in Puerto Rico, continued to be considerable despite the Dole rule. As seen with the attempts to regulate Mexico's maquila plants, MNEs were able to avoid losing their tax savings by the judicious use of two "safe harbors" or escape clauses from the Dole rule. To preserve most of their tax holiday, MNEs chose either the cost sharing safe harbor for intangibles or the profit split safe harbor for income from the intangible. The cost sharing safe harbor allowed the Puerto Rican affiliate to own the manufacturing intangibles in exchange for mandatory payments to the parent for a share of the MNE's worldwide R&D costs. Section 482 and its ALS is then used to set the transfer price of goods manufactured in Puerto Rico and sold to the U.S. parent. The profit split safe harbor called for a 50–50 division of the combined taxable income of the U.S. parent and the Puerto Rican affiliate on the basis of a separation of returns from marketing and from manufacturing (Eden, 1998).

Three other U.S. tax measures of note from the late 1970s and 1980s were Sections 861, 367 and 367(D). Section 861 regulated the worldwide allocation of R&D expenses by U.S. MNEs. Section 367 restricted tax-free transfers of intangibles by U.S. parents to overseas locations if tax avoidance was seen as the motive. Section 367(D) called for the calculation of imputed royalty payments for intangible transfers (Eden, 1998). These sections limited the ability of MNEs to use Section 351 in combination with the other generations of fiscal incentives to transform tax savings into a tax bonanza while engaging in outward FDI. The lessons learned over time with investment in Puerto Rico remain valid elsewhere: U.S. tax policy has been Janus-like, creating investment incentives and helping U.S. MNEs compete, while simultaneously attempting to close tax loopholes, minimize losses to the U.S. Treasury and maximize tax revenues from those same MNEs.

On a final note, it is interesting to observe that a relatively labor-intensive MNE such as General Electric progressively positioned Puerto Rico, with its changing level of investment incentives, wages and other locational advantages, as a strategic "turntable" or intermediary between the high-cost U.S. parent and affiliates in lower-cost Caribbean manufacturing locations such as the neighboring Dominican Republic (Nowicki, 1992). As overall costs rose in Puerto Rico, GE's most sophisticated manufacturing processes remained in Puerto Rico, while the lower value-added manufacturing and assembly activities were increasingly "handed off" to other, less developed locations. Regulatory change in Washington, in combination with fluctuating economic, financial, technological and geographic variables, has had a cascading effect on the offshore location of international business activities. The Puerto Rican evidence suggests that the "flying geese" model of economic development, as originally formulated by Akamatsu (1961) on the basis of the knowledge-intensive activities of the firm, has a supplementary "incentives" dimension to explain the transfer of business activity from the leading country to its "followers."

GENERAL CONCLUSIONS

A questionnaire of the United Nations addressed to developing countries and their relevant policy makers and tax administrators revealed that more than 60 percent of those surveyed believed that their own MNEs were engaged in income shifting through the use of outward FDI (UNCTAD, 1999). In addition, 70 percent of those surveyed considered the practice to be a significant problem. An even greater percentage of developing countries (more than 80 percent) felt that the affiliates of the foreign-based MNEs they were hosting were shifting income out of the country surveyed and back to the parent in order to avoid tax liabilities. Such statistics serve as an indicator of the importance of effective transfer pricing regulation. These numbers also suggest that many developing countries do not have the means for carrying out effective regulation. The evidence presented in this research, and especially for the Malaysian case, tends to confirm this observation.

Developing country governments may well have reason to suspect that some transactions with low-tax areas and zones with special investment incentives aren't conducted at arm's length, but documentation and APAs such as those being employed in Mexico can mitigate the doubts of government authorities. The existence and enforcement of a transparent, well-defined and rules-based taxation and transfer pricing framework that wins the support of both MNEs and government is needed to avoid discouraging inward FDI, everything else being equal. Two types of cooperation thus emerge as optimal policy alternatives: the cooperation that exists between MNEs and governments, e.g. as needed in order to reach APAs; and the cooperation needed between developed and developing countries for the purposes of information sharing and the avoidance of double taxation and unfair taxation.

REFERENCES

Akamatsu, K. (1961). "A Theory of Unbalanced Growth in the World Economy," *Weltwirtschaftliches Archiv*, 88, no. 2.

Chan, K. H., and L. Chow. (1997). "International Transfer Pricing for Business Operations in China: Inducements, Regulations and Practice," *Journal of*

Business Finance and Accounting, 24, nos. 9/10 (October and December), pp. 1269–1289.

Daubon, R., and J. Villamil. (1991). "Puerto Rico as an Enterprise Zone." In R. E. Green (Ed.), *Enterprise Zones: New Directions in Economic Development*. Newbury Park, CA: Sage.

Eden, L. (1998). *Taxing Multinationals: Transfer Pricing and Corporate Income Taxation in North America*. Toronto: University of Toronto Press.

Engle, H. S. (1997). "International Developments," *Journal of Corporate Taxation*, 10 (Autumn), pp. 313–321.

Lin, L., C. Lefebvre, and J. Kantor. (1993). "Economic Determinants of International Transfer Pricing," *International Journal of Accounting*, 28, pp. 49–70.

Marappan, A., and K. S. Jomo. (1994). "Japanese Multinational Intra-firm Trade Transfer Pricing Practices in Malaysia." In K. S. Jomo (Ed.), *Japan and Malaysian Development*. London: Routledge.

Nowicki, L. (1992). "Production Sharing in the Americas: Changing Issues and New Directions." In K. Fatemi (Ed.), *Economic Perspectives for the Americas: 1993–1997, Proceedings of the Second Annual Conference on Western Hemispheric Economic Issues* (pp. 17–34). San Jose, Costa Rica: University of the Americas and Texas A&M International University.

———. (1997). "New Lessons from Malaysia's Industrial Estates and EPZs." In S. M. Lee (Ed.), *Restrategizing the Asia-Pacific Region towards a New Millenium. Proceedings of the Pan-Pacific Conference XIV* (pp. 390–392). Pan-Pacific Business Association, University of Nebraska and Kuala Lumpur, Malaysia.

———. (1998). "Second Generation EPZs and the East Asian Firm." In D. Chang and S. M. Lee (Eds.), *Restructuring the Asia-Pacific Economic Systems towards the 21st Century. Proceedings of the Pan-Pacific Conference XV* (pp. 255–257). Pan-Pacific Business Association, University of Nebraska and Seoul, Korea.

Oman, C. (2000). *Policy Competition for Foreign Direct Investment. A Study of Competition among Governments to Attract FDI*. Paris: Organization for Economic Co-operation and Development (OECD), Development Centre Studies.

Organization for Economic Co-operation and Development (OECD). (1995). *Transfer Pricing Guidelines for Multinational Enterprises and Tax Administrations*. Paris: OECD.

———. (1997). *Taxing International Business: Emerging Trends in APEC and OECD Countries*. Paris: OECD.

Porter, M. E. (1998). "Clusters and Competition: New Agendas for Companies, Governments, and Institutions." In M. E. Porter (Ed.), *On Competition* (pp. 1234–1250). Boston: Harvard Business Review Book.

Sachs, J. (2000). "Globalization and Patterns of Economic Development." *Weltwirtschaftliches Archiv*, 136, no. 4, pp. 579–600.

Tang, R. Y. (1997). *Intra-firm Trade and Global Transfer Pricing Regulation*, Westport, CT: Quorum.

United Nations Conference on Trade and Development (UNCTAD). (1996). *Division on Transnational Corporations and Investment, Incentives and Foreign Direct Investment*. New York and Geneva: United Nations.

———. (1998). *World Investment Report 1998: Trends and Determinants*. New York and Geneva: United Nations.

———. (1999). *Transfer Pricing*. UNCTAD Series on Issues in International Investment Agreements. New York and Geneva: United Nations.

CHAPTER 12

Money, Exchange Rates, and Inflation: Evidence from Malaysia

Mohammed B. Yusoff and Lee Chin

INTRODUCTION

Currency depreciation has far-reaching effects on the world economic growth, interest rates, and inflation rates. It is often asserted by monetarists that inflation is a monetary phenomenon; no major inflation can take place without rapid money growth. Malaysia, on the average, was facing only a 5.5 percent inflation rate during the 1970s, except in 1973 and 1974. During the two-year period the prices of Malaysian exports were very favorable and coupled with the sharp rise in the price of oil, had triggered inflation rate to double digits at 10.6 percent and 17.3 percent, respectively (Figure 12.1). But since then the inflation rate had dropped to below the 5 percent level, mainly due to the effective government's efforts to reduce inflation through tight monetary, fiscal, and income policies (Yusoff, 1985). Malaysia experienced a second episode of inflationary pressure during the 1979–1981 period as a result of a sudden rise in oil prices by 47 percent in 1979 and 66 percent in 1981. At the same time, prices of raw materials and investment goods also increased rapidly accelerating inflation from 7.9 percent in 1979 to 12.5 percent in 1981. There was a sharp decline in oil and non-oil commodity prices in 1985 and 1986 during which Malaysia suffered negative growth of 1 percent in 1985 and a marginally positive growth of only 1.2 percent in 1986 and therefore the inflation rate in Malaysia decelerated accordingly. Thus, inflation was almost zero for three consecutive years from 1985 to 1987. However, inflation started to rise in 1988, when it increased by 2.5 percent and reached 4.7 percent in 1992 but fell to 3.6 percent in 1996.

Figure 12.1
Exchange rate changes and inflation rate in Malaysia.

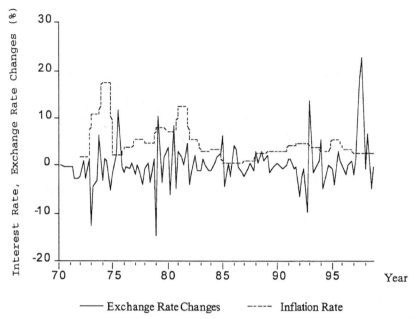

It has been argued that one of the causes of inflation is the depreciation of domestic currency; a ringgit depreciation increases the domestic price of imported raw materials resulting in inflation. Against the U.S. dollar, the monthly average ringgit (RM) nominal exchange rates appreciated from RM2.26 in 1975 to RM2.00 in 1979. After reaching RM2.28 in 1980, the rate remained stable around RM2.32 until 1985 when the ringgit began to weaken to RM2.58 after which the depreciation started to accelerate until the trend was reversed after the rate rose to RM2.74 in 1991. Then in 1993, the ringgit appreciated until the currency crisis in 1997 after which it began to slide.

Malaysia adopted a flexible exchange rate regime in 1973 and had pursued this policy for more than two decades. Before the currency crisis in 1997, Malaysia was considered as the best development model among the second-tier newly industrializing economies in East Asia. During 1987–1996, the Malaysian economy grew at an average annual rate of 8.8 percent, raising per capita income from US$1,850 to US$4,425. The economy was virtually at full employment with modest inflation at 4.5 percent. This impressive growth changed dramatically with the onset of the currency crisis. For five years prior to the July 1997 currency crisis, the exchange rate of Malaysia varied in the narrow band of 2.58 to 2.54 ringgit per

U.S. dollar. When the Thai baht came under heavy speculative attack in mid-May 1997, the ringgit also experienced heavy selling pressure. Then Bank Negara Malaysia (BNM) responded with massive foreign exchange market intervention, selling close to US$1.5 billion to prop up the ringgit but ultimately gave way to market forces on 14 July 1997 (Athukorala, 1998).

Between the first week of July 1997 and January 7, 1998 when the Malaysian ringgit exchange rate hit the bottom at RM4.88 per U.S. dollar, the ringgit depreciated against the dollar by almost 50 percent. After showing some signs of stability during February and March, the exchange rate continued to slide in the followings months until the government abruptly fixed the rate at RM3.80 per U.S. dollar on September 1, 1998. This financial crisis subsequently turned into economic turmoil as stock market collapsed, property market crashed, massive capital outflows, nonperforming loans increased and domestic market oriented industries were also affected by the contractionary impact of this unexpected currency depreciation.

The ringgit depreciation during the currency turmoil had resulted in a decade of high growth crumbled into stagflation–low-growth scenario. This study attempts to find out the relationship between exchange rate and inflation in Malaysia and also to explore the interrelationship among exchange rate and inflation with other macroeconomic variables, such as domestic output, money supply, and interest rate.

REVIEW OF LITERATURE

Economists have investigated empirically the effects of exchange rates on prices. Most of these studies find that exchange rate changes have caused inflation, while others have found otherwise or reported mixed results. Papell (1994) estimates the effects of exchange rates on domestic prices in the context of a semistructural model of exchange rate determination in which both exchange rates and prices are determined endogenously and find that exchange rates have relatively small effects on national price levels for the G7 (the United States, Canada, the United Kingdom, France, Germany, Italy, and Japan) countries. Kim (1998) studies the relationship between U.S. inflation and the dollar exchange rate by employing cointegration vector error-correction model and finds that U.S. inflation, exchange rate, money supply, income, and interest rate are cointegrated and that the dollar exchange rate Granger causes inflation.

For the developing countries, Deme and Fayassa (1995) investigate the inflationary effects of the rates of growth of money supply, gross domestic product, effective exchange rate, and imported inflation for Egypt, Morocco, and Tunisia. The results indicate that the long-run and short-run parameters of the exchange rates are positive and statistically significant for Morocco and Tunisia. For Egypt, the long-run parameter of the exchange rate is not statistically significant, but the interim parameter estimate of the exchange rate is negative and significant. Kyereme (1991) explores the dynamic interrelationships among the currency exchange rate, inflation, and real output growth in Ghana and find that there exists significant interrelationships between the exchange rate and inflation.

Deravi, Gregorowicz, and Hegji (1995) estimate the effects of exchange rate depreciation on the price level using a vector autoregressive model of exchange rates, the price level, and money and they find that exchange rates and prices are monetary phenomena, with the money supply Granger causes both variables. These results are further supported by the impulse response analysis, which indicates that a depreciated dollar leads to a higher rate of inflation over a two-year period. Rittenberg (1993) examines the relationship between exchange rate changes and price level changes in Turkey during the 1980s using Granger causality tests. During that period, Turkish exchange rate policy was characterized by considerable flexibility. The evidence from the study suggests that Granger causality runs from price level changes to exchange rate changes without feedback. In Malaysia, Tan and Baharumshah (1999) examine the dynamic causal chain among money, real output, interest rate, and inflation in Malaysia. The cointegration tests suggest a stable long-run equilibrium relationship exists among these macroeconomic variables while the short-run results based on vector error-correction modeling support the view that money is non-neutral in the short-run.

MODEL SPECIFICATION

In this study we shall employ the vector autoregressive error-correction model (VECM), which is a standard vector autoregressive (VAR) in first-differences augmented by error-correction terms, and cointegration technique to analyze the economic relationships among macroeconomic variables. Engle and Granger (1987) demonstrate that once a number of variables are found to be cointegrated, there always exists a corresponding error-correction representation which implies that changes in the dependent variable are a function of the level of disequilibria in the cointegrating relationship, which is captured by the error-correction term, as well as changes in other explanatory variable(s). If there exists comovements among exchange rate, inflation, domestic output, money supply, and interest rate and they trend together to find a long-run stable equilibrium, then by Granger representation theorem we may write our vector error-correction model:

$$\Delta CPI_t = \alpha_1 + \Sigma\beta_{1t} \Delta CPI_{t-i} + \Sigma\theta_{1t} \Delta ER_{t-i} + \Sigma\delta_{1t} \Delta IPI_{t-i}$$
$$+ \Sigma\gamma_{1t} \Delta M3_{t-i} + \Sigma\phi_{1t} \Delta INT_{t-i} + \Sigma\lambda_{1t} ECT_{t-i} + \mu_{1t} \quad (12.1)$$

$$\Delta ER_t = \alpha_2 + \Sigma\beta_{2t} \Delta CPI_{t-i} + \Sigma\theta_{2t} \Delta ER_{t-i} + \Sigma\delta_{2t} \Delta IPI_{t-i}$$
$$+ \Sigma\gamma_{2t} \Delta M3_{t-i} + \Sigma\phi_{2t} \Delta INT_{t-i} + \Sigma\lambda_{2t}ECT_{t-i} + \mu_{2t} \quad (12.2)$$

$$\Delta IPI_t = \alpha_3 + \Sigma\beta_{3t} \Delta CPI_{t-i} + \Sigma\theta_{3t} \Delta ER_{t-i} + \Sigma\delta_{3t} \Delta IPI_{t-i}$$
$$+ \Sigma\gamma_{3t} \Delta M3_{t-i} + \Sigma\phi_{3t} \Delta INT_{t-i} + \Sigma\lambda_{3t}ECT_{t-i} + \mu_{3t} \quad (12.3)$$

$$\Delta M3_t = \alpha_4 + \Sigma\beta_{4t} \Delta CPI_{t-i} + \Sigma\theta_{4t} \Delta ER_{t-i} + \Sigma\delta_{4t} \Delta IPI_{t-i}$$
$$+ \Sigma\gamma_{4t} \Delta M3_{t-i} + \Sigma\phi_{4t} \Delta INT_{t-i} + \Sigma\lambda_{4t}ECT_{t-i} + \mu_{4t} \quad (12.4)$$

$$\Delta TB3_t = \alpha_5 + \Sigma\beta_{5t} \Delta CPI_{t-i} + \Sigma\theta_{5t} \Delta ER_{t-i} + \Sigma\delta_{5t} \Delta IPI_{t-i}$$
$$+ \Sigma\gamma_{5t} \Delta M3_{t-i} + \Sigma\phi_{5t} \Delta INT_{t-i} + \Sigma\lambda_{5t}ECT_{t-i} + \mu_{5t} \quad (12.5)$$

where $\Delta X_t = X_t - X_{t-1}$ and X represents the logarithm of domestic price level, exchange rate, domestic output, money supply, and interest rate, respectively (that is, CPI_t, ER_t, IPI_t, $M3_t$, and $TB3_t$, respectively). ECT refers to error-correction term(s) derived from the long-run cointegration relationship using Johansen maximum likelihood procedure, and μ_{ht}'s (for $h = 1, 2, 3, 4, 5$) are serially uncorrelated random error terms with mean zero. Equations (12.1)–(12.5) will be used to test the causation from exchange rate, domestic real output, money supply and interest rate to the dependent variable. The optimal lag structure is selected based on the criterion of minimum Akaike's Final Prediction Error (FPE).

The Granger causality or endogeneity of the dependent variable, can be exposed either through the statistical significance of: (1) the lagged ECTs (λ's) by a t-test; (2) a joint test applied to the significance of the sum of the lags of each explanatory variables (β's, θ's, δ's, γ's, and ϕ's) by a joint F-test or Wald χ^2 test; or a joint test of all the set of terms just described in (1) and (2) by a joint F-test or Wald χ^2 test. The insignificance of both the t-test and F-test or Wald χ^2 test in the vector error-correction model (VECM) indicates econometric exogeneity of the dependent variable.

ESTIMATION METHODS

In this study we first test for the existence of cointegrating relations among the macroeconomic variables. If two variables are cointegrated, then there exists Granger causality in at least in one direction, which can be detected through the VECM. We also test for a unit root in the time series and if the constructed series do not have a unit root, these fundamentals move together in the long run.

Cointegration

Macroeconomic variables can be characterized as nonstationary processes that have no tendency to return to a deterministic path (Nelson & Plosser, 1982). Taking into consideration that the macroeconomic time series that we are going to study are the exchange rate, price income or output, interest rate, and money supply which possess trend structure that is nonstationary, the appropriate econometric method to be used to estimate the long-run relationship among them is the cointegration technique.

A necessary condition for the existence of cointegration is that all the variables to be integrated must be of the same order. Therefore the standard unit root test is applied to the series to ensure that they exhibit the same order of cointegration. Existence of unit roots in a series indicates nonstationary property. There are several tests for unit root such as the Dickey-Fuller (DF) test, the Phillips-Perron (PP) test, and the Augmented Dickey-Fuller (ADF) test. In this study, the PP test will be conducted to examine the existence of unit roots as the PP test is more powerful than the ADF test in a small sample. If the series are cointegrated of the same order, then we proceed from unit root test to cointegration test using cointegration approach developed by Johansen (1988, 1991) and Johansen and Juselius (1990).

The Granger causality test is then carried out after the variables are found to be cointegrated since if two or more variables are cointegrated, causality must exist in at least one direction. Engle and Granger (1987) demonstrated that once a number of variables (say, x_t and y_t) are found to be cointegrated, there always exists a corresponding error-correction representation which implies that changes in the dependent variable are a function of the level of disequilibrium in the cointegrating relationship (captured by the error-correction term) as well as changes in other explanatory variable(s).

The Data

All the data series (except Industrial Production Index) were obtained from various issues of the Quarterly Bulletin, Bank Negara Malaysia (1999–2000) while Industrial Production Index (IPI) data was obtained from various issues of the International Monetary Fund's International Financial Statistics Year Book (1994–2000). The data was collected at the quarterly frequency from 1970:1 to 1997:2 (before the currency crisis). Exchange rates are quarterly average in terms of RM/USD. Domestic price level is measured by the consumer price index (CPI). Interest rates are the quarterly averages of three-month treasury bill rates (TB3). The IPI was utilized as a proxy for domestic real output as quarterly GDP or GNP data was not available. The broad money stock (M3) was chosen to represent money supply.

RESULTS AND DISCUSSION

In this section we shall discuss the results of the unit root test, cointegration test, Granger causality test based on vector error-correction model, variance decompositions, and impulse response analysis.

Unit Root Tests

The results of the unit root test (with intercept and trend) on the level and its first-difference of the series are given in Table 12.1. In all the cases for the unit root tests on levels, the absolute value of test statistics are smaller than the absolute critical value of 4.04 which is tabulated in Mackinnon (1991) at 1 percent level of significance, suggesting that the null hypothesis of unit root cannot be rejected and all the series under study are nonstationary in their level forms. Since all the series are integrated of the same order, I(1), the series can be further tested for the existence of long-term relationships among them using the cointegration technique.

Cointegration Test

The results of the Johansen cointegration test (Table 12.2) indicate that, for the period 1970:1 to 1997:2, the variables are cointegrated with at most two cointegrating vectors suggesting that there is a long-run relationship among the five variables.

Granger Causality Tests Based on VECM

The VECM separates the short-term and long-term causality. When the variables are cointegrated, short-run deviations from the long-run equilibrium will affect the dependent variable forcing it back into equilibrium. Thus if the dependent variable does not respond to the long-run equilibrium error, then it only responds to short-run shocks. The endogeneity of a dependent variable is gauged by t-test of the lagged error-correction

Table 12.1
Philips-Perron Unit Root Test for Series

Series	Levels	First-Differences
CPI	-1.83	-6.92**
ER	-2.69	-14.73**
IPI	-2.73	-24.73**
M3	-1.71	-6.03**
TB3	-3.20	-8.74**

Notes: Lag truncation for all series is 6. ** indicates rejection at 99 percent critical value. All series are log-transformed.

terms (ECTs) and/or F-tests on the joint significance of the sum of the lags of each of the explanatory variables. If both the t-test and F-test are not significant, then the dependent variable is exogenous. The short-run causality is indicated by the significance of the differenced explanatory variables while the long-run effect is implied by the t-test of the ECTs). If the ECTs are not significant, then the dependent variables is termed as weakly exogenous. The F-tests from Table 12.3 suggest that for the inflation equation, all the explanatory variables: exchange rates, output, money

Table 12.2
Johansen Cointegration Test

Hypothesized No. of Cointegrating Equation(s) H_0	Maximum Eigenvalue	Critical Value (99%)
None $(r = 0)$**	245.74	96.58
At most 1 $(r \le 1)$**	103.37	70.05
At most 2 $(r \le 2)$**	49.88	48.45
At most 3 $(r \le 3)$	24.53	30.45
At most 4 $(r \le 4)$	8.14	16.26

Notes: ** denotes rejection of the hypothesis at 1 percent significance level. All series are log-transformed.

Table 12.3
Granger Causality Tests Based on VECM

Dependent Variables	Caused by				Error-Correction Terms			
	ΔCPI	ΔER	ΔIPI	ΔM3	ΔTB3	ECT_1	ECT_2	ECT_3
	F-statistics				*t*-test			
ΔCPI	—	2.33*	2.32*	2.29*	2.33*	-0.06	-1.58	-1.87
ΔER	0.25	—	0.80	— 16.80***	0.37	0.12	0.05	-0.22
ΔIPI	6.58***	2.16	—	33.38***	3.11**	— 4.68***	-2.71**	-0.65
ΔM3	5.22***	11.43***	13.95***	—	10.13***	0.53	-2.00*	— 4.39***
ΔTB3	0.14	4.84***	0.30	9.82***	—	2.31**	3.24**	2.56**

Notes: The asterisks indicate the following levels of significance: * = 10 percent, ** = 5 percent, and *** = 1 percent. Lags interval for all series is 6. All series are log-transformed.

supply, and interest rate could only affect inflation marginally (10 percent significant level) in the short-run. Feedbacks occur among inflation with money supply and inflation with output.

In the exchange rate equation, only money supply influences exchange rates where it is significant at 1 percent level. The ECTs are not significant in both inflation and exchange rate equations suggesting that these two variables are weakly exogenous. All the variables, except exchange rate, could explain the variation in national output at least at 5 percent significant level while in the money supply equation, all the explanatory variables are significant at the 1 percent level; but the effects are bidirectional among money, inflation, and output. In the case of interest rate equation, only the exchange rate and money supply cause the variation in the interest rate where it is significant at the 1 percent level and feedbacks occur between interest rate and money supply. At least two ECTs in these three equations are significant at the 5 percent level suggesting that these dependent variables adjust to the equilibrium level in the long-run.

CONCLUSION AND POLICY IMPLICATIONS

The main objective of this study is to investigate the interrelationship among Malaysian ringgit-U.S. dollar exchange rates, inflation, domestic output, money supply, and interest rates in Malaysia. The findings suggest that there exist a long-run relationship among them. The Granger causality test indicates that exchange rates have significant impacts on domestic price levels and the effect is unidirectional running from exchange rates to inflation. There exist feedbacks among inflation and money supply and output, inflation with output, and money supply with interest rate.

The unidirectional effect running from exchange rate to inflation suggests that depreciation of ringgit is inflationary. The study shows that inflation is caused by changes in exchange rates, money supply, interest rate, and domestic output (supply shocks) suggesting that in Malaysia, supply shocks such as oil price increases, excessive growth in money supply, and exchange rate depreciation are inflationary.

The significant relationship between money supply and output indicates that expansionary money supply lowers real interest rates, encouraging domestic investment and consumer spending which generate economic activities, employment opportunities and income. The Granger causality from output to price level suggests that supply constraints are inflationary, as advocated by the supply-side economics, especially in the light of the late 1980s and 1990s as Malaysia was virtually operating at full employment during the period. The government had partially resolved the problems of supply bottlenecks through investment in infrastructures and the imports of foreign inputs, including labor from neighboring countries. The study also finds that a rise in interest rates results in inflation as it will increase the cost of borrowing and thus the costs of production. All these factors support the view that we should employ monetary and fiscal policy and incomes policy to contain inflationary pressure.

REFERENCES

Athukorala, P. (1998). "Swimming against the Tide: Crisis Management in Malaysia," *ASEAN Economic Bulletin*, no. 15, pp. 281–289.

Bank Negara Malaysia, Quarterly Bulletin, various issues, 1992–2000.

Deme, M., and B. Fayassa. (1995). "Inflation, Money, Interest Rate, Exchange Rate and Causality: The Case of Egypt, Morocco, and Tunisia," *Applied Economics*, 27, no. 12, pp. 1219–1224.

Deravi, K., P. Gregorowicz, and C. E. Hegji. (1995). "Exchange Rates and the Inflation Rate," *Quarterly Journal of Business and Economics*, 34, no. 1, pp. 42–54.

Engle, R. F., and C. W. J. Granger. (1987). "Cointegration and Error Correction: Representation, Estimation, and Testing," *Econometrica*, 55, pp. 251–276.

International Monetary Fund, International Monetary Fund's *International Financial Statistics Year Book*, various issues, 1994–2000.

Johansen, S. (1988). "Statistical Analysis of Cointegration Vectors," *Journal of Economic Dynamics and Control*, 12, pp. 231–254.

———. (1991). "Estimation and Hypothesis Testing of Cointegration Vectors in Gaussian Vector Autoregressive Models," *Econometrica*, 38, no. 3.

Johansen, S., and K. Juselius. (1990). "Maximum Likelihood Estimation and Inference on Cointegration, with Applications to the Demand for Money," *Oxford Bulletin of Economics and Statistics*, 52, no. 2, pp. 169–210.

Kim, Ki-Ho. (1998). "US Inflation and the Dollar Exchange Rate: A Vector Error Correction Model," *Applied Economics*, 30, no. 5, pp. 613–619.

Kyereme, S. S. (1991). "Exchange Rate, Price, and Output Inter-Relationship in Ghana: Evidence from Vector Autoregressions," *Applied Economics*, 23, no. 12, pp. 1801–1810.

Mackinnon, J. (1991). "Critical Values for Cointegration Tests." In R. Engle and C. Granger (Eds.), *Readings in Cointegration* (pp. 267–276). Oxford, England: Oxford University Press.

Nelson, C. R., and C. I. Plosser. (1982). "Trends and Random Walks in Macroeconomic Time Series, Some Evidence and Implications," *Journal of Monetary Economics*, 10, pp. 139–162.

Papell, D. H. (1994). "Exchange Rate and Prices: An Empirical Analysis," *International Economic Review*, 35, no. 2, pp. 397–410.

Rittenberg, L. (1993). "Exchange Rate Policy and Price Level Changes: Causality Tests for Turkey in the Post-Liberalisation Period," *The Journal of Development Studies*, 29, no. 2, pp. 245–259.

Tan, H. B., and A. Z. Baharumshah. (1999). "Dynamic Causal Chain of Money, Output, Interest Rate and Prices in Malaysia: Evidence Based on Vector Error-Correction Modelling Analysis," *International Economic Journal*, 13, no. 1, pp. 1–18.

Yusoff, M. (1985). "Inflation and Controls: Malaysian Experience in 1970's," *Journal Ekonomi Malaysia*, 11, pp. 35–54.

CHAPTER 13

Impact of Pegging on Malaysian Ringgit after the Onset of the Asian Financial Crisis in July 1997

Che Ani Mad, Nik Kamariah bt. Nik Mat,
Nasruddin Zainudin, Nor Hayati bt. Ahmad, and
Engku Ngah Sayudin Engku Chik

INTRODUCTION

The International Monetary Fund (IMF) (1999) claimed that the fixing of the Malaysian ringgit (hereafter called the ringgit) to the United States dollar (USD), at RM3.80 per USD since September 1998, has prevented the ringgit from correcting itself to its true market value. IMF and Malaysian Institute of Economic Research (MIER) estimated that the ringgit remained undervalued by about 16 percent to 18 percent in 1999. On the other hand, market participants, that is, businessmen and investors largely perceived that the ringgit remained "undervalued" by a larger margin. They contended that the undervalued ringgit was instrumental in fostering Malaysia's export growth since it provided a competitive price advantage to Malaysia's exports against similar products and services of other Association of South East Asian Nations (ASEAN) economies (IMF, 1999).[1]

In contrast, Abidin and Mahmood (2000) argued that the recent surge in Malaysia's export was basically due to a natural phenomenon. As the domestic economy contracted during the crisis (Asian financial crisis [AFC]), export income became the main Malaysian source of economic growth. They rationally argued that as the weak domestic demand stalled most investments, Malaysian producers have no other alternatives but to export their commodities overseas. The export proceeds (regardless of the level of exchange rate) were then channeled into the domestic economy to provide liquidity and to sustain domestic consumption. The strong export expansion in 1999 was expected to absorb most of the excess export inventories and ultimately new investments would be made to meet the growing (domestic and overseas) demand since the economy was recovering.

They further argued that when the international capital began to flow into the region in the third quarter of 1998, some of the East Asian currencies such as South Korea, Thailand, and the Philippines (except Indonesia) appreciated against the USD. This was also a natural economic phenomenon because these countries did not exercise any significant control over the in- and outflow of funds, Malaysia meanwhile pegged its currency against USD, besides imposing selective capital controls in order to keep its currency stable, at least against USD. A stable ringgit reduces uncertainty, improves investors' confidence, promotes investments, and fosters economic growth.

In addition, many researchers began to argue that Malaysia's export and economic growth was also basically due to its ability to weather the crisis using its own "homegrown remedy." For instance, Eam, So, and Mithani (2000), using Impulse Response Function Analysis, empirically argued that Malaysia's growing export growth was due to the expected economic recovery by the year 2000, provided no external shock emerges. Mahbob and Govindan (2000) and Salleh and Radzi (2000) expressed a similar argument.

Against this backdrop, this study attempts to examine two major issues: the stability of the ringgit and the relationship between the real effective exchange rate (REER) of ringgit and Malaysia's export performance, especially after the Asian financial crisis of July 1997.

LITERATURE REVIEW

Evolution of Malaysia's Exchange Rate: An Overview (1980–1997)

Like many other ASEAN countries, Malaysia has experienced a consistent upward and downward market exchange rate pressure over the 1980–1997 period. The exchange rate of the ringgit fluctuated according to financial and economic environments. Historical data revealed that Malaysia's export and exchange rate of the ringgit normally had a negative relationship.[2] When the exchange rate of the ringgit increased, Malaysia's export performance declined. On the other hand, when the exchange rate of the ringgit declined, Malaysia had favorable export and economic performances, for instance, during 1980 to the end of 1983.

The expansion in the industrial sector during 1980 to 1983 brought a boom in the construction sector and further contributed to an expansion in the nontradable sectors. The expansion in the nontradable sectors subsequently caused domestic price to fluctuate (IMF, 1999) and led to eventual appreciation of the ringgit. This caused Malaysia's export commodities to be more expansive in the international market. Malaysia's terms of trade (TOT) began to deteriorate in early 1984. The deterioration that was initially expected to be temporary turned out to be permanent. Thus, the Malaysian authority decided to allow the ringgit to steadily depreciate in 1984. The ringgit exchange rate decreased in 1985, in terms of nominal and REER. It declined further, especially after the Plaza Accord when the U.S. dollar was allowed to depreciate. The ringgit proportionately depreciated because it had been kept fairly stable against the U.S. dollar and Singapore dollar. The depreciation of the ringgit was further exacerbated by the recession that hit Malaysia in 1985 to the first half of 1986. The recession caused Malaysia's terms of trade (export over import) and the Malaysian ringgit to deteriorate further in tandem with the economic performance.

Thus, owing to this relationship "export-lead-industrialization policy" was adopted to replace the old less effective "import- substitution policy" during the mid-1980s. Trade and exchange rate policies were gradually liberalized to support the new export-lead-industrialization policy. The policy reduces the international market prices of Malaysian commodities and significantly promotes Malaysia's export growth. As a result, Malaysia's export growth subsequently expanded the industrial sectors, particularly the manufacturing sector which subsequently was responsible for Malaysia economic growth (IMF, 1999).

Malaysia experienced a surge in capital inflows in terms of Foreign Direct Investment (FDI) and portfolio funds during the second half of the 1980s (1986) to the first half of the 1990s. This was due to its outward orientation policy, economic openness, infrastructure developments, the gradual elimination of export-import barriers and commitment under the Asian Free Trade Association (AFTA) and World Trade Organization (WTO).[3] The outward orientation policy led Malaysia to experience a consistent growth in gross domestic product (GDP) and export with an average growth rate of around 7.8 percent in GDP (Salleh and Radzi, 2000) and 17.2 percent in export. As a result, Malaysia's share in world merchandise exports rose from 0.75 percent in 1990 to over 2.0 percent in 1997.

The increasing capital inflows, on the other hand, put pressure on the ringgit to appreciate and this led to a huge buildup in Malaysia's foreign reserves. The ringgit gradually strengthened in REER terms by about 15 percent between the second half of the 1980s to July 1997 (IMF, 1999). However, the appreciation of the ringgit was quickly eliminated owing to a fast declining exchange rate since the onset of the AFC in July 1997.[4] The ringgit was undervalued by more than 47 percent against the U.S. dollar during the AFC period (IMF, 1999) (see Figures 13.1 and 13.2). It remained undervalued by about 23 percent at the end of the study period (December 1999).

Recent Development of the Malaysian Ringgit Exchange Rate

The average intratrade between ASEAN countries had decreased from an average of 47 percent in 1996 to an average of 23.2 percent in 1999. However, since the onset of AFC, Malaysia's contribution in terms of exports to ASEAN countries had also declined to 26 percent in 1999, while its imports had increased from 20.4 percent in 1997 to 22.9 percent in 1999 (Abidin and Mahmood, 2000; IMF, 1999). Abidin and Mahmood (2000) further noted that the United States was becoming one of Malaysia's significant trading partners since the fixing of ringgit to USD at RM3.80 in September 1998. Eam, So, and Mithani (2000), and Abidin and Mahmood (2000) argued that the growth on Malaysia's export and its economy were mainly due to its natural phenomenon. Malaysian producers have to export their commodities overseas as the domestic demand and the demand from ASEAN countries stalled. Thus, the IMF claimed that Malaysia's exports and economic growth were at the expense of ASEAN economies could be easily disputed for two reasons. First, Malaysia imported more than it exported to those ASEAN countries that experienced almost similar economic difficulties as Malaysia. Secondly, Malaysia was one of the founding members of the ASEAN and being one that adopted an international economic policy "enrich your neighbor" was unlikely to pursue such an unfriendly international trade policy.

Figure 13.1
Real exchange rate of Asian currencies (July 1997 = 100).

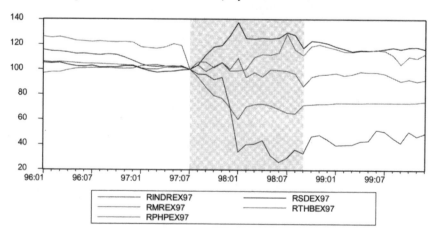

It was obvious that there were differences between Malaysia and the rest of the ASEAN countries in terms of the approaches taken to weather the AFC crisis. It was the only badly hit country that refused to adhere to IMF prescriptions on how to handle and to curb the crisis since Malaysia was not subjected to the regulatory framework imposed by the IMF "rescued policy." Although, Malaysia initially did attempt to use IMF prescriptions, it subsequently found that those prescriptions merely improved the economic distortions (Mahbob and Govindan, 2000) rather than addressing the real issues of the crises (Yoon and McGee, 2000). Owing to these factors, Malaysia formulated the National Economic Action Council (NEAC) to develop a short-term "homegrown" measure. Thus, on September 2, 1998, Malaysia pegged its exchange rate to USD and imposed selective capital controls, as the essence of the remedy, to tackle the crisis. The action was praised to be a workable remedy by businessmen, investors, and academicians alike (Salleh and Radzi, 2000) as well as by IMF itself.[5]

Against this backdrop, this study is organized as follows. The section entitled "Data" discusses data collection and interpolation. The section "Statistical Approach" examines the methodology and the approaches of the study. Finally "Conclusion" presents the findings, conclusion, and direction of future related studies.

Data

Published monthly data from January 1996 to December 1999 (48 timeseries data) was used in this study. The data was extracted from IMF

Figure 13.2
Real exchange rate of Malaysian ringgit to U.S. dollar, UK pound, and Singapore dollar (January 1996 to December 1999).

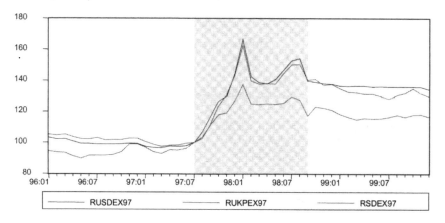

monthly bulletins and the Central Bank of Malaysia (CBM) quarterly and monthly bulletins. Data such as the amount of fiscal deficit and the population growth which were available only on quarterly basis were interpolated (using Lotus programs) into monthly series. This is executed to fulfill the statistical time series requirement that no data gap should exist between the series.

The input data was first verified manually against the sources to minimize input errors. The data was then converted into graphs, histograms, and simple statistics: mean, minimum, and maximum values to spot for possible input errors. The graphs and data series were then compared against earlier researchers' graphs and data series, for example, Tzanninis (1999a) whenever available before they were properly employed in the analysis.

Statistical Approach

Using Tzanninis (1999a) and IMF (1999) as the related studies and Figure 13.3 as the guide, this study:

1. divides the study period into three subperiods:

    January 1961–July 1997: pre-AFC period;

    July 1997–September 1998: AFC period;

    September 1998–December 1999: Pegging to USD period.

    Figure 13.3 clearly suggests that there was a structural change in between the study period: July 1997–September 1998. The existence of structural change served as the primary reason for the data series to be divided into the above three sub-periods. According to Enders (1995, pp. 243–250), the structural change must be accounted for, otherwise, the statistical results may be considered spurious or provide no economic value.

2. employs both descriptive and quantitative analyses to strengthen the arguments and the findings of this study.

Descriptive Analysis

Stability of Malaysian Ringgit

According to Valentine and Mennis (1980), there are various statistical measures that can be used to test stability or dispersion of data series. Among the statistical measures include range, variance, standard deviation, coefficient variation, and mean absolute deviation. Brigham (1995), like many other finance researchers, employed standard deviation and coefficient variation to measure risk and the stability of the variables. This study similarly uses standard deviation and coefficient variation to measure the stability of the ringgit over the study period and the three subperiods. The results are shown in Table 13.1.

Figure 13.3
The movement of real exchange rate of the Malaysian ringgit (January 1996 to December 1999).

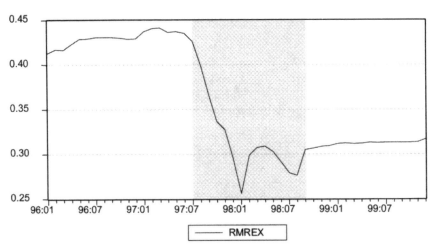

As expected, the impact of pegging and selective capital controls are found to be effective in stabilizing the Malaysian ringgit against USD. The standard deviations: σ, and coefficient variation (CV), as shown in Table 13.1 suggest that the volatility of the Malaysian ringgit in terms of REER after the pegging has been reduced by approximately half as compared to the pre-AFC period ($\sigma = 0.003/0.008 = 0.375$; $CV = 0.009/0.018 = 0.500$). Obviously, the ringgit was significantly more stable after the pegging to USD compared to the period during the crisis, July 1997 to September 1998 ($\sigma = 0.003/0.062 = 0.048$; $CV = 0.009/0.173 = 0.052$).[6]

The volatility of the ringgit, in terms of REER, after the pegging has also been significantly reduced against other ASEAN currencies (see Appendix 13.1). Thus, the statistical results clearly show that the pegging of ringgit to USD has significantly caused the ringgit to be more stable after the crisis period. The stable ringgit reduces exchange rate uncertainty, encourages businessmen and investors to invest, improves business confidence, promotes new investments, and subsequently stimulates export and economic growth in Malaysia. At this junction, this article will proceed to test the key economic determinants of REER before and after the AFC using quantitative analyses.

Quantitative Analyses

The Determinants of REER

Tzanninis (IMF, 1999) used 1979 to 1998 annual data such as EXIM, TOT, CAP, and BLS (see Appendix 13.2 for additional details). He employed

Table 13.1
The Stability of Real Malaysia Ringgit Exchange Rate to U.S. Dollar

	Study period	Prior to the AFC	During the AFC but before pegging and SCC [1]	After pegging and SCC to Dec. 1999
	1996:1–1999:12	1996:1–1997:7	1997:7–1998:9	1998:9–1999:12
	48 obs.	19 obs.	15 obs.	16 obs.
Mean	0.358	0.429	0.318	0.311
σ	0.062	0.008	0.046	0.003
CV	0.173	0.018	0.146	0.009
Changes in gap between the period				
σ	-	0.129	0.742	0.048
CV	-	0.104	0.844	0.052

1. Pegging refers to fixing exchange rate at RM3.80 per U.S. dollar on September 2, 1998 and SCC means selective capital control.

Standard deviation is calculated using E-View Statistical Package: $\sigma = \sqrt{\Sigma (x - x)_i^2 / N}$.

Coefficient variation (CV) is manually calculated. CV = σ/k; where k is the arithmetic average of the observations ≡ mean.

Changes in gap between the period are calculated by dividing the observed σ and CV of the sub-period by the study period, that is, σ for 1996: 1–1997: 7/σ over the studying period (0.008/0.062 = 0.129)

Augmented Dickey-Fuller statistics to test for unit root and subsequently conducted cointegration tests. His results suggests that:

1. Both the dependent and independent variables are stationary in the first difference, hence co-integration analysis among the level variable is therefore required,

2. the depreciation of the ringgit since the onset of the AFC has resulted in a gain in Malaysia's competitiveness,

3. the ringgit was undervalued by about 16 percent to 19 percent in 1998,

4. historically, misalignments of the ringgit has tended to correct by itself within two to three years.

This study offers no dispute. In fact, it provides evidence to support Tzanninis's findings. However, it should be noted that, although this study attempted to replicate the analysis using unit-root and cointegration tests similar to Tzanninis (IMF, 1999), it was unable to pursue the tests.[7] According to Enders (1995), the statistical results of the monthly time series would provide no economic value due to a structural change in

Malaysia's real effective exchange rate (REER) as shown in Figure 13.3 earlier. The unit-root and cointegration statistical results obtained are not shown here. In order to overcome this limitation, Box-Jenkins autoregressive moving average (ARMA) statistical procedures can be employed as one of the alternatives (Enders 1995, pp. 95–97). Nevertheless, Box-Jenkins ARMA statistical procedures may also provide no economic value if the data for the study period is analyzed in isolation since the statistical results may also provide no explanation property as shown in Table 13.2.

Although the regression result in Table 13.2 using Tzanninis (IMF, 1999) model shows a very high goodness-of-fit over the study period, the results, however, provide no economic value. Figure 13.4 suggests clearly that owing to the structural change, the residual of the regression does fluctuate beyond the acceptable bands, that is, during the crisis period: July 1997–September 1998.

The study proceeds to test the key economic determinants of REER using the Tzanninis (IMF, 1999) model below. The theoretical details of the variables are briefly described in Appendix 13.2.

Table 13.2
Dependent Variable: RMREX

Method: Least Squares
Date: 06/19/00   Time: 15:50
Sample(adjusted): 1996:03 1999:12
Included observations: 46 after adjusting endpoints
Convergence achieved after 16 iterations
Backcast: 1996:02

Variable	Coefficient	Std. Error	t-Statistic	Prob.
C	0.295089	0.155046	1.903236	0.064605
EXIM	-0.003655	0.018090	-0.202047	0.840958
TOT	-0.014912	0.022235	-0.670674	0.506485
FGOEGDP	-0.061575	0.104369	-0.589970	0.558703
BLS	-0.000460	0.000429	-1.073537	0.289801
M31B	0.013381	0.008380	1.596739	0.118608
AR(1)	0.960343	0.038496	24.94665	3.65E-25
MA(1)	0.357796	0.159963	2.236748	0.031249

R-squared	0.962506	Mean dependent var		0.355610
Adjusted R-squared	0.955599	S.D. dependent var		0.061942
S.E. of regression	0.013052	Akaike info criterion		-5.682944
Sum squared resid	0.006474	Schwarz criterion		-5.364920
Log likelihood	138.7077	F-statistic		139.3547
Durbin-Watson stat	1.911819	Prob(F-statistic)		0.000000

Inverted AR Roots	0.96	
Inverted MA Roots	-0.36	

Figure 13.4
Residual, actual, and fitted IMF model of real exchange rate of the Malaysia ringgit (January 1996 to December 1999).

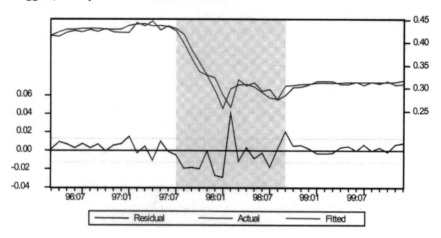

$$RMREX_t = \alpha + \beta_1 EXIM_t + \beta_2 TOT_t + \beta_3 FGOEGDP_t$$
$$+ \beta_4 BLS_t + \beta_5 M31B_t + \epsilon_t$$

Table 13.3 presents the selected statistical results using Box-Jenkins ARMA statistical procedures employing maximum likelihood and stepwise statistical processes. The results suggest that the REER's determinants are dynamic: they change over time, that is, over the various subperiods, due to the differences in the economic environments. The statistical results in Table 13.3 also suggest that:

1. The higher exchange rate of the ringgit leads to lower export (and subsequently decreases import because Malaysia's export commodities generally have a high percentage of import content). The inverse relationship holds true. Therefore, the Real Malaysian Ringgit Exchange Rate (RMREX) is found to have a negative relationship with the level of Malaysia's export and import, although the magnitude of the impact is small, as shown by the coefficient of $\beta_1 EXIM_t$.

   The deterioration of export (and import) prior and during the crisis was reflected by the overvaluation of the ringgit and hence provided a negative impact on the level of exchange rate of the ringgit. The exchange rate of the ringgit subsequently had to decline toward its market level to bring down the price of Malaysian commodities to competitive levels. During early 1998 the ringgit exchange rate declined to more than RM4.00 per USD. When it bounced back to RM3.80 per USD, Malaysia pegged the ringgit to USD in September 1998. At the same time, the exchange rate of other ASEAN currencies (except Indonesia), continued to appreciate. The pegging did not only help reducing entrepreneurs', businessmen's, and traders' uncertainty but also led the price of Malaysian commodities to remain relatively cheaper. Thus, the fixing of the ringgit to USD successfully spurred Malaysia's export growth and is partly

Table 13.3

$$RMREX_t = \alpha + \beta_1 EXIM_t + \beta_2 TOT_t + \beta_3 FGOEGDP_t + \beta_4 BLS_t + \beta_5 M31B_t + \epsilon_t$$

Variables Coeficient (1)	Study period (2)	Prior to the AFC (3)	During the AFC before pegging and SCC (4)	After the pegging and SCC to Dec. 1999 (5)
α	0.217** (2.122)	0.460*** (31.104)	1.078*** (16.722)	0.343*** (88.782)
β_1			-0.344*** (-9.103)	-0.006** (-2.931)
β_2			-0.176** (-2.407)	
β_3			-0.473*** (-4.618)	
β_4	-0.001* (1.815)	0.001* (1.901)		-0.001** (-2.385)
β_5	0.013 (1.633)	-0.005*** (-2.068)	0.040*** (3.491)	-0.003*** (-7.283)
AR(1)	0.960*** (26.056)	0.586*** (3.984)		0.282 (1.759)
MA(1)	0.403*** (2.750)	0.928*** (32.135)	-1.910** (-2.483)	-0.943*** (-12.398)
Adj. R^2	0.958	0.872	0.972	0.971
Se (ϵ_t)	0.007	0.001	0.001	0.001
D.W.	1.919	1.434	2.247	1.921
F Value	257.23	28.14	98.29	100.57

1. RMREX, EXIM, TOT, FGOEGDP, BLS, and M31B refer to the real Malaysian ringgit exchange rate to the U.S. dollar, total exports and imports over gross domestic product, total exports over total imports, federal government official expenditure over gross domestic product, the Balassa-Samuelson effect (per capita real growth in manufacturing over per capita real growth in services), and the difference between M3 (broad money supply), and M1 (based money supply) in billion Malaysian ringgits to reflect capital inflow, respectively.

2. The figure in parentheses are t statistics. ***, **, and * refer to 1 percent, 5 percent, and 10 percent level of significance, respectively.

3. AR and MA refer to autoregression or Cochran-Orcutt model and Moving Average (Markov model), respectively. The Multivariate Time Series Regression technique used in this study employs Advanced Box-Jenkins statistical technique, which is a combination of AR and MA models utilizing Maximum Likelihood and Stepwise procedures to select the best statistical results.

4. Adj. R^2, D.W., Se (ϵ_t), and F refer to adjusted R squared, Durbin-Watson statistics, standard error of regression, and F value, respectively.

5. The selection of the statistical results was based on:
   i. Durbin-Watson statistics, which are close to 2.0. The data can be assumed to be normally distributed.
   ii. The highest adjusted R squared and F value as well as the lowest standard error of regression where the results are expected to provide the best goodness-of-fit of the linear regression.

also responsible in steering Malaysian economy toward a speedier recovery from the crisis.

2. The terms of trade (TOT) and Federal Governments Official Expenditure over Gross Domestic Products (FGOEGDP) provided a significant impact during the crisis than during the stable economic environment. Both variables provide negative impact to the level of exchange rate of the ringgit as suggested by negative coefficients of $\beta_2 \, TOT_t$ and $\beta_3 \, FGOEGDP_t$, respectively. The results are justifiable at least for two reasons:

    i. during the crisis, Malaysia obviously experienced deterioration in TOT. The price of export commodities temporarily declined while the price of import commodities temporarily increased as the exchange rate of the ringgit declined.

    ii. the more the government spent, the higher the supply of fund in the economy as compared to the commodities available, hence the price of the commodities became more expensive while the value of money became cheaper as the market was willing to spend more on the limited supply of the available commodities. This led to a negative relationship between the FGOEGDP and the exchange rate of the ringgit.

3. The relationship between exchange rate of the ringgit and productivity may be positive or negative. It is positive if the growth in productivity increases. Productivity leads to cheaper production costs, and the commodities can be exported at competitive prices in the international market. Thus, the demand for the ringgit will be higher to provide a positive impact on its exchange rate. The opposite holds true. The negative relationship between Balassa-Samuelson effect (BLS) and RMREX after the pegging and over the study period, supports the contention suggested by the Abidin and Mahmood (2000) and Mahbob and Govindan (2000) analyses that the level of productivity in Malaysia has declined since early 1990s. Although the magnitude of the impact of BLS exhibited in Table 13.3 is small, its implication on the long-term impact of Malaysian export and economic growth performances warrant a serious concern.[8]

4. Theoretically, the amount of the available fund in the economy exerts a downward pressure on the commodity prices and hence the real exchange rate. However, during the crisis the amount of the available fund provides a positive impact on the real exchange rate. This may possibly be due to the "liquidity crisis and bank run." In other words, owing to the market uncertainty, the market expects that as the amount of the available fund declines in an economy owing to the liquidity crisis and bank run, the market confidence on the exchange rates of the ringgit also decline. However, the relationship between the real exchange rate of the ringgit became negative when there was no more liquidity crisis and bank run. The market confidence that had been built under the National Economic Recovery Plan (NERP) was restored to normal when the available fund in the economy exerted a downward pressure on the real exchange rate as shown by coefficient β_5 in Table 13.4.

Table 13.4 provides additional statistical evidence confirming the earlier literature that export and real exchange rate are negative related. In the case of Malaysia, the study shows that the lower exchange rate of the

Table 13.4

$$MALEXPT_t = \alpha + \beta_1 RMREX_t + \beta_2 MALIMPT_t + \epsilon_t$$

Variables Coeficient	Study period	Prior to the AFC	During the AFC before pegging and SCC	After the pegging and SCC to Dec. 1999
(1)	(2)	(3)	(4)	(5)
α	0189.743	19.482***	36.292***	80.945**
	(0.030)	(5.956)	(4.324)	(2.268)
β_1	-18.422**	-16.242**	-38.256**	-243.432*
	(-2.410)	(-2.108)	(-2.236)	(-2.057)
β_2	0.615***	0.248***	0.083	1.026***
	(5.001)	(3.345)	(0.315)	(7.696)
AR(1)	0.995***	-0.378**	0.736*	
	(32.821)	(-2.194)	(2.175)	
MA(1)	-0.701***	-0.977***	-1.925***	0.990***
	(-5.117)	(38.573)	(-3.102)	(58529-93)
Adj. R^2	0.941	0.858	0.918	0.908
Se (ϵ_t)	1.106	0.526	0.602	0.676
D.W.	**2.052**	**2.349**	1.992	2.480
F Value	183.78	26.70	40.30	50.10

Notes: See Table 13.3.

Sources of data: See Table 13.3.

ringgit has consistently been responsible for a higher export growth of Malaysian commodities over the study and subperiods, as evidenced by the coefficient of β_1 in Table 13.4.

The results presented in Table 13.4 further support the contention of the earlier literature that Malaysian export commodities contain a large proportion of import content, as signified by β_2. It is also interesting to note that the large magnitude of imports after the pegging of the ringgit suggests that the industries began to replenish their inventories to meet the increasing demand for exports. This further signifies a growing investors' confidence in the economic recovery. This confidence has been highlighted by Mahbob and Govindran (2000), Abidin and Mahmood (2000), and Eam, So, and Mithani (2000) through their descriptive and empirical analyses of the recovery of the Malaysian economy.

CONCLUSION

The pegging of the ringgit and selective credit controls on September 2, 1998 were not intended to provide a competitive advantage for Malaysia's export and economic growth. It was initially intended to insulate Malaysian economy from future speculative attack on the ringgit that might further distort the economy (Mahbob & Govindan, 2000). The undervaluation of the ringgit compared to other ASEAN currencies that did not undergo pegging made Malaysian commodity prices more competitive and the ringgit more stable, promoted investors' confidence, increased investment as a result, and improved current account balance. All of these resulted in the speedy economic recovery of Malaysia.

Malaysia, which practices an open-economic policy and intends to comply with its AFTA and WTO commitments, cannot rely on the undervalued ringgit to promote its exports and economic growth over a long period. Nor can it sustain the undervalued ringgit since the market will adjust the value of the ringgit accordingly in the long run. Thus, it needs to launch a policy of promoting productivity-enhancing measures to maintain it's long-run competitiveness as seriously proposed by Abidin and Mahmood (2000), Mahbob and Govindan (2000), and Salleh and Radzi (2000). Measures including investment and training in new technology, incentives to promote a larger usage of domestic components in its exports, innovations in product design, fostering additional export incentives, and ensuring credit availability are among other measures that must be seriously and immediately considered by the relevant authorities. Thus, additional studies of the impact of these measures will be essential as significant inputs to foster Malaysian long-term economic development.

NOTES

We wish to record our thanks to Professor Dr. Sudin Haron, the Dean of School of Finance and Banking, Universiti Utara Malaysia (UUM) for his consistent encouragement, support, and ideas for the completion of this chapter. A similar appreciation goes to Professor Mohammad Alias, from the School of Economics, UUM. We are also glad to record our appreciation to our research members, Puan Norafifah Ahmad and En. Khairul Anuar Adnan, for their support and assistance.

1. Some respectable businessmen in the street even argued that the ringgit remained undervalued by about 30 percent. The imposition of selective capital control (SCC) and pegging of the ringgit exchange rate to the U.S. dollar on September 2, 1998, has led the ringgit to remain broadly unchanged, while other ASEAN currencies continued to appreciate and further strengthened (owing to the gradual depreciation of the U.S. dollar). Thus, Malaysian commodity prices were cheaper than the rest of the ASEAN countries.

2. See Tzanninis (1999b) for detailed additional discussion.

3. See CBM (1999) for detailed additional discussion.

4. This was due to liquidity crisis and bank run as suggested by the recent literature.

5. Nominal One Malaysia Ringgit Exchange Rate to Nominal U.S. Dollar

	Study Period	Prior to the AFC	During the AFC Pegging and SCC**	After Pegging And SCC to Dec. 1999
	1996:1–1999:12	1996:1–1997:7	1997:7–1998:9	1998:9–1999:12
	48 obs.	19 obs.	15 obs.	16 obs.
Mean	0.320	0.398	0.281	0.263
σ	0.067	0.004	0.047	0.000
CV	0.210	0.010	0.166	0.001

6. It must be noted that owing to the annual data employed by Tzanninis (IMF, 1999), it is highly possible that this must have been overlooked and unintentionally ignored by Tzanninis. Nevertheless, the implications to the results are not serious since a long annual data time series was employed.

7. See Tzanninis (1999a), Abidin and Mahmood (2000), and Mahbob and Govindan (2000) for additional detailed discussions.

REFERENCES

Abidin, M. A., and A. Mahmood. (2000). "Export Competitiveness of Malaysian Manufacturing: An Assessment." Paper presented at the National Seminar Strengthening the Macroeconomic Fundamentals of the Malaysian Economy, Kuala Lumpur, June 5–6.

Brigham, E. (1995). *Fundamentals of Financial Management,* 7th ed. New York: The Dryden Press.

Eam, L. H., L. T. So, and D. M. Mithani. (2000). "The Shock Effect of Terms of Trade Fluctuations on Economic Growth: The Malaysian Case." Paper presented at the National Seminar Strengthening the Macroeconomic Fundamentals of the Malaysian Economy, Kuala Lumpur, June 5–6.

Enders, W. (1995). *Applied Econometric Time Series.* New York: John Wiley and Sons.

International Monetary Fund (IMF). (1999). Staff Country Report, no. 99186. Washington, D.C.

Khoon, G. S., and D. M. Mithani. (2000). "The Determinants of Real Exchange Rates: The Malaysian Experience: 1973–1997." Paper presented at the National Seminar on Strengthening the Macroeconomic Fundamentals of the Malaysian Economy, Kuala Lumpur, June 5–6.

Mahbob, S., and K. Govindan. (2000). "Macroeconomic Fundamentals of the Malaysian Economy: Before and After the Crisis." Paper presented at the National Seminar on Strengthening the Macroeconomics Fundamentals of the Malaysian Economy, Kuala Lumpur, June 5–6.

Meera, A. K., and H. A. Aziz. (November 2000). "The Malaysian Financial Crisis of 1997: Is the Monetary Sector the Culprit?" Working paper. Department of Business Administration, International Islamic University, Malaysia.

Salleh, K., and N. A. Radzi. (2000). "The Resilience of the Economy: Preparing for the Next Crisis." Paper presented at the National Seminar on Strengthening the Macroeconomics Fundamentals of the Malaysian Economy, Kuala Lumpur, June 5–6.

Tzanninis, D. (1999a). "Malaysian Exports and Competitiveness." In *Malaysia: Selected Issues, IMF Staff Country Report*, No. 99/86 (August), pp. 28–54. Washington, DC: International Monetary Fund.

———— .(1999b). *The Central Bank and the Financial System in Malaysia—A Decade of Change: 1989–1999*. Kuala Lumpur: Bank Negara Malaysia.

Valentine, J. L., and E. A. Mennis. (1980). *Quantitative Techniques for Financial Analysis*, rev. ed. Homewood, IL: Richard D. Irwin.

Yoon, Y., and R. W. McGee. (2000). "The Asian Financial Crisis: A Gratuitous Unnecessary Tragedy?" In *Managing Global Business in the Internet Age, The 5th International Conference in Global Business & Economic Development, New Jersey, Conference Proceeding*, Vol. 2 (pp. 925–932). Seton Hall University, South Orange, NJ.

APPENDIX 13.1

Stability of Malaysian Ringgit against Foreign Currencies: Real Foreign Exchange Rate of 100 Unit Foreign Currencies to One Malaysian Ringgit

		Study Period	Prior to the AFC	During the AFC Before Pegging and SCC[2]	After Pegging and SCC to Dec. 1999
		1996:1–1999:12	1996:1–1997:7	1997:7–1998:9	1998:9–1999:12
Selected ASEAN Countries		48 obs.	19 obs.	15 obs.	16 obs.
Indonesia	Mean	0.067	0.100	0.053	0.040
	σ	0.031	0.005	0.027	0.005
	CV	0.435	0.048	0.517	0.113[3]
Thailand	Mean	8.596	9.008	8.068	8.514
	σ	0.581	0.428	0.602	0.296
	CV	0.068	0.047	0.075	0.035
Philippines	Mean	8.547	8.879	8.511	8.120
	σ	0.425	0.184	0.454	0.283
	CV	0.050	0.021	0.053	0.035[3]
Singapore*[1]	Mean	1.824	1.644	1.959	1.904
	σ	0.169	0.039	0.160	0.040
	CV	0.093	0.024	0.082	0.021

1. RM per unit of foreign currencies.

2. SCC stands for Selected Capital Control executed on September 2, 1998.

3. An increase in the volatility of Indonesian rupiahs and Philippine pesos against MR may be due to the instability of those currencies, instead of MR. MR was found to be more stable after the pegging against other ASEAN currencies as well as selected developed countries' currencies: including United States dollar, United Kingdom pound and Japanese yen.

APPENDIX 13.2

**Stability of Malaysian Ringgit against Foreign Currencies: Real Foreign
Exchange Rate of One Unit Foreign Currencies to Malaysian Ringgit**

Selected Developed Economies (Major Trading Partners)					
United States	Mean	2.874	2.329	3.197	3.211
	σ	0.486	0.043	0.418	0.030
	CV	0.169	0.019	0.131	0.009
United Kingdom	Mean	4.664	3.703	5.268	5.244
	σ	0.857	0.110	0.699	0.147
	CV	0.184	0.030	0.133	0.028
Japan	Mean	2.422	2.073	2.464	2.775
	σ	0.349	0.145	0.223	0.176
	CV	0.144	0.070	0.091	0.063

1. RM per unit of foreign currencies.

2. SCC stands for Selected Capital Control executed on September 2, 1998.

3. An increase in the volatility of Indonesian rupiahs and Philippine pesos against MR may be due to the instability of those currencies, instead of MR. MR was found to be more stable after the pegging against other ASEAN currencies as well as selected developed countries' currencies: including United States dollar, United Kingdom pound and Japanese yen.

APPENDIX 13.3

DETERMINANTS OF MALAYSIA'S LONG-RUN EQUILIBRIUM REAL EFFECTIVE EXCHANGE RATE (REER)

An empirical model was developed to test the determinants of Malaysia's long-run Equilibrium Real Effective Exchange Rate (REER), based on the earlier reported model by Tzannis (IMF, 1999). The Tzanninis model is, however, built on some preexisting paradigms and the model has taken into account the available data and major factors affecting the REER.

CONCEPTUAL ISSUES

The Degree of Openness in Trade policy is proxied by the sum of exports and imports over GDP (EXIM). The relaxation of control is suggested to promote export competitiveness that eventually fosters both export and import. On the contrary, import control is suggested to lead to an overvalued exchange rate.

The External Economic Environment is proxied by terms of trade (TOT). TOT is the ratio of Malaysia's total export value over total import value. An increase in the ratio implies a greater growth in export as compared to import. This leads to a positive impact on current account and thus an appreciation of the REER.

Real Productivity of the Domestic Economy is proxied by per capita real growth in manufacturing less per capita real growth in services. The higher productivity growth in the tradable than in the nontradable goods (services) sector, eventually leads to raise in wages and prices of service sector, and eventually leads to a real appreciation of the REER. The impact is known as the *Balassa-Samuelson* (BLS) effect.

Fiscal policy is defined as the ratio of government consumption to GDP. In our case government consumption is defined as Federal Government Official Expenditure over GDP (FGOEGDP). Higher government expenditure increases the supply of money and thus pushes up the price of nontraded goods, which eventually promotes to an appreciation of the REER. Some scholars have already noted that fiscal policy provided a significant influence on REER while Tzanninis (1999b) observed the opposite.

Capital inflows would exert an upward pressure on the REER. In our case, the relevant data for net total capital inflows (capital outflows less capital inflows are not available). Thus, the difference between M3 less M1 [broad money less base money in the domestic economy (M31B)] was used as the proxy.

CHAPTER 14

Optimum Currency Area: Euro as a Practical Paradigm?

Elinda Fishman Kiss

INTRODUCTION

Several economists have argued that "Euroland" (the 12 countries that have adopted the euro) is not an Optimum Currency Area (OCA). One reason for this argument is that Robert A. Mundell (1961) indicated that an essential ingredient of a "currency area is a high degree of factor mobility."[1] At present there is neither a high degree of factor mobility within Euroland nor factor immobility outside Euroland. However, Mundell (1998a) has advocated that "Monetary union will do much to integrate Europe's commodity, factor, and capital markets. It will increase Europe-wide competition and revolutionize financial markets."[2] Labor and capital will move more freely in the future due to the existence of the European Monetary Union (EMU) today. As Frankel and Rose emphasize, "Trade patterns and income correlations are endogenous. . . . (A country) could fail the OCA criterion for membership today, and yet, if it goes ahead and joins anyway, as the result of joining, pass the OCA criterion in the future."[3] Is "Euroland" today an OCA under the strict criteria originally set forth by Robert Mundell? No; however, if trade patterns and income correlations are endogenous, it will be more likely to satisfy the OCA criteria in the future.

This chapter reviews the criteria of OCA and evaluates the performance of "Euroland" in its first 18 months of existence. The euro has had some successes but still furnishes evidence of some disappointments to its critics. One major achievement is the expansion of the European commercial bond market. The European System of Central Banks (ESCB) succeeded, in its conduct of monetary policy, in fostering a strengthening of demand that will result in a faster growth of output. The introduction of EMU has resulted in reduced fiscal deficits, inflation, and unemployment. To its critics (primarily in the United States) the major disappointment has been the depreciation of the euro, but that price should be market determined and a decline is *not* a failure. Effective 2002 the euro will be the only currency in Euroland, and much of the European objections to the euro have faded.

In the next section, entitled "Optimum Currency Area," we look at the theoretical description of an OCA. In the section "Benefits and Costs of Optimum Currency Areas and Monetary Unions," we examine the benefits and costs of Optimum Currency Areas and Monetary Unions. A brief description of the process that led to the creation of the euro and EMU is found in the section entitled "A Brief History of the Euro and EMU." The convergence criteria for membership in EMU are listed in the section entitled "Convergence Criteria for Membership in EMU." The Central Banking System of the EMU and its conduct of monetary policy is detailed in the section entitled "European System of Central Banks." The depreciation of the euro vis-à-vis the dollar and yen is discussed in the section "Exchange Rate Movement January 1, 1999–December 31, 2001." Some of the successes of the euro and EMU are found in "Successes for the Euro." The chapter's conclusions are found in the final section, "Conclusions."

OPTIMUM CURRENCY AREA

Traditional literature suggests structural criteria, for example, factor mobility (Mundell, 1961), trade integration (McKinnon, 1963), and regional production patterns (Kenen, 1969) to assess if a region is an OCA. Other literature (Marston, 1984) emphasized the importance of flexible exchange rates between regions experiencing asymmetric shocks or differences in shock-absorbing mechanisms. More recent literature has focused on which countries should participate in EMU (Frankel and Rose, 1997; von Hagen and Neumann, 1994) or whether there should be an EMU (Feldstein, 2000; Mundell, 1968, 1998a, 1998b).

In 1961 Robert A. Mundell defined the OCA as "a domain within which exchange rates are fixed." He indicated that an essential ingredient of a "currency area is a high degree of factor mobility." Ronald McKinnon expounded on this theory in 1963 by discussing the influence of the openness of the economy, that is, the ratio of tradable to nontradable goods, on the problem of reconciling external and internal balance, emphasizing the need for internal price-level stability."

There has been academic opposition to the idea of monetary union, from both Keynesians and monetarists. The Keynesians feared the removal of devaluation as a weapon of policy. The monetarists' objections range from the threat that the euro might bring the dollar to its knees to the political possibility that it will create civil war in Europe! Art Laffer (2001) warned that weakness in the euro "is putting the entire fabric of Euroland in harm's way," in a June 7essay entitled "A Note from the Doctor, Europe's Mad Duisenberg Disease."

Economists who have looked at Europe, ask, in the manner of Mundell, whether it is an OCA. Usually they answer "No." Factors are not sufficiently mobile between countries: this factor mobility makes the exchange rate a useful price-adjuster, under certain circumstances.

Mundell, however, believes that Europe is, in practice if not in theory, an OCA. He is an enthusiast for Europe's single currency. Although it may not fit the strict interpretation of an OCA, Mundell made a case for the euro (using the name "europa" rather than "euro") in 1969. At that time the Hague Summit was setting up the Werner Committee to develop a plan for an economic and monetary union. Mundell believes that the world is an OCA, and has long argued for a return to the gold standard, as the next best thing to a single currency for the world.

How can these positions be reconciled? Mundell indicates that his point all along was as follows. A flexible exchange rate is only valuable if shocks are felt across entire currency areas. In fact shocks tend to hit regions that lie within such areas (as when cheap oil hurts Texas and helps New England states). Taken to an extreme, the logic of the OCA approach would state that the world requires a proliferation of currencies, so that every area subject to shocks has its own currency. But Mundell argues against this proliferation of exchange rates for each subregion. Consequently, Texas, however far the price of oil drops, will never demand its own currency; likewise Yorkshire, England, even though the decline of the coal industry may have called for a devaluation. Similarly, in Italy, the industrialized Genoa-Milan region and the southern Mezzogiorno region can be in different phases of the business cycle, but they had not called for two separate lira. Flexible exchange rates will not help solve regional unemployment problems.

BENEFITS AND COSTS OF OPTIMUM CURRENCY AREAS AND MONETARY UNIONS

Benefits are the reduction in transactions costs that previously resulted from currency exchanges. Costs of a monetary union are the loss of the ability to operate separate monetary and exchange rate policies. The policy dilemma is that a country cannot simultaneously have: free capital flows, fixed exchange rates, and independent monetary policy.

Benefits of Monetary Union

The most direct and immediate benefits are reduced transaction costs and the elimination of exchange-rate uncertainty. A third benefit is enhanced efficiency and competitiveness of the European economy. There was a popular saying in Europe that if one traveled through all 15 European Union (EU) countries, changing money in each country but not actually spending it, he or she would return home with only half the original amount. With countries using the same currency, transaction costs are reduced; the consensus estimation is 0.4 percent of Europe's gross domestic product (GDP).[4] The elimination of exchange rate uncertainty will result in saved hedging costs for companies that previously hedged exchange rate risk. Consumers will benefit, as increased price transparencies will promote Europe-wide competition, resulting in less inflation. Reduced transaction costs and elimination of currency risk will promote cross-border investment and trade. By furthering economic integration of Europe, the euro will promote corporate restructuring via mergers and acquisitions, encourage optimal business location decisions, and ultimately strengthen the international competitive position. Utilizing the euro and coordinating monetary policy with the European System of Central Banks creates the development of European capital markets with depth and liquidity comparable to those of the United States.

Costs of Monetary Union

The main cost of a monetary union is the loss of national monetary and exchange rate policy independence. Let us examine a hypothetical example. Suppose Finland, a nation dependent on paper and pulp industries, faces a sudden drop in world paper and pulp prices. This price drop could hurt the Finnish economy, causing unemployment while scarcely affecting other Euroland countries. Finland faces an "asymmetric shock." An asymmetric shock is more likely to affect a country whose economy is less diversified and more trade-dependent (high ratio of traded to nontraded goods). If Finland had maintained monetary independence, the economy could lower domestic interest rates to stimulate the weak economy as well as let its currency depreciate to increase foreigners' demand for Finnish products. Since Finland has joined the EMU, it no longer has these policy options available. Furthermore, since the rest of Euroland is not affected by the paper industry problem, the ECB probably will not use monetary policy to address asymmetric economic shocks that affect only a particular country or subregion; it will use the policy for Euroland-wide shocks.

Although Finland cannot use monetary policy to solve the asymmetric shock problem, if wage and price levels in Finland are flexible, then lower wage and price levels in Finland would have economic effects similar to those of a depreciation of the markka. In addition, if capital flows freely across Euroland and workers are willing to relocate to where jobs are available, then much of the asymmetric shock can be absorbed without monetary adjustments. If there is not free movement of labor and capital and flexible prices, then the asymmetric shock can cause a severe recession. Unemployed workers in Helsinki may not wish to move to Rome or Vienna for job opportunities because of linguistic, cultural, or other barriers. The stability pact of EMU also constrains the Finnish government to restrict its budget deficit to 3 percent of GDP or less, preventing Finland from using fiscal stimulus to create domestic employment. Furthermore, Finland would not expect to receive a large transfer payment from another Euroland country since fiscal integration is low. These considerations suggest that EMU will involve economic costs. An empirical study by von Hagen and Neumann (1994) identified Austria, Belgium, France, Luxembourg, the Netherlands, and Germany as nations that satisfy the conditions for an OCA. It indicated that Denmark, United Kingdom, and Italy did not. Denmark and UK opted out of EMU. Denmark affirmed its decision not to adopt the euro in a referendum on September 28, 2000.

Does the United States of America approximate an OCA? It would be suboptimal for each of the 50 states to issue its own currency; however, prior to the adoption of the U.S. constitution the 13 original states did issue their own currencies, and argued against a common currency 225 years ago. Furthermore, asymmetric shocks can occur within a country. In the United States when oil prices jumped in the 1970s, oil-consuming regions such as New England suffered a severe recession while Texas, an oil-producing state, experienced a boom. In 1991, the United States suffered a recession in which it experienced regional differences in the severity and length of the downturn. The recession came as federal military expenditures were reduced, and regions such as southern California, which had a heavy concentration of defense contractors and military bases, were particularly hard hit. Consequently, unemployment in California was higher than in the rest of the country; by 1993, U.S. unemployment was only 6.5 percent while in California unemployment stood at 8.6 percent. The federal tax and transfer system aided unemployed Californians through unemployment benefits. The federal government also aided the region by subsidizing conversion of military bases to commercial use, the revenues for which came from more prosperous regions of the country. Labor-market flexibility also contributed to eventual recovery as workers migrated from California to neighboring states. Hence, the United States, with a 225-year history, acts more like an OCA than Europe does, at present.

Countries have managed their economies with a common national policy. Although asymmetric shocks may be more serious internationally, they are not an impediment to monetary union. Since the advent of the EMS (European Monetary System) in 1979, the EMU countries have restricted their monetary policies to maintain exchange-rate stability (the "snake inside the tunnel") in Europe. Since intra-Euroland trade accounts for 60 percent of foreign trade, benefits from EMU are likely to exceed the associated costs.

As a practical matter, the costs associated with giving up the possibility of independent monetary policy may be small for most European countries. As part of their effort to stimulate trade and investment, potential EMU members eliminated all barriers to international capital flows, which created a competitive multicountry financial market. Consequently, there was little or no difference in the cost of borrowing in the different countries so long as exchange rates between European currencies were kept fairly stable. Because this European interest rate was determined by the large European countries (primarily Germany), small countries in the EU did not have the ability to lower interest rates during recessions unless they were willing to see their currencies devalued. European financial and exchange rate treaties left small member countries effectively without the ability to conduct independent monetary policy. But all member countries have representation in monetary policy decisions under the monetary union. The EMU gives small countries some influence in determining the European interest rate even as it formally eliminates the possibility of using independent monetary policy and exchange-rate adjustments.

The EMU member countries also agreed to limit the use of fiscal policies. Consequently, when one or several countries within the currency union, but not all, face(s) recession or an overheated economy, adjustment must occur largely through changes in wages and prices or through the movement of workers from one country to another.

Monetary Policy

The biggest change in moving to a single currency is that each country relinquishes control over monetary policy to the new European central bank that issues the single currency for all the countries in the union. But what happens if a recession hits just one country, as in the hypothetical description of Finland and a recession in the paper/pulp industry? Prior to EMU, its central bank could have responded to the recession by increasing the money supply, thereby pushing interest rates downward and stimulating investment and economic recovery. The central bank for the EMU will be unlikely to use expansionary monetary policy to help one country, since doing so would cause inflation in those EMU countries not in recession.

Of course, if economic adjustment from recessions happens quickly, there is little cost associated with giving up interest- or exchange-rate policy and no need for federal redistribution. The speed of recovery depends greatly on the flexibility of the European labor market. If workers are highly mobile, Finnish workers who are unemployed or earning low wages during the recession will quickly relocate to Austria or other countries with a high demand for labor. This type of flexibility has an equalizing effect across the monetary union and makes for greater symmetry in policy objectives. In Europe, however, cultural and linguistic differences hinder labor movements across countries; consequently, this particular type of labor-market flexibility is not promising in the near future. A second form of labor market flexibility occurs through wage adjustments. If, in a recession, workers are willing to accept lower wages, employers will not only be able to maintain the same number of employees but also to pass on the reduction in payroll costs to lower output prices. Lower prices, in turn, spur exports and lead domestic consumers to buy fewer imports and more locally made goods. That increase in demand spurs economic recovery. In practice, however, although wages seem to go up during booms, they do not fall so readily during recessions.

Reducing the Costs and Preserving the Benefits

The keys to a currency union's ability to adjust to economic shocks are the degree to which wages and prices are flexible and the ease with which labor moves across borders. Although labor-market flexibility can substitute for a policy response, labor-market flexibility in Europe is clearly much lower than that in the United States. Compared with their U.S. counterparts, European workers are much more willing to remain unemployed rather than accept lower wages. They are also much less willing to move out of regions with high unemployment rates. This situation is only partly due to the language and cultural barriers that hinder cross-country movements; European workers are also less likely to move within their own countries in response to labor-market pressures. This reluctance may reflect the relatively high unemployment compensation in Europe.

European governments recognize the need for greater labor-market flexibility, but attempts at labor-market reform are controversial. There has been some progress. For instance, workers are now free to move across national borders, and this movement can reduce the cost of regional shocks. But it seems unlikely that European labor markets will be able to meet the demands for flexibility in the short run. Consequently this important shortcoming could limit the Euro's early success.

The costs associated with losing independent monetary and exchange-rate policy might be small if there were either little evidence of regional asymmetry or great evidence of labor market flexibility. In the European case, the opposite is true; Bayoumi and Eichengreen (1993) find not only that shocks are more symmetric across regions in the United States than in Europe, but also that labor markets in the U.S. regions stabilize much more quickly than labor markets in European countries. These findings seem to suggest that Europe will not form as successful a monetary union as that in the United States, since regional losses may be greater in Europe than the U.S. experience would suggest, but that conclusion might be premature.

Comparing the ability of U.S. and European labor markets to adjust to economic shocks, a la Bayoumi and Eichengreen, may not be appropriate because they were comparing asymmetries within an existing monetary union to those in a potential one. Since inauguration of the EMU, sources of asymmetry have been reduced. For example, the EMU has eliminated asymmetries in setting monetary policy. Furthermore, countries with fiscal deficits out of line with the European norm will be fined. In contrast, the U.S. federal income tax and welfare systems redistribute income from expanding to contracting regions; this leveling effect may make U.S. regions appear more symmetric in their cyclical movements than their European counterparts. As similar tax and welfare policies take hold within the EU, redistributive policies may create more symmetry across regions there as well.

Although a single currency should lessen fiscal and monetary sources of asymmetry, there are, at the same time, reasons to suspect that adoption of a single currency may increase asymmetry within the EMU. By reducing transaction costs, adopting a single currency may increase trade. Trade tends to encourage regional specialization in the production of goods. If regions specialize in the types of goods they produce, shocks to demand or to the production of any particular good will affect regions differently. If monetary union does increase trade, regions within the common-currency area may become less alike than they are now. It may be argued (as Mundell did in 1973a) that asymmetric responses to economic shocks may help smooth aggregate business cycles in optimum currency areas.

How Do Countries in Europe Compare with Each Other?

At one time economists referred to Europe as consisting of a "core" and a "periphery," with the core represented by the U.K., France, Germany, and perhaps Austria, and the periphery by the Mediterranean countries. Relatively large budget deficits and high inflation rates distinguished "peripheral" countries, as did the fact that their business cycles were rarely in sync with those in "core" countries. This breakdown is no longer as clear as it once was. Budget deficits in Germany and France have grown over the past nine years, while those in the once-peripheral countries have fallen, as have their interest and inflation rates. German reunification represented a large asymmetric shock, relative to the rest of Europe, from which Germany is still recovering. Nonetheless, Europe as a whole has undergone a period of dramatic convergence in interest and inflation rates and government budget deficits since the ratification of the Maastricht Treaty on monetary union in 1993.

A BRIEF HISTORY OF THE EURO AND EMU

The introduction on January 1, 1999 of the euro—the single currency adopted by 11 of the 15 countries of the EU—marked the beginning of the final stage of Economic and Monetary Union (EMU). This lengthy process began in March 1957, when six European nations—Belgium, France, Germany, Italy, Luxembourg, and the Netherlands—signed the Treaty of Rome, founding the European Economic Community (EEC).[5] The treaty came into effect on January 1, 1958, exactly 41 years before the euro.[6]

In 1971, a group of European experts developed a proposal for coordinated monetary policy among EEC members—the Werner plan. In 1979 a system of stable, but adjustable, exchange rates known as the European Monetary System (EMS), was established. The Single European Act, signed in 1986, set the objectives of establishing a European single market and a monetary union. In 1989, Delors Committee report detailed the specific stages toward achieving Economic and Monetary Union (EMU), and in December 1991 in the Dutch city of Maastricht, EU nations produced the Treaty on European Union.

The Maastricht Treaty also provided the legal basis for the European Central Bank (ECB) and protocols for the European System of Central Banks (ESCB) and the European Monetary Institute (EMI), the precursor to EMU. The ESCB comprises the European Central Bank and the 15 EU-member national central banks. During its transitory existence between January 1994 and July 1998, the EMI worked to strengthen cooperation and monetary policy coordination among national central banks and to facilitate preparations for the establishment of the ESCB. The ECB came into formal existence on June 1, 1998, and took over formal responsibility for the monetary policy of the EMU on January 1, 1999. The euro has replaced the national currencies of the Euroland and in 2002 the notes and coins that circulated in these countries ceased to be legal tender. During the transition period from January 1, 1999, to December 31, 2001, one could use the euro for noncash transactions, but euro notes and coins did not circulate. Anecdotal evidence that the euro is a success is that criminals tried to use counterfeit euros for cash purchases during the first week of circulation.

Overall, legislation governing the euro and transactions made with euros provides a framework to ensure acceptability of the new currency. The transition period proceeded without major difficulties, a situation that reflects the extensive planning that took place well before the EMU member countries entered into the union.

CONVERGENCE CRITERIA FOR MEMBERSHIP IN EMU

The Economics and Finance (ECOFIN) Council made recommendations to European Council (heads of EU governments) for membership decisions. ECOFIN Council set bilateral exchange rates. Euro (ECU) exchange rates were locked in January 1999. Denmark and United Kingdom opted out at present. Greece and Sweden were ruled ineligible in 1999, but Greece met eligibility criteria and joined the EMU in 2001.

The ratio of government debt to GDP must be less than 60, unless the ratio is sufficiently diminishing and approaching this value at a satisfactory pace. A government budgetary position should not have an "excessive deficit" (exceeding 3 percent) unless the excess over 3 percent is temporary or the ratio has declined substantially and reached a level close to 3 percent. For one year prior to examination, the inflation rate of the country cannot exceed by more than 1.5 percent the inflation rate of the three best-performing states in terms of price stability.

For one year before examination, a member state must have an average nominal long-term interest rate (long-term government bond or comparable securities) that does not exceed by more than 2 percent that of the three best-performing member states in terms of price stability.

EUROPEAN SYSTEM OF CENTRAL BANKS

As specified in the Maastricht Treaty, the primary objective of the ECB is to "maintain price stability." Without jeopardizing this objective, the ECB is also expected to support the general economic policies of the European Commission. In this respect, the mandate of the ECB is similar to that of the Bundesbank, which was charged with "safeguarding the currency." In practice, safeguarding the currency was interpreted to mean price stability. In comparison, the Federal Reserve Act states that U.S. monetary policy should seek "to promote effectively the goals of maximum employment, stable prices, and moderate long-term interest rates."

The ECB's published definition of price stability is inflation, measured as the 12-month change in the harmonized index of consumer prices (HICP) for the euro area, of below 2 percent, with no explicitly defined lower bound. Although the ultimate goal of Euroland monetary policy is clearly specified as price stability, the Governing Council of the ECB has also adopted a target for money growth. The reference value for M3 is derived from three assumptions: price stability as defined above; the trend rate of growth of real GDP is 2–2.5 percent; the trend rate of decline in M3 velocity is 0.5–1.0 percent per annum. The relevant reference value for the central bank's monetary growth target for 1999 was M3 growth of 4 1/2 percent, as measured by a three-month moving average of the 12-month percent change. The ECB also monitors other indicators. In January 1999, the ECB noted that, among other things, the mix of other indicators would include wages, bond prices, the yield curve, measures of real activity, business and consumer surveys, and the exchange rate.

While monetary policy decisions are centered in Frankfort, the operational aspects of monetary policy implementation (including open market operations, administration of the minimum reserve system, and management of the standing facilities) are undertaken in a decentralized fashion at the twelve national central banks. The main features of the Eurosystem's operating procedures are similar in many respects to those employed by the Bundesbank and other national central banks in the euro area in recent years: The ECB relies heavily on open market operations, especially term repurchase agreements, to control a short-term interest rate.

The Eurosystem also has two standing facilities to provide and absorb overnight money and to provide a "corridor" for the market-determined interbank rate: the marginal lending facility and the deposit facility. The marginal lending facility provides overnight credit to all eligible credit institutions with sufficient collateral, and its interest rate usually serves as a ceiling for the overnight interbank rate. There is no stigma associated with borrowing at the marginal lending facility. However, such borrowing takes place at a penalty rate, between 100 and 150 basis points above the official weekly refinancing rate. The overnight interbank rate usually trades close to the weekly refinancing rate, giving banks an incentive to borrow in the interbank market if possible. Intra-day credit that is not repaid by the end of the day automatically rolls over to overnight lending through the marginal lending facility.

The second standing facility, the deposit facility, usually provides a floor for the interbank rate. This facility is available for banks to deposit excess funds that earn interest, although excess funds are not automatically swept into it. Normally, the interest rate on the deposit facility is 100 basis points below the refinancing rate. Thus, in normal times, the corridor provided by the marginal lending and deposit facilities is quite wide, at 2 percent to 2.5 percent.

The ESCB is probably the most independent central bank in the world. The fact that the charter of the ESCB can only be changed with the unanimous consent of its signatories makes it difficult to exert political pressure on the ESCB. Independent central banks tend to deliver lower inflation rates without costing higher unemployment or slower growth in real output. The rate of inflation as measured by the HICP has been below 2.5 percent and declined in August. Higher oil prices and the lower euro have increased the inflation rate. Core inflation has remained constant.[7]

EXCHANGE RATE MOVEMENT JANUARY 1, 1999–DECEMBER 31, 2001

The critics have argued that the euro has failed because it has depreciated against the dollar and the yen. Prior to its introduction many predicted that the euro would rapidly appreciate against the dollar, given the relative current account positions of the United States and the euro area. On January 4, 1999, the euro traded at $1.18 and 133.82 yen, versus $0.89 and 116.17 as of December 31, 2001.

However, one could argue that the legal currencies that comprised the euro were over-valued in late 1998. The currencies of the euro experienced a strong appreciation against the dollar in late 1998. This appreciation resulted partially as a response to: Russia's default, the failure of the hedge fund Long Term Capital Management in the United States, and the "euphoria" between the announcement of the Brussels summit in May 1998 (announcement of the participation in EU) and the actual beginning of the euro. In fact, if we look at the U.S. dollar price of the ECU (precursor to the euro) from 1995 to present, we see that it has trended downward, except for the spike in late 1998.

The dollar value of the deutsche mark (another precursor of the euro) has shown similar volatility in its history. The current period of decline, which started in the Spring of 1996 is not a unique development. There was a similar period after the world debt crisis of 1981, bringing the dollar to 3.45 DM, which would be equivalent to a drop in the euro to $0.56; the lowest value to which the euro has fallen $0.84 in June 2001.

Another reason that the dollar appreciated vis-à-vis the euro in 1999 was that the U.S. economy continued to grow at a robust pace, while the euro area experienced a growth recession. GDP increased only 2.1 percent in Euroland in 1999 and 3.5 percent in 2000, while the United States grew at a 5.1 percent pace in 1999. Unemployment remained high in Euroland, declining from 10.6 percent in December 1998 to 9.6 percent in December 1999. Furthermore, uncertainty about the direction of economic policy in Germany, Euroland's largest economy, and confusion about ECB's attitude toward exchange rate developments detracted from market confidence in the first months of the euro. There is evidence that the slowdown in Europe has ended. Germany and Italy show signs of an upturn in economic activity. (The recession in Russia and Asia led to Germany's exports falling by 3.4 percent in late 1998 while Finland, Ireland, Spain, and Portugal continue to grow rapidly.) After reaching a low of $0.89 in early May 2000, the euro had appreciated as the ECB raised interest rates and the Federal Reserve did not increase its target for the federal funds rate. ECB raised the refinancing rate again in August.[8]

As the euro depreciated to $0.8438 and 90.04 in mid-September, the G-7 (the United States, Canada, the United Kingdom, France, Germany,

Italy, and Japan) central banks to intervene on September 22, 2000, to support the euro when it traded around $0.8630. Analysts estimate that the central banks spent $2.5–$5.0 billion to bolster the euro.

What has prompted that decline in the euro vis-à-vis the dollar was the demand for dollars by corporations. Approximately $58 billion flowed from the euro-zone in August 2000, due to merger-and-acquisition activity. Euroland acquisitions of non-euro-area companies are running at an annual rate of 7 percent of the region's GDP, up from 0.5 percent a few years ago.

The Euroland companies largely finance those acquisitions by borrowing euros and converting the euros to dollars to pay the sellers; hence, they have euro liabilities but dollar-denominated assets. The Europeans will convert dollar cash flows from their newly acquired American companies to euros to repay their euro debts, and that could prove to be another bullish factor for the euro. "If Euroland acquisitions fall from their 7 percent of GDP level—even if they remain large—the euro will rise," says Ray Dalio of Bridgewater. "And repaying their euro loans is bearish for the dollar and bullish for the euro."[9]

Another pressure on the euro is European purchases of foreign stocks, up fivefold since 1996. Portfolio investments showed net outflows of 5.1 billion euros in May 2000, mainly from Euroland residents investing in U.S. equities due to the strong U.S. economy and strong U.S. stock market. The gap between U.S. and European returns has widened from 2.1 percent in 1998 to 2.6 percent in the first quarter of 2001. Of the $155 billion net foreign purchases of U.S. securities in the 1st quarter of 2001, $100 billion originated with European residents; mostly from the euro zone. That is a substantial flow of capital out of euro and into the U.S. dollar. It is no wonder the euro had been weak. The increased European investment in U.S. securities was largely a product of the creation of the euro and of legal changes that freed pension funds and insurers to invest in stocks and also invest outside their home market. That makes it a one-time reallocation of assets. Since investors' portfolios have reached their allotted dollar allocations, the buying will cease, which should alleviate this pressure on the euro.

Billions of euros have been borrowed, converted into U.S. dollars and subsequently placed in dollar denominated investments. For several years there has been a net acquisition of American companies and assets by European firms and investors. Much of this was financed with euro denominated debt.

There were good reasons to borrow euro and buy dollars. Interest rates in Euroland were lower than those in the United States. A European investor could borrow euros as banks and other institutions were eager to lend euros. The euro loan proceeds were then easily converted into U.S.

dollars and easily used to buy American assets including marketable securities.

For two years this was a terrific trade. Since the interest rate in the United States was higher than on the euro loan, there was a positive carry. In addition, as the euro weakened against the U.S. dollar, there was a currency based capital gain. This trade is not as appealing since the Nasdaq bubble burst and since U.S. interest rates have changed. Positive carry is no longer available. U.S. stocks are no longer a one-directional investment; European investors saw their U.S. stocks fall in value just as Americans did.

Today, the condition of the global financial market reflects the cumulative euro denominated debt in place and massive U.S. investment by Europeans. When the currency reversal comes, this cumulative position has enormous investment ramifications. It amounts to a large euro short position; that is the precise recipe for a massive euro rally and a short squeeze.

Enormous amounts of cash hoards have been leaving the deutsche mark, lira, franc, etc. for the U.S. dollar. This transfer of both legal and "black" money must not be underestimated.

One rationale as to why the dollar is presently strong because monies flow to it for a temporary resting place and why they will flow into the euro as euro denominated bills become globally available, is that individuals turned their cash hoards of the old currencies into dollars. Residents of non-EMU countries, particularly those of "Eastern Europe" had been holding deutsche marks. Many "ordinary people" had heard that the deutsche mark would be abolished in 2002, and were afraid of sustaining a loss by continuing to hoard deutsche marks and began to hold dollars, which were free of this kind of uncertainty. This argument was put forth by Sinn and Westerman (2001).[10] EMU residents who had been hoarding cash for black or gray market transactions similarly may have changed their local currencies for dollars with the plan to switch to Euros in 2002.[11]

The cash exchange may trigger the euro rally but the economics of cost vs. gain will sustain it. ECB president, Wim Duisenberg, has affirmed estimates that the changeover to euro from the existing twelve currencies has a one-time cost of between "0.3 and 0.8 percent of GDP."

In 2002 the savings from a common currency will be fully seen. Estimates vary but seem to suggest a common currency will add at least 0.5 percent to EU countries' GDP growth rate. This is a recurring and productivity based addition, not a one-time event. The growth occurs because of the removal of financial friction in transactions; no more currency hedging cost among intra-EMU trading partners. Fees for bank transfers between countries (as high as 31 percent for Germans receiving bank transfers from Portugal) are eliminated. Another effect is transparency in prices. Anyone will be able to compare a price denominated in euro in any of the twelve

EMU countries. Existing open borders among countries mean transactions across borders are facilitated by the single currency.

Martin Feldstein (2000), who has not been an advocate of the euro, indicated that "there is no reason to be unhappy that it fell in value, especially since that has helped to strengthen aggregate demand by increasing Europe's net exports and has done so without any obvious increase in overall inflation."[12] The purchasing power parity value of the euro is above parity against the U.S. dollar and above 0.7 against the British pound.

Will the euro be a strong currency? Yes. The ECB has focused on fulfilling its primary mandate, achieving price stability. The Euroland current account registered a small (e1.3 billion) deficit in 2001. Once the euro establishes its credibility as a major global currency, the world's central banks, pension funds, and institutional investors will allocate a large portion of their portfolio and reserve holdings to euro assets.

Will the euro become a global currency rivaling the U.S. dollar, which has been the dominant global currency since the end of World War I, when it replaced the British pound? That dominance was possible due to the size of the U.S. economy and the relatively sound monetary policy of the Federal Reserve. Since Euroland is comparable in population, GDP and international trade share to the United States and since ECB is pursuing a sound monetary policy, the euro is likely to emerge as the second global currency in the near future, ending the dollar's sole dominance.

SUCCESSES FOR THE EURO

One major achievement is the expansion of the European commercial bond market. The volume of international bonds denominated in euros exceeded dollar-denominated issuance in 1999. The ability to borrow and lend in euros, obviating the need to hedge exchange rate fluctuations, has facilitated substantial cross-border lending. It also makes it easier to finance cross-border mergers and acquisitions. Cross-border bank acquisitions have become more common in the past four years.

The ECB also succeeded in 1999 in fostering strengthening demand that is producing a faster growth of output in 2000. EMU also succeeded in reducing fiscal deficits. The Maastricht Treaty required lower deficits and national debt as a condition for a country's admission to the EMU. Some countries achieved this goal by accounting manipulation and intrayear movements of spending and tax receipts or by treating asset sales as if they were a real source of revenue for the government, but all countries did substantially reduce their fiscal deficits. Much of the reduction occurred because interest rates paid on the national debt fell as inflationary expectations improved. No matter the reason, EMU has fostered lower deficits.

Euroland governments have undertaken initiatives to attract business by reducing taxes in the region by 60 billion euros, about 0.7 percent of GDP, which could result in another 0.5 percent increase in GDP annually.[13] At 46 percent of GDP in 1999, the tax receipts ratio is still large compared to the 31 percent of GDP in the United States.

While there were some differences in economic performance across Euroland over the past year, we did not see the kind of dramatic asymmetries the skeptics believe would cause EMU to collapse. Despite sluggish growth in two of the larger economies (Germany and Italy), unemployment continued to decline across Euroland and is at an eight-year low, although it does remain at unacceptably high levels. Manufacturing activity is at a record high. Germany, which accounts for about one third of Euroland economic activity, only experienced one quarter of negative growth (at the end of 1998) rather than a full-blown recession. How well the institutions of EMU will deal with more severely asymmetric cycles if and when they occur is an open question.

There are also signs of structural reform. The Spanish government is considering extending a plan to all employees that reduces the high cost of firing employees, resulting in greater efficiency and mobility in the workforce. Unemployment is down eight percent since the plan was enacted in 1997 (although it is the highest in the zone at 14 percent). The plan reduces the maximum severance pay for employees from 24 months to 12, in exchange for subsidies to company social security contributions. Structural changes like this will contribute to a more stable euro.

Another measure of the success of the euro is that other countries wish to join the EU and adopt the euro. Several candidate countries expect to convert their own currencies to the euro two years after becoming EU members. At their summit in Laeken in December 2001, the 15 EU leaders said that Cyprus, the Czech Republic, Estonia, Hungary, Latvia, Lithuania, Malta, Poland, Slovakia, and Slovenia could join the Union in 2004. Bulgaria and Romania are excluded from the calculation because they are not expected to be ready before 2008, while Turkey is expected to join the EU even later due to the vast amount of reforms that still need to be implemented.

CONCLUSIONS

Monetary union has not eliminated the unemployment problems of Europe, which are due to excessively high tax rates, overregulation of the labor market, and the social safety net. However, there will be direct effects arising from the increase in transparency of pricing in the labor market, which will lead to increased awareness of Europe-wide labor market conditions and increased labor mobility and will create pressures for convergence in pensions, unemployment benefits, and taxes on labor.

There are both costs and benefits associated with forming any monetary union. The benefits of monetary union stem from reducing transaction costs and eliminating exchange-rate uncertainty. Falling transaction costs mean fewer barriers to trade, which should increase competition and reduce prices. Eliminating exchange-rate uncertainty will spur still more trade; it may also lower interest rates, therefore making it cheaper to borrow to finance new investment. In the European case, the benefits may be greater still because when each country had its own currency, speculative pressures heightened the risk of costly exchange-rate movements.

Whatever the costs of EMU, mechanisms other than domestic monetary or exchange rate policy will have to bear the burden of economic adjustment after adoption of the single currency. Legal barriers to movements of labor have been removed, which should encourage that adjustment process. Further labor-market reforms may be necessary to increase labor markets' speed of adjustment. In addition, member countries may find it necessary to institute international tax and redistribution policies to allow for regional differences in policy stimulus or restraint.

Robert Mundell indicated, in "The Case for the Euro" (1998a), "A good exchange rate is an old exchange rate. After countries have been in a currency area for a long time, wages, prices and interest rates become harmonized to a common level."[14]

The changeover to a new currency is not a simple process. Each of the 375 million people in the EU must learn a new way of comparing and thinking about prices. The residents must also relinquish their emotional attachment to their national currencies, an emotional trauma akin to the loss of national heritage.

These costs are real, but the European residents gain a currency that spans a continent. The benefits will derive from transparency of pricing, stability of expectations and lower transactions costs, as well as a common monetary policy.

As Mundell advocated in 1998, "Monetary union will do much to integrate Europe's commodity, factor and capital markets. It will increase Europe-wide competition and revolutionize financial markets. It will spur rationalization, mergers and takeovers in the European banking industry and commercial firms. Perhaps most important of all, EMU will change the way Europeans think about themselves and about a multi-regional continental market that has become the largest in the world."[15]

NOTES

1. Mundell, R. A. (1961). "A Theory of Optimum Currency Areas," *American Economic Review*, Vol. 51 (September), pp. 657–665.

2. Mundell, R. A. (1998). "The Case for the Euro, Part I," *The Wall Street Journal* (March 24, 1998), p. A22.

3. Frankel, J. A.., and A. K. Rose. (1997). "Economic Structure and the Decision to Adopt a Common Currency," *Institute for International Economic Studies, Stockholm University, Seminar Papers,* No. 611 (November 5).

4. European Commission. (1990). "One Market, One Money: An Evaluation of the Potential Benefits and Costs of Forming an Economic and Monetary Union," *European Economy,* Vol. 44.

5. The Treaty of Rome was preceded in 1951 by the Treaty of Paris to which the same six European nations were signatories; the Treaty of Paris established the European Coal and Steel Community, which aimed at the more-limited objective of pooling the coal and steel resources of member countries.

6. Over the years, membership in the EEC, which was renamed the European Union, grew from the initial 6 countries to 15, with Denmark, Ireland, and the United Kingdom becoming full members in 1973, Greece in 1981, Spain and Portugal in 1986, and Austria, Finland, and Sweden in 1995.

7. According to Eurostat, the European Commission's statistical agency, August inflation rates were highest in Ireland, at 5.7 percent, and Spain and Portugal, both at 3.6 percent. They were lowest in Germany, at 1.8 percent, and Austria, at 1.9 percent. The inflation rate increased in two countries, decreased in six, and stayed the same in three.

8. The ECB made its first rate moves, lowering the repurchase agreements rate from 3.0 percent to 2.5 percent in April 1999, and then raising it back to 3.0 percent in November. On August 31, 2000, the ECB raised the refinancing rate 25 basis points to 4.50 percent, effective September 6. A chronology of monetary policy measures of the ECB is detailed in Table 14.8.

9. Sesit, M. R. (2000). "Time for a Wild and Crazy Idea? Some Make Bet on Ailing Euro," *Wall Street Journal* (September 22), pp. C1, C6.

10. Sinn, H-W., and F. Westermann. (2001). "Why Has the Euro Been Falling? An Investigation into the Determinants of the Exchange Rate," *National Bureau of Economic Research Working Paper* 8352 (July 2001), p. 29.

11. Kotok, D. R. (2001). "Italy–4 The Mafia" (June 27). http://www.cumber.com/comments/062701.htm. "The conversion of lira and other currencies is causing a problem for organized crime. Vast amounts of currency will be invalid by the middle of next year. The conversion to the euro has specific timeframes. That means organized crime has to find a way to either launder money quickly or convert it. The euro will not be available in paper form until January 1, 2002, and then there will only be a few months of conversion time before the old currencies are completely withdrawn. Organized crime has a difficult task because large currency transactions would call attention to the criminal. Several economists speculate that the way they are choosing to get around this problem is to convert those currencies to the U.S. dollar. Intuitively that makes a lot of sense. Could it explain the continuing strength in the dollar at a time when the dollar seems overvalued against the euro?

"We should know the answer to this question within a year when the euro has completed its transition from a virtual to a real currency. We think the answer is 'yes' and that means the euro should start to strengthen as this one-time transition is completed.

"An additional technical aspect of the currency conversion involves the denomination of bills. The European Central Bank intends to issue a 500 euro denominated note. The largest size mass circulated U.S. dollar denomination is the $100 bill. Some experts speculate that organized crime will favor the larger 500 euro bill over the $100 because it will allow them to make cash payments in smaller containers. If this speculation proves accurate, a potential worldwide shift of billions of dollars into euros is possible with the transfers starting early next year. Presently those $100s which are printed by our Federal Reserve amount to an interest free loan to the U.S. government from the worldwide holders of that paper. Substitution of the euro would mean the interest free loan will be to the European Central Bank and that our Fed will have to offset this shift out of our currency."

12. Feldstein, M. (2000). "The European Central Bank and the Euro: The First Year," *National Bureau of Economic Research Working Paper* 7517 (February), p. 2.

13. "Following Germany's landmark tax reform passed last month, France is set to respond Thursday by unveiling its own ambitious plan. The bill, which would amount to the country's deepest cuts since World War II, is expected to lop off 120 billion francs ($16.48 billion or 18.29 billion euros) from the annual tax burden during the next three years beginning in 2001. Italy has promised to move ahead with a plan that would match the German reform. And Belgium's finance minister earlier this week proposed reducing income taxes across the board. . . . Tax receipts as percentage of GDP, 1999: France 50.4, Finland 49.4, Austria 48.7, Belgium 47.2, Italy 46.4 Euro zone 45.6, Germany 44.6, Netherlands 43.7, Portugal 42.8 U.K. 40.4, Spain 37.5, Ireland 33.2, Japan 31.1, U.S. 31.1."

Rhoads, C.R., and D. Woodruff. (2000). "European Countries Make Moves to Reduce a Heavy Tax Burden," *The Wall Street Journal Interactive Edition*, (August 31).

14. Mundell, R. A. (1998). "The Case for the Euro, Part I," *The Wall Street Journal* (March 24), p. A22.

15. Mundell, R. A. (1998). "The Case for the Euro, Part I," *The Wall Street Journal* (March 24), p. A22.

REFERENCES

Alberola, E., S. G. Cervero, H. Lopez, and A. Ubide. (1999). "Global Equilibrium Exchange Rates: Euro, Dollar, 'Ins,' 'Outs,' and Other Major Currencies in a Panel Cointegration Framework." IMF working paper WP/99/175, (December), Washington, D.C.

Bayoumi, T., and B. Eichengreen. (1993). "Shocking Aspects of European Monetary Union." In F. Torres, F. Giavazzi, and F. Giavazzi (Eds.), *The Transition to Economic and Monetary Union* (pp. 193–240). Cambridge, England: Cambridge University Press.

Cleeton, D. L. (1999). "Economic and Monetary Union Is Off on the Right Foot," *Brown Journal of World Affairs*, 6 (Summer/Fall), pp. 163–172.

Dowd, K., and D. Greenaway. (1993). "Currency Competition, Network Externalities and Switching Costs: Towards an Alternative View of Optimum Currency Areas," *The Economic Journal*, 103 (September), pp. 1180–1189.

European Central Bank. (1999). *Annual Report*.

———. *Monthly Bulletin*. August 2000, September 2000, January 2001.

European Commission. (1990). "One Market, One Money: An Evaluation of the Potential Benefits and Costs of Forming an Economic and Monetary Union," *European Economy*, 44.

Feldstein, M. (2000). "The European Central Bank and the Euro: The First Year," National Bureau of Economic Research working paper 7517 (February), Cambridge, MA.

Frankel, J. A., and A. K. Rose. (1997). "Economic Structure and the Decision to Adopt a Common Currency," Institute for International Economic Studies, Stockholm University, Seminar Papers, no. 611.

Johnson, H. P., and R. Lovelady. (November 1955). "Migration between California and Other States: 1985–1994," California Demographic Research Unit Research Paper.

Kenen, P. B. (1969). "The Theory of Optimum Currency Areas: An Eclectic Vie." In R. A. Mundell and A. K. Swoboda (Eds.), *Monetary Problems of the International Economy*. Chicago: University of Chicago Press, pp. 299–332.

Kotok, D. R. "Italy-4 The Mafia." Retrieved June 27, 2001, http://www.cumber.com/comments/062701.htm.

Laffer, A. (2001). "A Note from the Doctor, Europe's Mad Duisenberg Disease," 7 June, *The Wall Street Journal*.

LeBaron, B. A., and R. McCulloch. (2000). "Floating, Fixed, or Super-Fixed? Dollarization Joins the Menu of Exchange-Rate Options," *American Economic Review*, 90 (May), pp. 32–42.

Marston, R. C. (1984). "Exchange Rate Union as an Alternative to Flexible Exchange Rates: The Effects of Real and Monetary Disturbances." In J. F. O. Bilson and R. C. Marston (Eds.), *Exchange Rate Theory and Practice*. Chicago: University of Chicago Press, 93–105.

McCallum, B. T. (1999). "Theoretical Issues Pertaining to Monetary Unions," National Bureau of Economic Research working paper 7392.

McKinnon, R. I. (1963). "Optimum Currency Areas," *American Economic Review*, 53 (March), pp. 717–725.

Mundell, R. A. (1961). "A Theory of Optimum Currency Areas," *American Economic Review*, 51 (September), pp. 657–665.

———. (1968). *International Economics*. New York: Macmillan.

———. (1971). *Monetary Theory: Inflation, Interest and Growth in the World Economy*. Pacific Palisades, CA: Goodyear.

———. (1973a). "Uncommon Arguments for Common Currencies." In H. G. Johnson and A. K. Swoboda (Eds.), *The Economics of Common Currencies* (pp. 114–132). Cambridge, MA: Harvard University Press.

———. (1973b). "A Plan for a European Currency." In H. G. Johnson and A. K. Swoboda (Eds.), *The Economics of Common Currencies* (pp. 143–172). Cambridge, MA: Harvard University Press.

———. (1997). "Updating the Agency for Monetary Unio." In M. I. Blejer, J. A. Frenkel, L. Leidern, and A. Razin (Eds.), *Optimum Currency Areas: New Analytical and Policy Developments* (pp. 29–48). Washington, D.C.: International Monetary Fund.

———. (1998a). "The Case for the Euro, Parts I and II," *The Wall Street Journal*, 24–25 March, p. A22.

———. (1998b). "Making the Euro Work," *The Wall Street Journal*, 30 April, p. A18.

———. (1999). "The International Impact of the Euro and Its Implications for Transition Countries." In M. I. Blejer and M. Skreb (Eds.), *Central Banking, Mon-*

etary Policies and the Implications for Transition Economies (pp. 403–427). Norwell, MA: Kluwer Academic Publishers.

Sinn, H-W., and F. Westermann. (2001). "Why Has the Euro Been Falling? An Investigation into the Determinants of the Exchange Rate," National Bureau of Economic Research working paper 8352 (July), Cambridge, MA.

Sesit, M. R. (2000). "Time for a Wild and Crazy Idea? Some Make Bet on Ailing Euro," *Wall Street Journal*, 22 September, pp. C1, C6.

von Hagen, J., and M. J. M. Neumann. (1994). "Real Exchange Rates within and between Currency Areas: How Far Away Is EMU?" *Review of Economics and Statistics*, 76, (May), pp. 236–244.

Wynne, M. A. (1999). "The European System of Central Banks," *Economic Review Federal Reserve Bank of Dallas* (First Quarter), pp. 2–14. Dallas, TX: Federal Reserve Bank of Dallas.

———. (2000). "EMU at 1," *Economic and Financial Review Federal Reserve Bank of Dallas* (First Quarter), pp. 14–28. Dallas, TX: Federal Reserve Bank of Dallas.

APPENDIX

CHRONOLOGY OF MONETARY POLICY
MEASURES OF THE EUROSYSTEM

December 22, 1998

The Governing Council of the ECB decides that the first main refinancing operation of the Eurosystem will be a fixed rate tender offered at an interest rate of 3.0 percent a level that it intends to maintain for the foreseeable future. This operation will be initiated on January 4,1999, while the allotment decision will be taken on January 5, 1999, and settlement will take place on January 7, 1999. In addition, the first longer-term refinancing operation will be announced on January 12, 1999 (with a settlement date of January 14, 1999) and will be conducted through a variable rate tender using the single rate allotment procedure.

The Governing Council furthermore decides that the interest rate for the marginal lending facility will be set at a level of 4.5 percent and the interest rate for the deposit facility at a level of 2.0 percent for the start of Stage Three, that is, January 1, 1999. As a transitional measure, between January 4 and 21, 1999, the interest rate for the marginal lending facility will be set at a level of 3.25 percent and the interest rate for the deposit facility at a level of 2.75 percent. The Governing Council intends to terminate this transitional measure following its meeting on January 21, 1999.

December 31, 1998

In accordance with Article 1091 (4) of the Treaty establishing the European Community, the EU Council, acting with the unanimity of the Member States of the European Community without a derogation, upon a proposal from the European Community and after consultation of the ECB, adopts the irrevocable conversion rates for the euro, with effect from January 1, 1999, 0.00 a.m. (local time).

The ministers of the euro area Member States, the ECB and ministers and central bank governors of Denmark and Greece decide, in a common procedure involving the European Commission and after consultation of the Monetary Committee, to fix the central rates against the euro for the currencies participating in the exchange rate mechanism which comes into operation on January 1, 1999. Further to this decision on the euro central rates, the ECB, Denmark National Bank and the Bank of Greece establish by common accord the compulsory intervention rates for the Danish krone and the Greek drachma. A fluctuation band of + /– 2.25 percent will be observed around the euro central rate for the Danish krone. The standard fluctuation band of + /– 15 percent will be observed around the euro central rate for the Greek drachma.

January 7, 1999

The Governing Council of the ECB decides that for the two main refinancing operations to be announced on January 11 and 18, 1999, respectively, the same conditions will apply as for the first such operation, which was settled on January

7, 1999, that is, they will be fixed rate tenders conducted at an interest rate of 3.0 percent.

January 12, 1999

Following the decision of the Governing Council of the ECB on December 22, 1998, the ECB announces that the first longer-term refinancing operation for the Euro-system will be conducted as variable rate tenders using the single rate method of allotment. With a view to phasing in the longer-term refinancing operations, the first such operation is conducted through three parallel tenders with three different maturities, namely February 25, March 25, and April 29, 1999. The ECB also announces that the intention is to allot an amount of 15 billion in each of these parallel tenders. For the subsequent longer-term refinancing operation in the first three months of 1999, the intention is to allot an unchanged amount of 15 billion per operation.

January 21, 1999

The Governing Council of the ECB decides to revert to the interest rates on the Eurosystem's two standing facilities which it had set for the start of Stage Three, that is, to set the interest rate for the marginal lending facility at a level of 4.5 percent and that for the deposit facility at a level of 2.0 percent with effect from January 22, 1999. Furthermore, it decides that for the two main refinancing operations to be settled on January 27 and February 13, 1999, respectively, the same conditions will apply as for the first three such operations settled earlier in January, that is, they will be fixed rate tenders conducted at an interest rate 3.0 percent.

February 4, 1999

The Governing Council of the ECB decides that for the main refinancing operations to be settled on February 10 and 17, 1999, the same conditions will apply as for the first such operations settled earlier in the year, that is, they will be fixed tenders conducted at an interest rate of 3.0 percent. In addition, the interest rate on the marginal lending facility continues to be 4.5 percent and the interest rate on the deposit facility remains 2.0 percent.

February 18, 1999

The Governing Council of the ECB decides that for the main refinancing operations to be settled on February 24 and March 3, 1999, the same conditions will apply as for the first such operations settled earlier in the year, that is, they will be fixed tenders conducted at an interest rate of 3.0 percent. In addition, the interest rate on the marginal lending facility continues to be 4.5 percent and the interest rate on the deposit facility remains 2.0 percent.

March 4, 1999

The Governing Council of the ECB decides that for the main refinancing operations to be settled on March 10 and 17, 1999, the same conditions will apply as for the first such operations settled earlier in the year, that is, they will be fixed tenders conducted at an interest rate of 3.0 percent. In addition, the interest rate on the marginal lending facility continues to be 4.5 percent and the interest rate on the deposit facility remains 2.0 percent. The Governing Council also decides that for forthcoming longer-term refinancing operations of the Eurosystem the multiple rate method of allotment will be applied (starting from the operation with a settlement date of March 25, 1999) until otherwise indicated.

March 18, 1999

The Governing Council of the ECB decides that for the main refinancing operations to be settled on March 24 and 31 and April 7, 1999, the same conditions will apply as for the first such operations settled earlier in the year, that is, they will be fixed tenders conducted at an interest rate of 3.0 percent. In addition, the interest rate on the marginal lending facility continues to be 4.5 percent and the interest rate on the deposit facility remains 2.0 percent.

April 8, 1999

The Governing Council of the ECB decides to reduce the interest rate on the main refinancing operation by 0.5 percentage point to 2.5 percent, starting with the operation to be settled on April 14, 1999. In addition, it decides to lower the interest rate on the marginal lending facility by 1 percentage point to 3.5 percent and the interest rate on the deposit facility by 0.5 percentage point to 1.5 both with effect from April 9, 1999.

April 22, 1999, May 6, 1999, June 2, 1999, June 17, 1999, July 1, 1999,
July 15, 1999, July 29, 1999, August 26, 1999, September 9, 1999,
September 23, 1999, October 7, 1999

The Governing Council of the ECB decides that the interest rates on the main refinancing operations, the marginal lending facility and the deposit facility will remain unchanged at 2.5 percent, 3.5 percent, and 1.5 percent respectively.

November 4, 1999

The Governing Council of the ECB decides to raise the interest rate on the main refinancing operations of the Eurosystem by 0.5 percentage point to 3.0 percent, with effect from the operation to be settled on November 10, 1999. In addition, it decides to increase the interest rates on both the marginal lending facility and the deposit facility by 0.5 percentage point to 4.0 percent and 2.0 percent respectively, both with effect from November 5, 1999.

November 18, 1999, December 2, 1999, December 15, 1999

The Governing Council of the ECB decides that the interest rates on the main refinancing operations, the marginal lending facility and the deposit facility will remain unchanged at 3.0 percent, 4.0 percent, and 2.0 percent respectively.

The Governing Council also decides to confirm the reference value for monetary growth, namely an annual growth rate 4.5 percent for the broad monetary aggregate M3. This decision is taken on the grounds that the components underlying the derivation of the reference value, namely the Eurosystem's definition of price stability (an annual increase in the HICP for the euro area of below 2 percent), the estimate for the trend of real GDP growth (2 percent to 2.5 percent) and that for the trend decline in M3 income velocity (0.5 percent to 1 percent per annum), have basically remained unchanged. As before, the Governing Council will assess monetary developments in relation to the reference value on the basis of a three-month moving average of annual growth rates. The Governing Council also decides to review the reference value henceforth on a regular annual basis. The next review will take place in December 2000.

January 4, 2000

The ECB announces that on January 5, 2000, the Eurosystem will conduct a liquidity-absorbing fine-turning operation with same-day settlement. This measure aims at restoring normal liquidity conditions in the money market after the successful transition to the year 2000.

January 5, 2000, January 20, 2000

The Governing Council of the ECB decides that the interest rates on the main refinancing operations, the marginal lending facility and the deposit facility will remain unchanged at 3.0 percent, 4.0 percent, and 2.0 percent, respectively.

February 3, 2000

The Governing Council of the ECB decides to raise the interest rate on the main refinancing operations of the Eurosystem by 0.25 percentage point to 3.25 percent, with effect from the operation to be settled on February 9, 2000. In addition, it decides to increase the interest rates on both the marginal lending facility and the deposit facility by 0.25 percentage point to 4.25 percent and 2.25 percent respectively, both with effect from February 4, 2000.

February 17, 2000, March 2, 2000

The Governing Council of the ECB decides that the interest rates on the main refinancing operations, the marginal lending facility and the deposit facility will remain unchanged at 3.25 percent, 4.25 percent, and 2.25 percent, respectively.

March 16, 2000

The Governing Council of the ECB decides to raise the interest rate on the main refinancing operations of the Eurosystem by 0.25 percentage point to 3.5 percent, with effect from the operation to be settled on March 22, 2000. In addition, it decides to increase the interest rates on both the marginal lending facility and the deposit facility by 0.25 percentage point to 4.5 percent and 2.5 percent respectively, both with effect from March 17, 2000.

March 30, 2000, April 13, 2000

The Governing Council of the ECB decides that the interest rates on the main refinancing operations, the marginal lending facility and the deposit facility will remain unchanged at 3.5 percent, 4.5 percent, and 2.5 percent, respectively.

April 27, 2000

The Governing Council of the ECB decides to raise the interest rate on the main refinancing operations of the Eurosystem by 0.25 percentage point to 3.75 percent, with effect from the operation to be settled on May 4, 2000. In addition, it decides to increase the interest rates on both the marginal lending facility and the deposit facility by 0.25 percentage point to 4.75 percent and 2.75 percent, respectively, both with effect from April 28, 2000.

June 8, 2000

The Governing Council of the ECB decides to raise the interest rate on the main refinancing operations of the Eurosystem by 0.50 percentage point to 4.25 percent and to apply this in the two operations (which will be conducted as fixed rate tenders) to be settled on June 15 and 21, 2000. In addition, it decides to increase the interest rates in both the marginal lending facility and the deposit facility by 0.50 percentage point, to 5.25 percent and 3.25 percent, respectively, both with effect from June 9, 2000.

It also announces that, starting from the operation to be settled on June 28, 2000, the main refinancing operations of the Eurosystem will be conducted as variable rate tenders, applying the multiple rate auction procedure. The Governing Council decides to set a minimum bid rate for these operations equal to 4.25 percent. The switch to variable rate tenders in the main refinancing operations is not intended as a further change in the monetary policy stance of the Eurosystem, but as a response to the severe overbidding that has developed in the context of the current fixed rate tender procedure.

June 19, 2000

In accordance with Article 122 (2) of the Treaty establishing the European Community, the ECOFIN Council decides that Greece fulfils the necessary conditions on the basis of the criteria set out in Article 121 (1) and abrogates the derogation of Greece with effect from January 1, 2001. The ECOFIN Council took its decision, taking account of the reports of the European Commission and the ECB on the progress made in the fulfillment by Sweden and Greece of their obligation regarding the achievement of Economic and Monetary Union, after consulting the European Parliament, and after a discussion in the EU Council meeting in the composition of Heads of State or Government.

The ECOFIN Council, acting with the unanimity of the Member States of the European Community without a derogation and the Member State concerned, upon a proposal from the European Commission and after consultation of the ECB, also adopts the irrevocable conversion rate between the Greek drachma and the euro with effect from January 1, 2001. Following the determination of the euro conversion rate of the Greek drachma (which is equal to its prevailing central rate against the euro in the exchange rate mechanism, ERM II), the ECB and the Bank of Greece announce that they will monitor the convergence of the market exchange rate of the Greek drachma against the euro toward its euro conversion rate, which should be completed at the latest by December 29, 2000.

June 21, 2000

The Governing Council of the ECB decides that the interest rates on the marginal lending facility and the deposit facility will remain unchanged at 5.25 percent and 3.25 percent, respectively. It reiterates that, as announced on June 8, 2000, the forthcoming main refinancing operations of the Eurosystem will be conducted as variable rate tenders, apply the multiple rate auction procedure, with a minimum bid rate of 4.25 percent.

The Governing Council also announces that, for the longer-term refinancing operations to be conducted in the second half of 2000, the Eurosystem intends to allot an amount of 15 billion per operation. This amount takes into consideration the expected liquidity needs of the banking system of the euro area in the second half of 2000 and the desire of the Eurosystem to continue to provide the bulk of its refinancing of the financial sector through its main refinancing operations.

July 6, 2000, July 20, 2000, August 3, 2000

The Governing Council of the ECB decides that the minimum bid rate on the main refinancing operations and the interest rates on the marginal lending facility and the deposit facility will remain unchanged at 4.25 percent, 5.25 percent, and 3.25 percent, respectively.

August 31, 2000

The Governing Council of the ECB decides to raise the minimum bid rate on the main refinancing operations of the Eurosystem by 0.25 percentage point to 4.50 percent, with effect from the operation to be settled on September 6, 2000. In addition, it decides to increase the interest rates on both the marginal lending facility and the deposit facility by 0.25 percentage point, to 5.50 percent and 3.50 percent, respectively, both with effect from September 1.

September 14, 2000, October 5, 2000, October 19, 2000, November 2, 2000, November 16, 2000, November 30, 2000, December 14, 2000

The Governing Council of the ECB decides that the minimum bid rate on the main refinancing operations and the interest rates on the marginal lending facility and the deposit facility will remain unchanged at 4.50 percent, 5.50 percent, and 3.50 percent, respectively.

In addition, on December 14, 2000, it decides to reconfirm the existing reference value for monetary growth, namely, an annual growth rate of 4 1/2 percent for the broad aggregate M3. This decision is taken on the grounds that the available evidence continues to support the assumptions underlying the initial derivation of the reference value in December 1998 (and its confirmation in December 1999), namely that, over the medium term, M3 income velocity declines at a trend rate in the range from 1/2 percent to 1 percent per annum and potential output grows at a trend rate between 2 percent and 2 1/2 percent per annum. The Governing Council will undertake the next review of the reference value in December 2001.

January 2, 2001

On January 1, 2001, the euro was introduced in Greece. Greece thus became the twelfth EU member state to adopt the single currency and the first to do so since the start of Stage Three of Economic and Monetary Union (EMU) on January 1,1999.

January 18, 2001, February 1, 2001, February 15, 2001, March 1, 2001,
March 15, 2001, March 29, 2001, April 11, 2001, April 26, 2001

The Governing Council of the ECB decides that the minimum bid rate for the main refinancing operations and the interest rates on the marginal lending facility and the deposit facility will remain unchanged at 4.75 percent, 5.75 percent, and 3.75 percent, respectively.

May 10, 2001

The Governing Council of the ECB decides to lower the minimum bid rate on the main refinancing operations by 0.25 percentage point to 4.50 percent, with effect from the operation to be settled on May 15, 2001. In addition, it decides to lower the interest rates on both the marginal lending facility and the deposit facility by 0.25 percentage point, to 5.50 percent and 3.50 percent, respectively, both with effect from May 11, 2001.

May 23, 2001, June 7, 2001, June 21, 2001, July 5, 2001, July 19, 2001,
August 2, 2001

The Governing Council of the ECB decides that the minimum bid rate on the main refinancing operations and the interest rates on the marginal lending facility and the deposit facility will remain unchanged at 4.50 percent, 5.50 percent, and 3.50 percent, respectively.

August 30, 2001

The Governing Council of the ECB decides to lower the minimum bid rate on the main refinancing operations by 0.25 percentage point to 4.25 percent, with effect from the operation to be settled on September 5, 2001. In addition, it decides to lower the interest rates on both the marginal lending facility and the deposit facility by 0.25 percentage point, to 5.25 percent and 3.25 percent, respectively, both with effect from August 31, 2001.

September 17, 2001

The Governing Council of the ECB decides to lower the minimum bid rate on the main refinancing operations by 0.50 percentage point to 3.75 percent, with effect from the operation to be settled on September 19, 2001. In addition, it decides to lower the interest rates on both the marginal lending facility and the deposit facility by 0.50 percentage point, to 4.75 percent and 2.75 percent, respectively, both with effect from September 18, 2001.

September 27, 2001, October 11, 2001, October 25, 2001

The Governing Council of the ECB decides that the minimum bid rate on the main refinancing operations and the interest rates on the marginal lending facility and the deposit facility will remain unchanged at 3.75 percent, 4.75 percent, and 2.75 percent, respectively.

November 8, 2001

The Governing Council of the ECB decides to lower the minimum bid rate on the main refinancing operations by 0.50 percentage point to 3.25 percent, starting from the operation to be settled on November 14, 2001. In addition, it decides to lower the interest rates on both the marginal lending facility and the deposit facility by 0.50 percentage point, to 4.25 percent and 2.25 percent, respectively, both with effect from November 9, 2001.

December 6, 2001

The Governing Council of the ECB decided to leave the minimum bid rate on the main refinancing operations of the Eurosystem, conducted as variable rate tenders, unchanged at 3.25 percent. The interest rates on the marginal lending facility and the deposit facility were also left unchanged at 4.25 percent and 2.25 percent, respectively.

In addition, it decides that the reference value for the annual growth rate of the broad monetary aggregate M3 will remain at 4 1/2 percent.

The current level of key ECB interest rates is considered appropriate to maintain price stability in the euro area over the medium term. This assessment is based on the analysis of the information provided under the two pillars of the ECB's monetary policy strategy. Starting with the analysis under the first pillar of the ECB's monetary policy strategy, the three-month average of the annual growth rates of M3 rose to 6.8 percent in the period from August to October 2001, from 6.2 percent in the period from July to September. This was significantly above the medium-term reference value for annual M3 growth of 4 1/2 percent.

The Governing Council confirmed the reference value of 4 1/2 percent at its meeting on December 6. This decision was taken on the grounds that the evidence continues to support the medium-term assumptions underlying the derivation of the reference value, namely those for trend potential output growth of 2–2 1/2 percent per annum and for a trend decline in M3 income velocity of 1/2–1 percent per annum in the euro area.

Ongoing Dynamic Growth of M3

In the period from August to October 2001, the three-month average of the annual growth rates of M3 (which are corrected for holdings by nonresidents of the euro area of money market paper and debt securities with a maturity of up to two years) increased to 6.8 percent, from 6.2 percent in the period from July to September 2001. The annual growth rate of M3 stood at 7.4 percent, up from 6.9 percent in September, which was significantly above the ECB's medium-term reference value for M3 growth.

Having shown a decline in 2000 and early 2001, to levels well below the reference value (3.8 percent in the first quarter of 2001), the annual growth rate of M3 increased significantly in the course of this year. This acceleration of M3 following a period of subdued growth can to some extent be seen as a normalization process through which economic agents brought money holdings back into line with desired levels. In addition, the higher price level reached as a consequence of increases in energy and food prices observed in 2000 and early 2001 fuelled the demand for transaction balances in 2001.

CHAPTER 15

Asian Financial Crisis: Whence and Whither?

Dilip K. Ghosh

Then the unexpected happened. The Asian miracle was shattered almost overnight and suddenly once-fawning economists argued that all it really had been was a bubble, overinflated by corruption, cronyism, and bad loans. Asians were not only impoverished but were blamed for impoverishing themselves.

Mahathir Mohamed (1999)

INTRODUCTION

Asian financial crisis: was it a crisis, chaos or absence of confidence? Many pundits and professional experts have pondered over the issue, and most politicians in the region certainly cried out loud on the fall of the currencies and the drop of the markets. People indeed suffered enormously, and economies did bleed, and still some of these countries are suffering beyond measure. Financial institutions came into disarray, and restructuring either dictated by international rescuers and/or by domestic governments had taken hold in all of these countries. Asia is a continent with a large mass of land with the highest population as a region. The question is: which countries in this continent came to the so-called crisis situation, and at what point in time did the economic malady hit them? Was the virus crippling and catastrophic, or was it made to look real fatal?

THE COUNTRIES UNDER CRISIS

When we talk about Asian crisis, we invariably refer to Thailand, Indonesia, Korea, Malaysia, and Philippines because these were the countries directly hit by the collapse of their financial architecture. The stock market fell, currency values plummeted, and nonperforming loans escalated in all those countries. But it is not correct to select only those countries as crisis-ridden. A larger set must be chosen, although the severity and the panic were not as great. Normally, the existing literature points to the fact that the Asian crisis started in Thailand, and then it spread like a wild fire throughout southeast Asia, and particularly in the countries just noted. But a closer look at the region should reveal that the crisis indeed started brewing from the early 1980s and in Japan—the second largest economy of the world, stemming from the bubble it created with its financial liberalization. Massive flotation of government bonds in the wake of the oil crisis in 1973, and the unconstrained flexibility in the exchange rate along with surplus in the current account balance, and almost unrestricted international capital flows made the economy buoyant. But the late 1980s began to unravel the economic weakness and presaged the collapse. The Nikkei 225 average peaked at 38,926 yen on December 29, 1989. It dropped to 23,849 yen in a year, and in April 1998, it came around 16,000; the total value of national wealth in the form of nonreproducible fixed capital, Kenjiro Hirayama (2000) notes, fell from 2420 trillion yen in 1990 to 1840 trillion yen in 1995—a loss greater than Japan's annual gross domestic product. In 1995 two rather small credit unions in Tokyo and another in Osaka failed, and then a very large regional bank (Hyogo) went under. In that rolling downward spiral came Nissan Life with its insolvency and it got liquidated. Later Hokkaido Takusho—one of the city banks—with deposits exceeding 6 trillion yen failed, and then came the closure of Yamaichi Securities—one of the big four—in Japan. That is where it all started.

HISTORICAL PERSPECTIVES—A GLOBAL VIEW

Our history is a chronicle of events, often marred by chaos, confusion, crisis and attack on confidence. The recent Asian financial crisis is a series of those episodes, piled up on each other. Financial crisis in Asia in 1997–1998 is not an endemic problem, not an idiosyncratic development of this region. It is a sad tale of mismanagement in banking and misalignment in currencies. Let us review some historical facts to gain a better perspective on the crisis and cure thereof. Note that at the end of the eighteenth century banks in the United States had serious failures creating miseries all around. To solve such problems the First Bank of the United States was established to serve as the central bank of the country. It did not do much good, and its charter expired after 20 years, and it simply died. Soon the Second Bank of the United States came into being, but it also became defunct after its 20 years of existence. Many banking failures plagued the nation throughout the nineteenth century, and so finally to address the problem effectively, the U.S. Congress established a Monetary Reform Commission under the chairmanship of Aldrich Vreeland whose recommendation created the Federal Reserve System in 1913. Soon the war ravaged every economy. In the aftermath of World War I, Britain had a difficult time to keep the external value of pound sterling pegged to the value of gold, and so Britain had to step out of the gold standard in 1925–1926 under the-then Chancellor of the Exchequer, Winston Churchill. But soon the country restored the gold standard to uphold the sanctity and prestige of pound sterling, and yet in the midst of the Great Depression 1929–1933 England bade final goodbye to the gold standard. The Pre-Poincaré French episode of franc's continuous tumbling in 1925–1926 is another historical anecdote of foreign exchange debacle. "The Peso Problem," which occurred later in the late 1970s, 1980s, and 1990s, was the replay of the French experience. Examination of those experiences prompted Ragnar Nurkse—one of the most renowned economists of the twentieth century—to make the following remarks often quoted in the literature:

anticipations are apt to bring about their own realization. Anticipatory purchases of foreign exchange tend to produce or at any rate to hasten the anticipated fall in the exchange value of the national currency, and the actual fall may be set up or strengthen expectations of a further fall. . . . Exchange rates in such circumstances are bound to become highly unstable, and the influence of psychological factors may at times be overwhelming (Nurske, 1944, p. 144)

The Asian crisis is the corroboration of this set of observations. The U.S. economy, although it suffered enormously in the Great Depression, and was bruised badly by the "run on banks," got back swinging by creating Federal Deposit Insurance Corporation (FDIC) and entering into gold standard by pegging the U.S. dollar to gold at $35 per each troy ounce of fine gold with the U.S. government's unlimited and unqualified commitment of convertibility of dollar into gold and *vice versa*. The world, however, was distrustful of U.S. commitment or ability. So the 1930s became the regime of unbounded floating exchange rates with cycles of competitive currency devaluations that almost wrecked the international financial transactions and commodity trade. Under a serious threat of a complete collapse of monetary system, a tripartite agreement among three nations—the United States, United Kingdom, and France—was reached, and the result was the establishment of the International Monetary Fund (IMF) upon a compromise of the White Plan and the Keynes Plan. The IMF was set up to maintain stability without exchange rigidity of the Gold Standard and to promote exchange flexibility with some controls. Let us briefly bring out the chronological records of the international monetary structures that the United States went through:

1. 1834–1861: a *de facto* gold standard in a largely bimetallic international monetary system

2. 1862–1878: the greenback standard

3. 1879–1914: a gold standard without a central bank, and a fractional reserve banking system, as part of an expanding international gold standard

4. 1914–1933: a managed gold standard, under the Federal Reserve System, which was legally obliged to maintain minimum gold reserves against its monetary liabilities, in a short-lived postwar international gold exchange standard

5. 1933–1934: a floating dollar in an international monetary system spilt between a depreciated sterling area and a gold bloc clinging to parity

6. 1934–1948: the interwar and World War II and immediate postwar managed gold standard, in a fragmented international monetary system

7. 1948–1968: the Bretton Woods dollar/gold standard system, with progressive dilution of the gold restraints on U.S. monetary conduct.

8. 1968–1973: the breakdown of the Bretton Woods system.

9. 1973–1981: the United States on an inconvertible paper dollar standard

Note that the U.S. economy experienced the exchange flexibility of the 1930s, and again in 1970s in the wake of oil embargo of the OPEC. Located next to this largest economy of the world, Mexico—the second largest Latin American nation—experienced a process of painful adjustments for almost the last quarter of the past century since the devaluation of the peso in 1976. Its financial situation, owing to its gargantuan foreign debt, intractable rates of inflation, and the plummeting value of the peso had brought real and fundamental economic disequilibrium. It was quite ironic that when the peso was greatly depreciating in the market, it was often getting overvalued in reality by the combined effects of *Fisher Open Principle* and the *Purchasing Power Parity*. This sort of turn or twist causing the paradox of appreciation in the midst of depreciation probably further sustained the plunging condition of the Mexican currency. Some analysts argued that since the foreign exchange market was not always efficient, even a low probability of an event might cause a large change in exchange rates, and that is what happened in the Mexican case and in Asian economies later. It was, unlike a speculative bubble, an exchange rate dynamics of disequilibrium in which expectation of expansionary policy menu induced an actual erosion in the current exchange rates and thus forced current inflationary pressures ahead of any expansion. Salant and Henderson recognized that as a generic problem of asset markets where speculators were actively over-reacting, or to put it in the words of Dornbusch (1982), "it is a problem where asset market-oriented adjustment of exchange rate works with an overkill."

Historians will remember the early 1980s as a period of systematic crisis in the emerging world. The Latin American countries, with their high debt burdens, fell like dominoes into an abyss of successive devaluations, banking crises, and deep and protracted recessions. Several countries in Asia were also deeply shaken. Yet, possibly, because much of the blame was placed on poor domestic policies and high real interest rates in the United States, little attention was given at the time to the possibility that financial crises could be contagious. After the Tequila crisis of 1994–1995, the Asian flu of 1997, and the Russian virus of 1998, not to mention the Exchange Rate Mechanism Crisis of 1992 and 1993, economists are now producing a growing volume of research on the "new" subject of contagion.

Yet, contagion has been understood to be different things across different studies. Crises could be synchronous across countries because of a common adverse shock (i.e., a rise in world interest rates). But symmetric shocks are usually not included in most definitions of contagion. In an early study on the subject, Calvo and Reinhart (1995) distinguish between fundamentals based contagion, which arises when the infected country is linked to others via trade or finance, and "true" contagion, which arises when common shocks and all channels of potential interconnection are either not present or have been controlled for. Most often, true contagion is associated with herding behavior on the part of investors—be it rational, as noted in Calvo and Mendoza (1996), or not.

Few studies have attempted to examine empirically the channels through which the disturbances are transmitted. By examining the role of various creditors, including international banks and mutual funds, traders' potential cross-market hedging, and bilateral and third-party trade in the propagation of crises, the following conclusions emerge:

- While interregional trade in goods and services has not increased markedly in the past few years (a notable exception is Chile's rising trade with Asia), interregional trade in assets has skyrocketed. This makes it more likely that if Korean asset prices fall, so too will Brazilian asset prices.

- Second, susceptibility to contagion is highly nonlinear. A single country falling victim to a crisis is not a particularly good predictor of crisis elsewhere, be it in the same region or in another part of the globe. However, if several countries fall prey, then it is a different story. That is, the probability of a domestic crisis rises sharply if a core group of countries are already infected.

- Third, observational equivalence is a serious obstacle in understanding the channels of transmission. Is the regional complexion of contagion due to trade links, as some studies have suggested, or is it due to financial links particularly through the role played by banks? As it appears, it is difficult to distinguish among the two, because most countries that are linked in trade are also linked in finance. In the Asian crises of 1997, Japanese banks played a similar role in propagating disturbances to that played by U.S. banks in the debt crisis of the early 1980s.

- Fourth, an analysis of two potential victims of contagion, Argentina after Mexico and Indonesia after Thailand, indicates that financial linkages were the more likely culprits, given that both bilateral and third-party trade links with the infected country were weak. In the case of Indonesia, it was also part of the same Japanese commercial bank borrowing cluster as Thailand.

In an interesting study of 80 currency crises episodes from 1970 to 1998, Kaminsky and Reinhart (2000) present the following list where currency crisis took place:

Industrial countries: Denmark, Finland, Norway, Spain, Sweden;

Developing countries: Argentina, Bolivia, Brazil, Chile, Colombia, Indonesia, Israel, Malaysia, Mexico, Peru, the Philippines, Thailand, Turkey, Uruguay, Venezuela.

They show that probability of crisis conditioned on crisis elsewhere increases sharply as the number of casualties rises, and they further conclude that when the proportion of infected countries increases over the 50 percent hurdle, conditional probability of crisis increases from 27 percent to 67 percent in Asia, and from 29 percent to 69 percent in Latin America. For Europe the increase is from 28 percent to 35 percent. It is instructive that we take a close look at the growth rate of different economies, taxonomically given as follows in Table 15.1.

Let us now focus more directly on the Asian situations. Look at the basic data on the financial conditions, as exhibited by Table 15.2.

The dramatic collapse of Asian currency and stock market values in 1997–1998 was triggered by a currency crisis in Thailand, and it then spread to its neighbors. The Philippines, Indonesia, Malaysia, and South Korea shared to a lesser degree some but not all of Thailand's weaknesses: an overvalued fixed exchange rate, large and growing current account deficit and domestic asset bubble, heavy dependence on short-term

Table 15.1
Growth in Real GDP (Annual Percentage)

Region	1965–1980	1980–1990	1990–1997
High Income	3.7	3.2	2.1
East Asia	7.3	7.8	9.9
South Asia	3.6	5.7	5.7
E. Europe and C. Asia	—	2.9	-5.4
Latin America	6.0	1.8	3.3

Source: World Bank 1998/1999.

Table 15.2
Percentage Change in the Stocks and Currencies in 1997

	Stock	*Currency*
Japan	-16.7%	-10.9%
Thailand	-35.4%	-51.9%
Indonesia	-44.7%	-69.3%
Korea	-33.3	-44.7%
Hong Kong	-42.8%	0.0%
Malaysia	-52.4%	-54.4%
Philippines	-41.1%	-53.4%

Source: Institute of International Finance, Inc. and IMF: International Financial Statistics, various issues, 1995–1998, Washington, D.C.

external debt, and an unstable government unwilling or unable to take the tough deflationary measures necessary to correct these problems.

While downward adjustments in individual exchange rates were expected, especially after Thailand, an export competitor devalued by over 25 percent the extent of the other countries' devaluations and the depth of their ensuing domestic recessions were quite unexpected. The severe collateral damage to the well-managed economies of Hong Kong and Singapore, which did not suffer from the same weaknesses, and to other emerging economies around the world, was also largely unanticipated.

There are three interrelated explanations for the unanticipated severity of the Asian crisis. First, economists underestimated the extent of "contagion" that could and would occur as a result of liberalized capital markets. Foreign money had flocked to their open capital markets when these economies were the fastest growing in the world—investing in high-return short-term loans and portfolio investments that fed their overvalued exchange rates and current account deficits.

This money could, and did, leave even more quickly—either because foreign capital market actors lacked full information about the security of their loans and investments, thus erring on the side of excessive pessimism and risk-aversion, or because they knew their loans and investments were highly risky, so pulled out "at the first sign of trouble."

Some argue that lenders and investors knowingly made these risky loans and investments because they expected to be bailed out by local governments or the IMF should the risks actually materialize (or "moral hazard"). When these expectations were not realized (e.g., because governments changed or refused to accede to IMF conditions), the foreign capital fled. The actions of speculators, and the "herd instinct" of much more numerous nonspeculative investors, both domestic and foreign, aggravated this capital flight.

A second explanation for the unexpected severity of the crisis is that economists, including those of the IMF, failed to recognize that the weakness of immature domestic financial systems rendered them extremely vulnerable to both speculative attack and a widespread loss of confidence in local investments.

Inadequate prudential regulation, banking supervision accounting standards, financial transparency, legal protection, and accountability in corporate governance, combined with pervasive market imperfections, government interventions in business, and the common (and locally rational) practice of relying on political or personal relationships to advance and protect one's business ventures ("crony capitalism")—all led to a high proportion of "bad loans" and "bad investments." The easy availability of capital—from high domestic savings and eager foreign lenders and equity investors—only exacerbated its unproductive use. The subsequent collapse of domestic asset bubbles when capital withdrew then undermined the health of financial institutions and highly leveraged local corporations. Otherwise healthy local businesses were hurt as well by the resulting liquidity crunch and ensuing recession.

The third explanation for the unexpectedly massive exodus of domestic and foreign capital rests in the realms of locally specific politics and mass psychology, which were little considered by economists. Governmental changes, which accompanied or were precipitated by the financial crisis, and the social unrest, which followed economic collapse, increased country political risk and further reduced local as well as foreign confidence in governments' abilities to manage both the crisis and its social and political consequences.

Recovery policies focused initially on conventional responses to currency crises: depreciation of overvalued currencies, deflation of domestic demand through fiscal and monetary austerity (with higher interest rates necessary to dampen imported inflation, compensate for higher risk, discourage speculation and capital outflow, and attract new capital inflow), and rebuilding of depleted foreign exchange reserves with IMF funds that were awarded on condition of accompanying financial and corporate sector reforms.

These policies were initially less effective than expected, in part because their implementation was delayed by government and private sector resistance, which in turn delayed disbursements of IMF funds and further damaged the confidence of private financial market actors. By the time austerity policies were implemented, heightened political risk, social unrest, and broadening regional contagion had exacerbated the ongoing market-induced economic downturns, and these policies became "too contractionary." Fiscal austerity was then relaxed.

The openness of these Asian economies that had contributed so much to their previous rapid growth did little to foster recovery. Exports were highly dependent on imported inputs, the prices of which rose with devaluation, and on the Japanese market, which fell back into a prolonged recession. Exports were also hurt by increased interest costs, difficulties in obtaining trade credits, transportation bottlenecks and the "competitive devaluations" of neighbors with similar export structures. Current accounts turned rapidly from deficit into surplus largely due to a collapse in import demand.

But by late 1998, the crisis-hit economies appeared to have "hit bottom," with currencies stabilizing and even strengthening, and interest rates dropping dramatically. As IMF funds poured into Thailand, Korea, and Indonesia, bank recapitalization began, and a start was made on financial and corporate sector restructuring to reduce debt burdens and increase transparency and efficiency. Malaysia, which had not asked for IMF funding, went on a different route by imposing foreign exchange controls that had allowed it to reflate the domestic economy through stimulative fiscal and monetary policy. This was likely to improve growth in the short run, but at the expense of long-term financial sector reforms that were necessary both to improve efficiency and attract back capital from foreigners and local residents who had already parked their assets overseas. Dornbusch (2001a, 2001b), although maintained that controls were often justified, raised the question of the timing of the controls imposed by the Malaysian government. It appeared that controls were imposed when economic statistics were already on the rebound. The IMF has noted, as Dornbusch (2001a) aptly points out, that "at the time the capital controls were imposed, markets had already settled in Asia, interest rates had been coming off and would soon do so everywhere under the impact of Fed rate cuts and a reduction in jitters. In fact, in Korea and Thailand rates had fallen by August to half their June level. And the same was true in Malaysia."

As Japan appeared to make a serious effort to solve its financial crisis and stimulate its domestic economy, and the U.S. Federal Reserve started cutting interest rates to prevent its economy going into recession, the dollar started depreciating significantly against the yen. This development, if sustained, would have helped the Asian countries recover by improving the price competitiveness of their exports to Japan versus Japanese companies in third markets, by increasing Japanese and maintaining U.S. demand for their exports, by reducing their dollar debt burdens, by increasing their ability to attract new loan and investment capital from Japan, and by reducing the likelihood that other big emerging market competitors—most notably China—would feel the need to devalue, which would risk setting off a renewed round of "contagion." Japan's offer of $30 billion in trade finance and credit guarantees that would enable the Asian countries to borrow at Japanese sovereign rates would further boost their exports and bring in new capital flows.

While the external environment has improved and the currency crisis is probably over, the Asian countries' economic recovery is likely to be slow, fragile, and continuously vulnerable to external and domestic shocks. The event on September 11, 2001, and the international terrorism have dealt a devastating blow to all these economies, and it once again has proven how international linkages work toward economic growth, financial stability, or the lack thereof. Financial sector reforms will take time and painstaking effort to implement, even with the strongest political will in the world, because they require money and expertise that are not present in large enough amounts to tackle the problem swiftly. Reforms in business practices that contributed to the crisis—such as "crony capitalism"—will also be slow, not only because they will impose severe hardships on both business and labor through mass bankruptcies and layoffs, but also because they require a degree of political and cultural change that both is difficult and will take much time to realize.

The danger is that, because structural reforms are so difficult, and the Asian countries' long-term macroeconomic fundamentals so favorable—particularly their high domestic savings rates and wage and price flexibility which have held unemployment and inflation below double-digit levels despite massive devaluations and severe recessions—recovery in the short run could reduce the incentive to persist with such reforms.

WHAT WENT WRONG IN ASIA?

Let us review in a nutshell what caused or exacerbated the chaos and crisis (for extensive discussion see Dufey, 1999; Ghosh, 1994; Haggard, 2000; Haggard & Low, 2000; and Lee & Park, 2000). The list of factors responsible for the downturn of the economies can be given as follows:

- Persistently widening current account deficits
- Lack of invoicing ingenuity
- Mounting accumulation of short-tem foreign debt by both private and public sectors
- Overvaluation of exchange rates, weak macroeconomic policy menu, infirm financial institutions, and poor transparency
- Speculative attacks on these currencies

Banks and financial systems provide three basic services:

1. they provide an effective system of payment services;
2. they provide credit, moving funds from savers to investors in real assets; and
3. they allocate risk.

The risk allocation is accomplished by banks and other financial institutions by transforming the riskiness of their assets vis-à-vis their liabilities through information processing, including monitoring and portfolio diversification. In Asia and particularly in South East Asia, crisis sprang from systemic weaknesses in the capital allocation process. In the end, there were too many investments that did not yield positive rates of returns on a risk-adjusted basis. The *Chicago Fed Letter, Special Issue, December 1998* spells out correctly that Asian financial institutions and markets failed to allocate risks and evaluate returns adequately in the later stages of the Asian boom. In the wake of the crisis, the Malaysian government introduced the National Economic Recovery Plan (NERP), and instituted the pegging of the ringgit (RM3.80 = USD1.00), put capital control, and called for a massive restructuring of its financial services. The Malaysian prime minister, Dr. Mahathir, called for a new system in which speculators could be ostracized, and in fact he called for a ban on currency trading (September 13, 1997, Hong Kong); the IMF, while flirting with mandatory capital account convertibility, could not deny some role for short-run ad hoc capital controls.

Was Dr. Mahathir wrong? The tone was wrong, but the policy was right. A more magical and mystifying invoicing structure on export import bills could alleviate the intense problems Malaysia faced. Pegging was ad hoc and abrupt when it came loaded with "fire sales" to foreigners.

But note that capital controls, taxes, and other barriers to asset trading had been gaining popularity since Chile's taxes and timing restrictions on inflows and outflows of short-term capital, which were put in place since the early 1990s. Malaysian policy was an extension of the Chilean experiment. If controls were applauded for Chile, if it is all right for the New York Stock Exchange (NYSE) to halt trading in extreme case of market swings, why could it be a wrong recipe for Dr. Mahathir's prescription? The introduction, like the Tobin tax, probably could not stem the capital flight, but it could lengthen the horizon of stay of the foreign capital. Malaysia could initiate some exit tax on capital outflow. A more direct talk and persuasion by the government on the fate of certain and no-loss roundtripping with some sequencing in the spirit of McKinnon and Pill (1996) under some nongovernmental organization (NGO) could change the Malaysian situation significantly. The statements of two leaders—Dr. Mahathir (prime minister) and Mr. Anwar (finance minister)—in the IMF-

World Bank Meeting in Hong Kong, created more confusion and engendered more political risk than possible clarification. Foreign portfolio investors took the preemptive stand to pull their funds out and parked them outside the infected region because of the fear that they could lose even their original principal if they did not do so. The government did not allay that fear at all. There was no exit barrier. NERP was a pious document, but its implementation was flawed.

Despite all these, Malaysia was recovering well, and the value of the ringgit almost came back to the precrisis level in August 2000, as shown by the purchasing power of the ringgit. It has slipped again; the stock market is down again. Although capital control is lifted, and Morgan Stanley has put Malaysia back in the Morgan Stanley Capital Index (MSCI), foreign capital is not coming for the same reason for which it left. More capital infusion is needed, and the government must bury its hatchet and make good friends with IMF, World Bank, and Western treasuries. Western investors need returns, and Malaysia can provide those returns once it is fully back in sound economic health. All Asian economies need the coordinated policy menu with the strongest determination to invite foreign capital back and a defined commitment to protect it.

REFERENCES

Calvo, G. A., and E. G. Mendoza. (1996). "Mexico's Balance-of-Payments Crisis: A Chronicle of a Death Foretold," *Journal of International Economics*, 41, pp. 235–264.

Calvo, S., and C. M. Reinhart. (1995). "Capital Flows to Latin America: Is There Evidence of Contagion Effects?," mimeographed, World Bank, Washington, D.C.

Choi, J. J. (2000). "The Asian Financial Crisis: Moral Hazard in More Ways Than One," *International Finance Review*, 1, pp. 3–14.

Dornbusch, R. (1982). "Equilibrium and Disequilibrium Exchange Rates." *Zeitschrift fur Wirtschafts und Sozialwissenschaften*, 102, no. 6: 573–599.

———. (2001a). "A Primer on Emerging Market Crises." Retrieved July 27, 2001, www.mit.edu/~rudi.

———. (2001b). "Malaysia: Was It Different?" National Bureau of Economic Research, working paper 8325, Cambridge, MA.

Dufey, G. (1999). "Asian Financial Markets: A Pedagogic Note," *Journal of Asian Business*, 15, no. 1.

Ghosh, D. K. (1994). "Foreign Exchange Dynamics, Debt and the 'Peso Problem'." In D. K. Ghosh and E. Ortiz (Eds.), *The Changing Environment of International Financial Market* (pp. 125–138). London: Macmillan Press; New York: St. Martin's Press.

Haggard, S. (2000). *The Political Economy of the Asian Financial Crisis*. Washington, D.C.: Institute for International Economics.

Haggard, S., and L. Low. (2000). "The Political Economy of Malaysian Capital Controls." Unpublished manuscript. Cambridge, MA: Harvard University.

Hirayama, K. (2000). "Japanese Financial Markets in Turmoil: Liberalization and Consequences." In D. G. Dickinson et al. (Eds.), *Finance, Governance and Economic Performance in Pacific and South East Asia* (pp. 91–111). Cheltenham, MA: Edward Elgar.

International Monetary Fund (IMF). (2000). *International Capital Markets.* Washington, D.C.: International Monetary Fund.

Kaminsky, G. S., and C. M. Reinhart. (2000). "On Crises, Contagion, and Confusion," *Journal of International Economics,* 51, pp. 145–168.

Lee, P-S., and K. S. Park. (2000). "Origins and Policy Implications of the Asian Financial Crisis," *International Finance Review,* 1, pp. 45–78.

McKinnon, R. I., and H. Pill. (1996). "Credible Liberalization and International Capital Flows: The 'Overborrowing Syndrome' " In Takatoshi Ito and A. O. Krueger (Eds.), *Financial Deregulation and Integration in East Asia.* Chicago: University of Chicago Press.

Mohamad, M. (1999). *A New Deal for Asia.* Kuala Lampur, Malaysia: Pelanduk.

Nurske, R. (1944). *International Currency Experience: Lessons from the Inter-War Period.* Princeton, NJ: League of Nations.

World Bank. (1998, 1999). *World Bank Data Book.* Washington, D.C.: World Bank.

Index

About the Editors and Contributors

DILIP K. GHOSH is the KLSE Chair Professor of Finance at Universiti Utara Malaysia (UUM) and Rutgers University. He is the Editor-in-Chief of *The International Journal of Finance, The International Journal of Banking and Finance,* and he sits on a number of editorial boards of academic journals. He is an author of numerous books and articles in academic journals. His major research interests are in foreign exchange markets, corporate finance, investment and financial engineering.

SHYAMASRI GHOSH is the Vice President of Forex Partners, Inc. Her research interests are in investment and financial economics.

NOR HAYATI BT. AHMAD is the associate dean of the School of Finance and Banking, and a lecturer at Universiti Utara Malaysia (UUM). She has an active research agenda on financial markets.

MOHAMED ARIFF is a Bumi Commerce Bank Endowed Chair Professor of Banking at Universiti Utara Malaysia (UUM), the head of Finance at Monash University in Melbourne, Australia. He has authored numerous books and journal articles. His basic research interests are in banking and financial markets.

MOHD NORDIN ASUDALLI is a lecturer in finance at Islamic International University of Malaysia. He is in the research field of banking, and other financial institutions.

OBIYATHULLA ISMATH BACHA is the senior lecturer of finance at Islamic International University of Malaysia, and Director of Research. He works on all areas of finance, but in the recent past he has been focusing on derivatives and financial engineering.

JOHN T. BARKOULAS is the associate professor of economics at University of Tennessee. He has extensive research interests in different areas of financial economics, and widely published in various academic Journals.

CHRISTOPHER F. BAUM is an associate professor of economics at Boston College in Massachusetts. He is a prolific researcher in economics and finance.

MICHEL-HENRY BOUCHET is a professor of CERAM in France. He works on distressed economies in particular, but he has wide interests in international financial markets.

MUSTAFA CAGLAYAN is an assistant professor at Boston College in Massachusetts.

ATREYA CHAKRABORTY is an assistant professor of finance at Brandeis College in Massachusetts, and a consultant to Brattle Group. He does work on small business finance, banks, and foreign exchange.

ENGKU NGAH SAYUDIN ENGKU CHIK is a lecturer in Finance and Banking at Universiti Utara Malaysia (UUM).

LEE CHIN is a lecturer in economics at Universiti Utara Malaysia (UUM). He studies markets, exchange rates and inflation.

EPHRAIM CLARK is a professor of finance at Middlesex University in London, U.K. He is the founding Editor of European Journal of Finance, and currently is the Editor of Frontiers in Finance and Economics. He writes in international finance, and recently he is doing a series of papers on the political risk analysis. He is the author of many books and journal articles.

VINCENT DROPSY is a professor of economics at California State University at Fullerton. His research interests are in emerging markets, and finance.

BERTRAND GROSLAMBERT is a professor of CERAM in France. He works on different areas of financial economies. He is often a participant in international conferences.

ELINDA FISHMAN KISS is a professor of finance at University of Maryland. She teaches corporate finance, but does research on European Union and common currency unit.

CHE ANI MAD is a senior lecturer in Finance and Banking at Universiti Utara Malaysia (UUM). He has a wide range of interest in financial economics.

NIK KAMARIAH BT. NIK MAT is a lecturer in Finance and Banking at Universiti Utara Malaysia (UUM).

LAWRENCE W. NOWICKI is an associate professor at Long Island University. He works on transfer pricing, and other international financial issues.

DENNIS OLSON is a professor of Finance at American University at Sharjah. His area of research is in foreign exchange trading and efficiency of the market. He is a frequent participant of international conferences.

BALA RAMASWAMY is a professor of Finance at Universiti Malaysia (UM). He is involved in research on the foreign exchange market.

SHAHIRA ABDEL SHAHID is the Vice President of Cairo and Alexandria Stock Exchanges in Egypt, and previously, she was the Director of Research of the same Stock Exchanges. Her research interests are on globalization and capital market integration.

MICHAEL T. SKULLY is a professor of Banking at Monash University at Melbourne, Australia. He is the former head of the Department of Banking and Finance. He came to Monash from the University of New South Wales. His research interests are mostly in banking.

RADU TUNARU is a consultant in the finance industry. Previously, he held the faculty position at Middlesex University in London, U.K.

MOHAMMED B. YUSOFF is a professor of economics at Universiti Utara Malaysia (UUM). He has research work and research interest in foreign exchange issues.

NASURUDDIN ZAINUDIN is a senior lecturer in the School of Finance and Banking at Universiti Utara Malaysia (UUM). He is the former associate dean of the School. He teaches and does research on corporate finance and international finance.